A William Condry Reader

Bill Condry at Ynys Edwin in 1962, on the day Eric Hosking commissioned him to write the first of his New Naturalist series books, on the Snowdonia National Park. He looks as delighted as the book still makes us feel.

A William Condry Reader

Jim Perrin

Gomer

Published in 2015 by
Gomer Press, Llandysul, Ceredigion, SA44 4JL

ISBN 978 1 84851 883 4

A CIP record for this title is available from the British Library.

© Text copyright: Penny Condry, 2015 (William Condry's writings)
Gwyneth Lewis, 2015 (Foreword)
Jim Perrin, 2015 (Introduction, selection and notes)

Penny Condry asserts her moral right under the
Copyright, Designs and Patents Act 1988
to be identified as the author of this work.

This book is published with the financial support of the
Welsh Books Council.

Printed and bound in Wales at
Gomer Press, Llandysul, Ceredigion
www.gomer.co.uk

For Penny Condry,

as Bill would have wished,
in gratitude, friendship and admiration.

'Let a man have thought what he will of Nature
in the house, she will still be novel outdoors.'

Thoreau, *The Journal*
November 4th, 1852

Contents

Foreword

I'm writing this in the rainy Green Mountains of Vermont, Robert Frost country. This morning, delicate stoles of mist are draped round the slopes, to be discarded if the sun comes out later. I've bought an intriguing book, a pictorial chronicle of Frost's time in Vermont. In it, Kathleen Morrison wrote: 'When asked, "How did you become a poet?" R.F. answered. "I followed the procession down the ages."' I see little distinction between the skills needed to be a good writer and a good naturalist. There's a lifetime of learning about and waiting for sights and sounds which are not under our control. This requires humility and knowing that, even though we might be alone at any one time, we follow in the train mentioned by Frost.

As I've learned to look at and listen to the Welsh wilderness, I've caught glimpses of William Condry. First, in his Collins New Naturalist Series volume, *The Natural History of Wales*, which I found in a Hay-on-Wye bookshop. Next, as I researched an opera for children about the red kite, I read the minutes of the Kite Committee, of which Condry was a member. He cycled miles across the Cambrian Mountains from Ponterwyd to Rhandirmwyn and back again the same day for its meetings. His vitality has been given to the red kite and other parts of the Welsh ecosystem. We are deeply in his debt.

Even though I never met him, William Condry's attention to the world around him has shaped my sense of the Welsh landscape. Such clarity and depth of field continues to be a force today. In collecting these writings together, Jim Perrin has brought this quality of awareness into a renewed focus. I see William Condry cresting the brow of a hill ahead, Jim Perrin halfway up and I'm still in the foothills. Thank God for such guides.

Gwyneth Lewis
July 2015

Introduction

In the real nature tradition

As I write this – in a foothills valley of the Pyrenees where nature is still as abundant and varied as it was in the Welsh countryside of half-a-century ago: where the woodlark still carols out its exquisitely inventive song; wrynecks hiss in a tree-hole nest at the bottom of my garden; a black woodpecker drums loudly in the same copse; red squirrels scamper along the telegraph wire where black redstarts perch; clusters of purple broomrape stain the bright tapestry of a wildflower meadow; and a thorn-thicket behind the hamlet's church reveals the gruesome natural sight of a red-backed shrike's larder – I count the time since dear old Bill Condry, who would have rejoiced to see all of these, passed on. Tomorrow, I realize, it will be seventeen years since he died, unexpectedly at the age of eighty in Morriston Hospital on the thirtieth of May, 1998.

I had just returned home from a walk up Cnicht and received the phone call from *The Guardian*, telling of what had happened, asking for a thousand words by lunchtime next day. The news left me reeling. Many others would have felt thus or worse, Penny Condry – his friend, partner and wife of fifty-two years – most of all. In the words of Arthur Chater, one of his long-time botanizing companions, 'for many of us he was a touchstone in his attitude to the natural world.' Years on, to remain conscious of the date of his going tells of how special was the man. In that response lies one reason for publication of this book (the first, I hope, of a pair; the present volume dealing with published sources and a forthcoming one to be devoted to material from the notebooks and journals). Bill – any other appellation than the familiar would seem false for this least stuffy of men – is someone whose life and work are as worthy of celebration as anyone I have ever known. Yet he was the most modest, self-deprecating, unassuming of men, and one who was entirely captivated by a lifelong passion for nature.

It is surely best to turn from sadness to the living memories of those who are gone from us. Mine of Bill are so clear, so distinguished. In the main, they're of botanizing among the Welsh hills. A spring day under the great cliff of Clogwyn Du'r Arddu on the northern flank of Snowdon, for example, when he showed me one of his prize exhibits – a boulder close to an old mine adit, one side of which was entirely covered in moss campion, the other with purple saxifrage; both in their full flowering glory. In return – and a paltry one it was – I took him to a ledge where I knew *Lloydia serotina*, the Snowdon lily, rarest of the rare, bloomed in its season. He instantly pointed it out despite its inconspicuousness when not in flower: as I could not.

He talked also, at length and wonderfully, his scholarship lightly worn but of serious depth. (This was a man who held Classics, French and History degrees, in the days when they counted for something in terms of erudition, from Birmingham, London and Aberystwyth universities). He held forth about the early botanists, travellers and guides on Snowdon; brought their characters, individual interests and approaches vividly alive for me; displayed all the tact, imagination and insight that underpinned his gift as a teacher; and made clear that he too was working within a continuing and still vital tradition of writing about the natural environment that has flowed limpid and uninterrupted for a millennium, firstly in the British Isles and later also in America: from the elegiac lyricism of the

Anglo-Saxon *Seafarer* and *Wanderer*; from early Welsh gnomic poetry; from the *Buile Suibhne* and the *cywyddau* of Dafydd ap Gwilym through middle-English alliterative verse of the Gawain Poet; from the neo-pastoral tradition of Thomas Carew and Robert Herrick through to John Clare; from Richard Jefferies and Henry Williamson to the present day; including early naturalists such as Ray, Willoughby, Lhuyd and Thomas Pennant; including too significant figures from environmental science like Rachel Carson and Derek Ratcliffe, and by way of significant American contributions particularly in recent times: Emerson and Thoreau, John Muir and Aldo Leopold, Ed Abbey, Edwin Way Teale (his 'American Seasons' tetralogy a neglected and sprawling masterwork[1]), Annie Dillard, Cormac McCarthy (read *The Crossing* if you think his name out of place here), Peter Matthiessen, Barry Lopez, Robinson Jeffers, Mary Oliver, George Schaller, Bernd Heinrich.

It's a list that leaves you as short of breath as a walk up Yr Wyddfa. Since the earliest stirrings of the Renaissance, under the pervasive influence of Virgil and in long-loved and culturally complex classics like *The Compleat Angler* and *The Seasons, The Natural History of Selborne, The Story of My Heart* and *Tarka the Otter*, the energy and relevance of nature writing, with all its social, symbolic and valuative dimensions have been maintained. This is the long context of Bill's writing. If you wish to establish his close knowledge of it at a glance, take a look at the range of reference in his very early essay 'Spring in the high woods' (included here in Part Two). James Thomson, William Cowper, Shakespeare, Scott, Virgil, Tennyson – is there a present-day nature writer with the retained knowledge to cite classic sources

---

[1] It was also one that Bill hoped to use as model for a book of his own on a nature-focused journey north through the seasons – something we can now only wish to have seen.

like these? As a worker within the nature-writing tradition, to my mind Bill Condry, both in content and style, was one of the twentieth-century masters. Now, when the meretricious, the ignorant, the inauthentic, the derivative, the cynically assimilative, the metropolitan and the exhibitionist have colonized the genre and the better writers on natural themes have been marginalized, it is time he received the informed and intelligent recognition that's his due.

More on this literary side in due course. I have another recollection (and can put a date to this one – the 9th of January, 1992) of a hill excursion we shared. It was to a mountain particularly precious and familiar to him, Cadair Idris near Dolgellau. As we approached it along the Foxes' Path, he told me that he'd not used this route to reach or descend from the summit since 1923 and didn't intend doing so now. Grateful to be spared a coming ordeal (for this is the worst of all paths to Penygadair, through a vile block-scree of a thousand feet), I did my sums. He would have been five. I pressed him for more information and in that teasing, mild accent of his, still tinged with the rounded vowels of Brummagem even after the greater part of a lifetime away from that city, he vouchsafed that his first experience of the Foxes' Path had been a bad one, ending in him being carried down with a turned ankle on the back of one of the adults in the party; and that at the summit his father had been distinctly grumpy about the price to be paid for a cup of tea – sixpence when everywhere else the going rate was a penny. Then, all negatives cleared away, he started to give me an account of his background and family and the intellectual influences that formed his diffident and remarkable character. Of this too I'll tell you more later, for it was one of those resonant and wide-ranging conversations that stay with you always: but let me first conclude the account of our wanderings on Cadair.

He had a plan for the day – a cold one, with snow on the tops – which was to head for Llyn Gafr, a plain and open sky-reflecting pool the quiet charm and solitude of which grow in attraction by contrast with the scenic melodrama and the crowds not far above. When he explained the plan, it was my turn to tease him, for any time spent with Bill, who was generally the most good-humoured of men, inevitably devolved to playful banter.

A mutual friend, Dewi Jones of Pen-y-groes, had found purple saxifrage flowering on Snowdon as early as the 26th of January. This saxifrage grew on the little bluffs above the lake for which we were heading, and if it were in flower, we would have beaten Dewi by more than a fortnight! I hooted with laughter, and suggested that the genteel pursuit of botany was as riddled with competitiveness as the activity of climbing, for my participation in which he would constantly berate me as a dangerous vandal jeopardizing the relict arctic-alpine flora of Welsh mountain cliffs.

He slapped me down for my levity and called me over to look closely at something among tangles of thyme that grew profusely over the rocks. There was the purple saxifrage, though none of it was yet in flower. It didn't matter to him. His hands were like a lover's, cupping the plant, caressing it, parting the leaves, probing, turning to view.

'See here,' he said, pointing to minute white specks on the leaves and offering me a hand-lens to view. 'Lime, exuded they say...'

I studied also his face. His eyes shone in witness of this smallest thing, his response radiant, communicating wonder; as only the most gifted teachers can.

'Look for the habitat, and you will find your plants,' he continued, after a few moments of silent contemplation. 'Or you may, if you're lucky and don't give up too soon,' he added, with another of those hovering expressions of amusement.

When I think of Bill, which is often for he was one of the crucial mentors in my life, one thing that invariably slips into mind is a piece he wrote on a man who loved curlews. In his late and delectable volume of autobiography, *Wildlife, My Life* (Gomer, 1995), he gives us a little more information about this man. His name was E.H.T. Bible. Bill and Penny first met him when they were living in a primitive, woodlark-chorused cottage called Glygyrog Ddu above Aberdyfi, on the edge of the woods halfway between the estuary and Llyn Barfog. They frequently visited him at his estuary-side home, 'a Gilbert White who is now remembered only by the oldest inhabitants' (and in our time not at all, but for Bill's record).

In *Wildlife, My Life* Bill offers the following elliptical tribute:

> In an ideal world every parish would have its naturalist, someone of long duration in the place, who keeps an eye on the ever-changing woods, fields, streams and their plants and animals; and who faithfully chronicles the events of nature day by day and year by year until the mind dims, the handwriting falters and it is time for a younger scribe to carry on the annals.

Bill was that younger scribe, and the connection was made explicit (though in the gentlemanly fashion of the time names were elided), in one of those delightful country diaries he produced every other Saturday for the *Guardian* newspaper between 1957 and 1998:

> MACHYNLLETH: A man I used to know had a passion for curlews. His house overlooked the estuary of the Dovey river so closely that the tide washed against his garden wall and curlews were his constant neighbours. He saw other creatures too. Sometimes with the tide came grebes, divers, mergansers, or big leaping fish with porpoises or grey seals

after them. And when the tide ebbed off the mud-flats he would watch the wader-flocks gather for the worm-harvest. Sometimes he slept badly and would lie awake listening to the estuary: the gentle lap-lapping of a neap tide under his wall; or the urgent hissing and gurgling of the great springs. But on some nights even the estuary would be quite without sound, the whole vast expanse of mud and water lying in absolute silence through the sleepless hours.

But sooner or later, lying there he would be sure to hear the deep wailings and liquid bubblings of the curlews and this gave him intense delight. When he died he left behind him several scrapbooks in which he had collected a mass of curlew lore; poems and bits of prose clipped out of innumerable books and magazines, every one of them about curlews. Clearly he was not the world's only curlew devotee. And now I live near the estuary and at times I wake in the night and hear the curlews crying in the darkness. Then I remember my old friend.

There is a dream-like mastery of prose-rhythm here, an underlying metricality as smoothly flowing as the tide itself, allied to limpid evocative simplicity. It's often suggested that when we write about others, the qualities we discern in them are our own, reflected. Certainly for me this piece of writing from forty years ago captures precisely the character of its author as well as that of its subject. If we were to take this sketch as Bill's brief self-portrait, then it's a very apt and accurate one, self-effacing, its focus entirely on the external world and its haunting beauties and rhythms.

Let me take you back now to that walk we shared on Cadair, and the information he imparted then of his family background and early experiences of Wales. Bill was born in the outer south-western suburbs of Birmingham, aptly for a man who was to spend the greater part of his life in Wales on *Gŵyl Dewi Sant* (St. David's Day), 1918. His father was a craftsman-jeweller – a diamond-setter – and an admirer and follower of Keir Hardie; his mother had strong connections with the Society of Friends and in her youth attended Meeting in Bournville. From this source comes the plain Quaker sobriety, which need not and does not preclude quiet exultation in the beauty and wonder of creation, that is so distinctive a characteristic of Bill's work: 'Much of the beauty of the mountain birds and their surrounding is made up of such quiet colours.' (This on the meadow pipit – see Part Four below.) Both his parents were pacifists and members of the Independent Labour Party. Also they were Clarionites. Which means they were subscribers to Robert Blatchford's weekly newspaper, *The Clarion* – one of the major precursors to the foundation of a political Labour Party in Britain. In Tredegar the paper was taken by David Bevan and was thus a crucial presence in the childhood home of Aneurin Bevan – another name to be remembered in this current time of political meddling with Bevan's great legacy, the National Health Service. *The Clarion* newspaper influenced the whole outdoor movement that grew so significantly in the first half of the last century, particularly through the proliferation of Clarion rambling clubs, Clarion cycling clubs, Clarion guest houses and cafes – a very few of the latter still proudly extant in the north of England. The holy scripture of Blatchford's *Clarion* was Thoreau's uncategorizable masterpiece *Walden: or Life in the Woods*, first published in 1854. *Walden* did rather more than merely influence Bill's writing – and Thoreau, one of the pre-eminent stylists as well as one of the closest observers of nature in American literature, was a very sound model for the young naturalist. He – 'my friend Thoreau' as Bill frequently refers to him – was also, and perhaps even more importantly, a man around whose values and social and moral tenets Bill was to construct the simple and sturdy framework of his adult life.

The most obvious early manifestation of this was his involvement in the outdoor aspect of the Clarion movement. For the dispossessed of the vast British industrial cities the dark and toxic bloom of which had spread across the land in the space of a few decades through the nineteenth century and was still spreading, this flocking back in precious leisure time to the countryside offered a lifeline to re-connect them with a lost rural tradition. There is a sense of yearning for this quite early in Victorian literature. A remarkable passage, for example, occurs in the Manchester novelist Elizabeth Gaskell's 1848 novel *Mary Barton*:

> There is a class of men in Manchester... who yet may claim kindred with all the noble names that science recognizes. ... the more popularly interesting branches of natural history have their warm and devoted followers among this class. There are botanists among them, equally familiar with either the Linnaean or the Natural system, who know the name and habitat of every plant within a day's walk from their dwellings; who steal the holiday of a day or two when any particular plant should be in flower, and tying up their simple food in their pocket handkerchiefs, set off with single purpose... There are entomologists... the two great and beautiful families of Ephemeridae and Phryganidae have been so much and so closely studied by Manchester workmen... Such are the tastes and pursuits of some of the thoughtful, little understood, working men of Manchester.

As with Manchester, so also with Birmingham – it is not merely fanciful to assume this was a tradition into which the Condry family connected on their Sunday rambles into the surrounding countryside. The proof exists. Bill had an elder brother Dennis, who died at the age of fourteen when Bill was two. His bent too had been for natural history, and from him Bill inherited two cases of specimens, one of butterflies and moths, the other of seabirds' eggs:

> Not that Dennis had made those collections himself. They had come into the family from some now forgotten relative who had evidently been a naturalist and collector in the Victorian tradition.

This helps in part to explain the sense of a fingertip and encyclopaedic natural knowledge present throughout Bill's writing, right from the earliest notebook examples. *Wildlife, My Life* carries in its 'author's preface' a telling disclaimer:

> Despite its title this book can hardly claim to be an autobiography. The story of my unadventurous life would not be of the slightest interest to anybody and I have written instead about the world of nature as I have witnessed it, finding it convenient to use the passing years as a series of pegs on which to hang a succession of wildlife pictures and experiences as they are recorded in my memory or in the diaries I have kept since the days of my youth.

Note the terminology there, and its Quaker resonance: '…the world of nature *as I have witnessed it*'. The preface continues thus:

> Certainly it is out of doors that I have always felt most at ease, well away from what Richard Jefferies called 'the endless and nameless circumstances… of house life'. What I have written here has been conceived in the open air and I pray that a fresh wind still blows through it. As time passes I become ever more convinced that it is in the wild places that

we have the best hope of finding such little sanity as survives in the world.

In that last sentence is the clear echo of Thoreau, as strongly present here in one of his last books as it was in the first (a 1954 biography of his major precursor). He continues: 'In the preface to *The Natural History of Selborne* Gilbert White wrote that even if the book was not a success he would still be able to console himself that his pursuits, "by keeping the body and mind employed, have, under Providence, contributed to much health and cheerfulness of spirits, even to old age". I cannot wish more for my own book.'

The influences are crowding in to help us understand the distinctive tenor of Bill's work: Thoreau, Jefferies, Gilbert White, the urban autodidact tradition, Quakerism, Clarionite and I.L.P. political views – all these add perspective, range, depth and integrity to the mature author's responses and preoccupations. This is no ordinarily bourgeois and complacent solipsist, but a committed social and political idealist ready to live out his own uncompromised truth, and speak out for a cause: 'Quite often I have ventured into controversial issues and said my say about access to moorlands, forestry, farming, reservoirs, mining in national parks, atomic power stations, the urbanization of the countryside, the excesses of tourism, low-flying aircraft, over-population, the pet-trade, blood sports and so on.' So take note! Our genial country writer with his front of mild affability had a radical, fierce morality with which to tax his timid editors from time to time (and I fear their descendants would still find his views often stronger than their delicate metropolitan constitutions can countenance.)

There are two threads to be unravelled at this point. The first concerns Bill's childhood environment as a boy growing up on the fringes of Birmingham. Crowded present-day Britain can give us little impression of what this was like. But the sense of it, fortunately for us, permeates Bill's journals, diaries, recollections: that around his home in Harborne he saw (or heard) – as these days you never would – sand martins, turtle doves, waxwings, corncrakes. Almost on his doorstep was the Moorpool with its mallards and dabchicks. Through the adjacent Hillyfields flowed 'a stream, crystal and unpolluted, where we turned the stones and found bullheads, loaches, lampreys, and best of all crayfish.' In the wildflower meadows alongside flew the small blue butterfly. On the nearby Clent Hills the woodlark still sang. The stream debouched into the 'willow-shaded, reedy paradise at the shallow end of the Harborne reservoir (memories of summer swimming and winter skating)', where 'there were darting shoals of minnows and occasionally some huge fish (they must have been every bit of six inches long) which an angler told us were gudgeon.' One year a pair of great crested grebes nested here and the Condry family's next-door neighbour, Billy Turner – like Bill's parents a rambler, gardener, swimmer and keep-fit enthusiast – became their self-appointed guardian and saw them safely through the breeding season:

> …one day in the autumn he arrived at the reservoir and met a sportsman, a gun under his arm and in his hand a pair of great crested grebes he had just shot. Billy exploded. Not waiting for any argument he picked the sportsman up and dumped him in the reservoir.

Pacifist though he was (throughout the Second World War as a conscientious objector he worked in forestry in Herefordshire), Bill's approval of the action thrills through his account of it.

His early horizons were not limited to the still-vestigially-rural suburbs of Birmingham. There were holidays, when his

mother would take the children off to the coast camping for
weeks on end, living in primitive fashion with their cooking
done on open fires, their water carried in buckets half-a-mile
from the nearest farm, his father joining them for the scant ten
days of annual holiday a craftsman was allowed:

> ...though life was not always comfortable there were huge
> compensations. For getting to know the natural history of
> any wild place, nothing is so good as camping there for weeks.
> Soon I was well acquainted with marram grass, sea spurge,
> sea holly, marsh orchids, ragwort, cinnabar caterpillars,
> burnet moths, oystercatchers, ringed plovers, banded snails,
> razor shells, winkles, shore crabs and a crowd of other forms
> of life I had not met with before. At the age of five I didn't
> know many of their names but they were my intimate friends
> all the same.

These early holidays spent in Ardudwy with the Rhinogydd
as rough and alluring backdrop were succeeded by summer and
Easter stays on the Blue Lias coast of Dorset, the paleontological
marvels of which induced an entirely new dimension of wonder.
From 1928 onwards, the limestone country of south Devon, so
rich of flora, buzzards constantly mewing overhead, became
their regular holiday destination. From his home in Harborne,
too, he was reaching out farther and farther into the Shropshire,
Worcestershire and Herefordshire countryside, abetted and
accompanied now by a close friend, Harold Wright, who shared
his birdwatching passion, their wanderings enabled by possession
of bicycles. His writing stores the fruit collected in the course of
all this wandering and observing. Read, for example, the set of
seven early nature essays included here as Part Two, and you
can understand how their range of experience, sureness of first-
hand knowledge and freshness of observation derive from his

youthful explorations. The same characteristics were there from the outset in his early nature diaries. Here's an entry from one of the voluminous and marvellous collection of notebooks held in the William Condry Archive at the National Library of Wales. It's by the sixteen-year-old Bill. I think it's not entirely fanciful already to detect in its movement from precise observation to implied moral comment the influence of Thoreau:

> Very fine cock Bullfinch, very conspicuous white patch at tail base in flight, in garden feeding on Snapdragon seeds, which it removes while fluttering in the air. A bird fond of sitting motionless for prolonged periods…

You come across passages like this time and again in Thoreau's *Journals*[2], which are essential reading for any budding naturalist. The prose-rhythm, the close quality of observation, the tonal shift, the elliptical concluding comment in Bill's diary entry are all thoroughly and delightfully Thoreauvian. We might also pick up here on the implied duty the final sentence places on the naturalist and would-be nature writer – for like the cock bullfinch, these poor mere humans must perforce be 'fond of sitting motionless for prolonged periods' – and thus emphasize a presiding characteristic of Bill's writings: one that has slipped away from the work of popular exponents of the genre in the years since his death.

Attentiveness.

Once you become alert to the significance of this crucial quality the exemplary nature of Bill's work, its wholehearted absorption in the natural scene, its complete lack of ego and posturing, emerges ever more clearly into view.

---

[2] The NYRB Classics selection, edited by Damion Searls and introduced by John R. Stilgoe, is the best popular selection from these – a crucial naturalist's bedside book.

Before moving to consideration of Bill as nature-writer, where the latter point will come up again, I want to give you an impression of the young Bill Condry from the fine autobiography[3] of a remarkable woman, the writer and mountain guide Gwen Moffat. She encountered Bill just after the war when Penny was youth hostel warden of Cae Dafydd at the foot of Nantmor:

> Bill was an enthusiastic ornithologist; walks with him were sheer delight. He seemed to know where nests were by instinct. Birds had just been birds [to me] before, although I knew a curlew now and coloured ones like woodpeckers, but most of the others were little brown birds, or big brown ones, just flashes across the landscape. Now I started to distinguish between them, to see shades of colour and observe behaviour. A whole new world was opening before me.

So it is with the great teachers – they show you how to use your senses, and reinforce the truth of Thoreau's great precept that 'It is not what you look at, but what you see'.

I hope you'll gain an impression through the selections from Bill's writings contained in this book of how fortuitous it was to be young and alive and in Wales during the 1940s and 1950s – the time in which the young teacher of classics and his new wife (Bill and Penny were married 'on a day of perfect April sunlight' at the Registry Office in Pwllheli in 1946), with her intense botanical interest and knowledge, became a part of the cultural landscape of our jewelled country. This was the time also in which Bill's life took up the second of those threads mentioned above, and in following it he found the vocation through which he will endure in the appreciation of those who want to know about the wild places of Wales of which he's the finest celebrant

---

[3] *Space Below My Feet* (Hodder & Stoughton, 1961).

in their every aspect. It was in this period that he became a writer – the pre-eminent writer on the natural history of Wales.

We have followed him briefly through that necessary apprenticeship to subject which the current 'Program Era'[4] creative writing creed would hold to be inessential (believing that 'finding your voice', however imitative and uninformed that may be, is of far greater importance than mere knowledge-in-depth of what you're writing about – a very attractive proposition to seekers-of-fame with inflated senses of entitlement); but without which writing on nature, or anything much else besides, is inevitably derivative and nugatory. In doing so, perhaps echoes have begun to sound in your mind, chiming with your knowledge of how other major naturalist-writers came to their subject?

Is not Bill Condry's post-Great War Harborne a version of Richard Jefferies' Coate Farm on the outskirts of rapidly-expanding Victorian Swindon? Are not his experiences with Harold Wright of hearing woodlarks on the Clent Hills, or warblers in the Shropshire countryside, or watching sparrowhawks nest in Ell Wood near Stourbridge, like themes re-visited from the magnificent early volumes of that war-damaged man and great writer Henry Williamson's monumental novel-cycle, *A Chronicle of Ancient Sunlight*, where he too describes youthful journeys out from urban, London-fringe Bromley into the Weald of Kent to seek the life and heart of the wild?

Bill belongs firmly within a great tradition of English nature writing, which he acknowledges and to which he refers throughout his own work. If he were alive today, he would

---

[4] See Mark McGurl's *The Program Era and the Rise of Creative Writing* (Harvard, 2009) for a partisan view of this modern cultural-industry phenomenon, which has now notably subsumed nature writing – to the latter's benefit in terms of commercial promotion rather than any enhancement of quality, originality and achievement.

recognize kinship with its modern masters – Mark Cocker, Jim Crumley, Paul Evans: *real* rather than 'New' nature writers, time-served craftsmen of the genre rather than dilettantes and ivy-tower excursionists – as surely as he pays tribute to those in whose debt he stood: Gilbert White, Thoreau, George Borrow, Richard Jefferies, W.H. Hudson, Henry Williamson:

> In the library I found another book that entranced me: *Bevis: the story of a boy* by Richard Jefferies. Bevis was a country lad (Jefferies as a child in fact) who revelled in simple, rural pastimes that appealed to me far more than the usual boys' adventure stories. At ten years of age I felt very close to Bevis though the book had been written nearly fifty years before. Not many years later I was to soak up all that Jefferies ever wrote about nature and the countryside.

Or again, he writes of his last family holiday in the anxious summer of 1939, before the Second World War, in the early part of which his mother died. They went to Croyde in north Devon, camped in Braunton Burrows which is the setting of Henry Williamson's early masterpiece (and concluding part of 'The Flax of Dream' novel-tetralogy), *The Pathway*:

> For me that north Devon holiday was partly redeemed by finding myself in well-known territory. This was 'the country of the two rivers' (Taw and Torridge) with which I was thoroughly familiar through reading *Tarka the Otter* and other stories by Henry Williamson to whose writing I was then devoted. The Richard Jefferies of his generation, Williamson was second only to Jefferies in helping to create that popular sympathy for wildlife which after the war was to lead to the nature conservation movement that is still growing in strength. Other memories of Croyde are of walking out to the end of Baggy Point, a windswept, wave-

lashed, raven-croaking headland; and of wandering among the plant-rich dunes of Braunton Burrows.

There are two points to be made here. Firstly, in Jefferies and Williamson, Bill has unerringly chosen the two supreme prose masters in the English nature-writing canon. There is a lyricism, a fecundity, a density, a vast store of first-hand experience and an easy familiarity of observation in their work that no other English writers on nature (with the possible exception of W.H. Hudson) had attained. These qualities, combined with Thoreau's example of how to meld a stringent social and philosophical outlook with the same traits, give a clear lead into appreciation of the quality and authenticity, the freshness and urgency of Bill Condry's writing.

My second point is on Bill's character. Not only was he an excellent field naturalist, renowned as one of the best all-rounders of his generation; he was also a good reader and critic, as you'll see particularly from his essays here on Thoreau and George Borrow, which home in so precisely on their defining qualities – the exemplary nature of Thoreau's project; the merrily fictive, proto-Sebaldian element in Borrow's writing that the Victorian age had somehow managed to miss. More than that, Bill was a forbearing and compassionate judge of literature, unafraid to challenge contemporary animus or to live outside the stockade[5] of unthinking, jingoistic, conformist response. In the assessment of Henry Williamson given above

---

[5] This phrase, 'outside the stockade', that I've also used as sub-title to the present introduction, comes from a postcard Bill sent me as the first contact between us. I had written an article berating the National Trust for leasing to a subsidiary of the MoD a stretch of coastline recently bought by public subscription. The backlash from this was vicious. Out of the blue came Bill's postcard: 'You have chosen to live your life outside the stockade. It is not always an easy place, but it is the only place to be.' I still feel intense gratitude for Bill's intuitive act of kindness.

he was espousing what had become a very unpopular cause. Williamson's sentimental flirtation with Hitler's Germany, his association with Oswald Mosley's British Union of Fascists, allied to certain unwise remarks and dedications, had given him pariah status in the eyes of the British literary mob, instead of the understanding and serious critical attention that was this major writer's due.

From my conversations with him, it's evident that Bill saw through what might be considered as Williamson's obtuse and wrong-headed behaviour to its unpolluted source in his presence at the Christmas Day Truce of 1914. Unlike the vast majority of his critics Williamson had lived through an entire war, in the first days of which he had enlisted and in the course of which he was twice seriously wounded. That camaraderie, those gifts exchanged in no-man's-land between the trenches, gave Williamson a hieratic belief in the brotherhood and not the enmity of man. However misguidedly he may have interpreted this at times, it is one of the tragedies of twentieth-century culture that animus came so fiercely to be directed against him, driving him and his work into a defensive insularity which affected its later quality and from which only flashes of the former genius gleamed. Of all this, Bill – despite his own pacifism, which might have resulted in a moderation of sympathy – was keenly aware. He did not allow received opinion and ignorant calumny to shift him an inch from a true estimate of Williamson's stature as a nature writer. (An intriguing greatness, incidentally, across which the shadows and patterns of war and other forms of debased human conduct fall in darkest projection. I can scarcely bear to read *Tarka* these days, masterpiece though it is and one that I've known for sixty years, for just this reason. Psychologically, there is as much of the war-book as the nature-book in it – a view in which Bill concurred.)

We should look cursorily at the two other writers whose presences infuse Bill's work, both of whom have already been mentioned. Gilbert White's *Natural History of Selborne* of 1789 is an enduring classic of our literature, written in the form of letters to the eighteenth century's foremost Welsh naturalist Thomas Pennant, and to Daines Barrington, both of them Fellows of the Royal Society. Bill recognized the formal aspect of White's project and – all too aware himself of the hold taxonomy retained upon the nature-writing genre – wrote about it thus:

> ...in their way his journals are wonderful too. Their cleanly chiselled, staccato utterances stand out from the page and have more force than many of the beautifully turned sentences of other writers. Possibly as he thumbs back through his daily log it may sometimes seem to him that he has merely accumulated a mountain of trivialities. But among them are observations of a new and brilliant kind. For he was looking at nature in a living, dynamic way that was being neglected by the leading scientists who were then preoccupied with classification and were studying mainly dead specimens of plants and animals. Of this difference White was fully aware.

He goes on to comment on how White gives us 'the facts cleanly and frankly without trying to sell them to us in a wrapper of fine writing' (an apposite sally against current fashion in the genre), and continues by thanking him for 'chatting with us so amiably and teaching us so much without for a moment giving the impression that he is trying to teach us anything. And for communicating the delight of finding things out for ourselves. And for so subtly appealing to our sense of wonder about the world of fields, woods, hills, swamps, stars, planets and all the winds that blow.'

Again, we recognize much of Bill himself in this characterization of another. The influence of Richard Jefferies and of Gilbert White upon Bill's work is very obvious in his searching curiosity, his painstaking attention to detail and to behaviour, his capacity for wonderment and surprise. But it's the fourth guest at this intertextual feast who takes the place of honour. As noted above, he's to be found in the crucial sentence which reads as follows:

> As time passes I become ever more convinced that it is in the wild places that we have the best hope of finding such little sanity as survives in the world.

The voice? The gravity? The apophthegmatic style? You cannot escape from it in Bill's writing. It is his constant touchstone. It belongs to the subject of his first book, and it permeates every worthwhile piece of 'nature writing' from 1850 to the present day. It's that of Thoreau, the greatest of all nature writers, of whom Bill wrote the elegant and gracious biography already mentioned as being published in 1954. The sentence I've just quoted is a knowing allusion to, a paraphrase of, the famous one, 'In wildness is the preservation of the world', from Thoreau's posthumously-published essay 'Walking' of 1862. Once you begin to search out the wholly benign and useful influence of Thoreau on Bill's writing, you are mining a very rich seam. And I'll leave you to chase the phantom presences of these four – White, Jefferies, Williamson and above all Thoreau – throughout his work with no further need to comment, because we need now to look at the writing itself.

What might catch your attention as you scan through these representative excerpts? The passion ('I heartily detest...')? The particular prejudices ('...a loathsomeness of conifers') that you may well share? The vivid brief glimpses into the intimate life of nature ('…a long-tailed tit guides a huge white feather into a blackthorn')? The longer descriptive vignettes: '…a dozen curlews come high across the sky. In silence they head out to the estuary and seem to be about to cross over when, dramatically, the flock explodes and each curlew comes yelping earthwards in a wild power-dive, corkscrewing down like a stricken aeroplane, with a violent sound as of tearing feathers. All land simultaneously on the sands, immediately fold away great beaks under their back feathers and stand in silence to wait for the tide'?

Or will you seize on the more subtle textures here? In the first chapter, Jenkins, for example, from the top farm in Cwm Einion, 'a sack pinned at his breast by a four-inch nail' – does he not bear family resemblance to the Iago Prytherch of R.S. Thomas's poetry (and we know that Thomas knew Tom Jenkins from his time as vicar of Eglwysfach)? And what of the extraordinary tone of the piece in which he appears? If 'creative writing' is a term both valid and meaningful, surely it is applicable to this? How about his masterful description of the hen sparrowhawk at her nest (and consider the watchful patience over hours, days and weeks invested here)? Or of the peregrine falcon who 'came flickering off a ledge to chatter with deep, angered notes as she hurled herself about the sky'? What of his dawn vigil for the blackcock lek – 'it was getting dimly light and the wind was cold' – and the moral he draws about the way most would be content to see this ritual: 'We can sit at home and see close-up films of it all on television and hear the wonderful noises that go with it. And both vision and sound may well be clearer than we can experience in the field. But it does not live as it lives in the greyness of dawn.'

There's all the appeal, too, of his sturdily Luddite vein: '…a bit of former wilderness that not even busy-fingered twentieth-

century man has found fit for his use.' There is the fury – Billy
Turner would have approved! – in his reactions to caged birds,
a cooped-up lynx, hooded falcons tethered to blocks of wood[6].
More positively, you'll find here the sly comedy of Bill's trip to
the Coto Doñana in southern Spain with R.S. Thomas, who
unconcernedly raises his binoculars and remarks 'woodchat
shrike!' as he and Bill are being arrested by French military
authorities in Les Landes. The affectionate characterizations –
R.S. Thomas disappearing off into the sand dunes 'like some
Old Testament prophet' – are balanced by exuberant, marvelling
descriptions of the birdlife, of flora, of fauna: as when the family
of wild pigs pass unconcernedly within feet of him. Birds are
vividly depicted too in his African writing – the memorable
strangeness of black herons and their hunting ritual; the bizarre
colony of vulture-like Marabou storks at Kalambo falls. Nearer
to home, you'll find innumerable exact insights into the wildlife
of Wales: squirrels, polecats, ravens, owls. There's his major
essay too – a conservationist *credo* to rank with the work of
Aldo Leopold, and as practically focused, pithily argued, core-
value-infused and finely expressed – on managing the Ynys-hir
nature reserve; and his sense of wonder at a night spent watching
migrants flying through the beams of Enlli lighthouse: 'hours
of dream-like experience'; which is finely balanced with his
night sleeping out on uninhabited Cardigan Island, listening to
'sounds you miss in daytime'.

All this variety and wealth of subject-matter is expressed in
a lucid classical style that is exact, unafraid of apt colloquialisms

---

[6] The latter makes me wonder how he might have viewed the metroliterati's
uninformed adulation for Helen Macdonald's *H is for Hawk*, which may be
many things but a nature book it assuredly is not, as the author herself, to her
credit, freely acknowledges. If you want a clear indication of Bill's views on
the subject of this book, see p. 181

('dimmit light', 'fossicked'), and puts none of the obstacles in the path of comprehension and vital prose-rhythm that are the hallmarks of much recent nature writing, where subject is demoted to a lesser place behind display of the writer's cleverness, register is ill-judged if considered at all, and the strained lexis frequently comes over as that of an academy of constipated lexicographers. Perhaps we should take an amused look now at the currently inescapable 'New Nature' phenomenon and its antecedents?

There's a curious mirroring – though without the intellectual rigour that she observed – of the Victorian autodidact naturalist tradition that Mrs. Gaskell wrote about in recent signs of a cultural yearning for renewal of a close relationship with nature. A question is implied by this for which we have yet to formulate an adequate answer. It runs thus. What measure of compensation can be found in contemporary life for the loss of connection with process and the natural cycle which was woven through the whole human life-fabric in a pre-industrial world, the disappearance of which has left us with a kind of psychic insubstantiality by comparison with those who, in a marvelling and resonant phrase from Barry Lopez, 'radiate the authority of first-hand encounters' (of whom Bill was assuredly one)? It is into the vacuum of that psychic insubstantiality that the 'New Nature' writers make their journeys. The term was first popularized by the publicity department of the publishing company *Granta* and the London literary editors who uncritically regurgitated its press releases. Bearing in mind T.S. Eliot's insights into the vitalizing role of historical precedent, we might be well advised to drop the misconception that this writing is 'new' in the sense of marking a radical departure from the practice and preoccupations of its antecedents. We might also consider that however much contemporary culture may insist on novelty, it is proper and courteous to acknowledge[7] the living influence of what has gone before. Which brings me to consideration of issue 102 (Summer 2008) of the periodical *Granta*, dedicated to *The New Nature Writing*. Jason Cowley's 'Editor's Letter' begins thus:

> When I used to think of nature writing, or indeed the nature writer, I would picture a certain kind of man, and it would always be a man: bearded, badly dressed, ascetic, misanthropic.

So far, so much tosh – and it gets worse:

> He would often be alone on some blasted moor, with a notebook in one hand and binoculars in the other, seeking meaning and purpose through a larger communion with nature: a loner and an outcast.

The crude mockery here, the tokenist genuflection to gender politics (just how tokenist you can establish simply by scanning through his list of contents and authors), the implicit dislike of nature ('some blasted moor'), as well as the narcissistic preoccupation with personal style rather than study of nature, is as discourteous as it is implicitly vain – though it does reflect the frequent substitution of 'Look at me!' stridency for serious and original writing in the field. What makes this mocking little tirade against traditional nature writers rather more disturbing, and perhaps even arrogant, is its author's confessed ignorance of his subject. The only 'nature books' Cowley admits to having read are Lopez's *Arctic Dreams*, Krakauer's *Into the Wild*, and Remarque's *All Quiet on the Western Front*.

---

[7] Participants in current literary discourses might dispute this. But then, they are unafraid of the charge of plagiarism that the more scrupulous within the writing community might level against them, viewing this as a valid tool of *intertextuality* which does not require acknowledgement of source. Careers have been built by those prepared to squirm through this moral loophole.

Puzzle that out for yourselves – and puzzle out too what all this has to do with the kind of luminous, knowledgeable, authentic and evocative accounts of the natural world with which Bill Condry enthralled us for so many decades. Whilst you're doing so, here are some relevant thoughts on the 'new nature writing' (if you thought the term encompassed nothing original you were absolutely right) of sixty years ago from a truly authoritative naturalist and writer on nature, James Fisher[8]. In the third issue of a short-lived eponymous journal that accompanied the 1945 launch of Collins' magisterial publishing project, the *New Naturalist* series, Fisher wrote tersely of the bucolic effusions of his day:

> Others are… by authors whose excessive consciousness of the exquisite nature of their prose, and the distinction conferred on the reader by a peep at their personalities, are so grotesque as to baffle description.

Application of that formula pins many of our current nature writers, with their unwavering commitment to style over substance, firmly to the specimen-board. Fisher again, with perfect rigour that needs intelligent consideration rather than dismissal as merely Gradgrindian:

> Do these people really believe that the search for truth is less important than the search for poetry or art or aesthetic satisfaction or 'happiness'? Do they not understand that the

---

[8] James Fisher (1912-1970) was one of the leading naturalists in the post-war period. He was a founding editor of the Collins *New Naturalist* series to which Bill contributed two important volumes – as did Fisher, whose monograph on *The Fulmar* (1952) is regarded as one of the most detailed and authoritative bird studies ever published: a true classic of the genre. It is also, in that vacuous phrase beloved of the *metroliterati*, book-prize judges and members of readers' groups, 'beautifully written!' Though these latter may not think so, it being rather rigorous.

purest source of these imponderables is in the realms of fact, and that the establishment of facts is most simply done by the ancient methods of logical science? Once facts are despised, fancies replace them; and fancies are poisonous companions to the enjoyment and appreciation of nature.

In the following issue of *The New Naturalist*, another important field naturalist of the day, Brian Vesey-Fitzgerald, gave a salutary description of what is crucial if you wish to be a naturalist. Welsh readers will, I am sure, recognize the following as an excellent working definition of 'dyn neu ferch y filltir sgwâr' ('a man or woman of his or her own square mile'):

...first, the local naturalist must know his country. Knowing a country, even a small area, takes time. It is not a matter of knowing merely the boundaries or the footpaths over fields and through woods. To be a really good local naturalist you must know the geography of your district as well as you know the geography of your own house; not just the paths through the woods, but the woods themselves; not just the paths across fields, but every fold in the ground in every field; not the hedges alone, but the lie of the hedgerows to the compass, their 'set' to the prevailing winds (if you had to live on what you could trap, you would soon realize the supreme importance of that point); the streams and their depths and eddies; the local weather and the local signs foretelling it; and so on and so on. A working knowledge of these things is acquired only slowly and over years, and at the same time the keen local naturalist will be learning the movements of the animals in his district. It is not often, in this country, that one may see a wild animal in person and by chance, but no animal can move over ground without leaving some sign of its passing. Too little attention is paid to such signs in this country. Of course, all these things will not be learnt by any one man in a lifetime (the man interested in spiders will find spiders which would be overlooked by another naturalist, equally observant, but interested in some other animal) but a good all-round working knowledge can be gained with just a little trouble taken.

A good, working *credo* there for all who are interested in natural history, evidence for the practice of which is little apparent between the covers of *Granta* 102. Bill Condry knew that, as Edward Thomas had it, nature writing should not be 'books written about books written about other people's books'. He understood and accepted that the best nature writing has always been founded on two crucial principles – applied knowledge and close, disciplined attention – allied to a willingness to be in the right place at the right time, however uncomfortable that may be and for however long it takes. You see that simple truth borne out time and again in the writings included here:

> I stand in a tree-sheltered spot where the wood meets the marsh, my gumboots in water from the melting snow. In the square mile of rushes and flood pools between the wood and the estuary nothing moves, nothing lives. It is dismal, cold and wet and there is nothing. But I wait. For this is the barn owl's hunting ground where he makes a careful patrol several times a day during winter, though in summer he is so nocturnal. So I wait, expecting every minute to see his white shape come floating lightly over the watery fields. But though I wait long he does not come and I wonder why.
>
> Then I happen to turn round and I find the reason: he is there already, not thirty yards away just inside the wood, staring at me from a branch, a pure white owl on the red branch of a pine.

Though there is literary artistry here (the cumulative effect of that repeated 'I wait'), there is also perfect, graphic simplicity: 'a pure white owl on the red branch of a pine'. There is effortless knowledge: 'he makes a careful patrol several times a day during winter, though in summer he is so nocturnal.' Bill's work is born of deep love and long knowledge. Can you imagine any current popular nature author writing, for example, a book for the *New Naturalist* series?

A single-species monograph, say – the acid test of a total commitment to nature? Robert Macfarlane on the *parasitic jaeger*[9], perhaps? That we are forced to answer 'no' to that proposition tells us how very far the rigour of the real naturalist and the self-indulgence of most popular practitioners of nature and outdoor writing have drifted apart.

Bill produced two very highly regarded volumes for the *New Naturalist* series, and would have added a third[10] had his subject not inconveniently declined to extinction as a breeding species in Wales. He wrote at a time when nature in Britain already faced grave threats from agri-industry, from habitat loss, from shooting. Read through the pieces collected here and you can hear the urgency of his response, and admire his concern and the directness and fearlessness with which he expressed it. Any nature writer worth his or her salt would pick up that challenge and carry on the tradition – as the real and worthwhile writers on nature still do.

I read today on the news of *Birdlife International*'s revised red list of endangered species: lapwing, puffin, curlew, oystercatcher,

---

[9] Otherwise known as the Arctic skua (*Stercorarius parasiticus*) – a sleek seabird of piratical habits.

[10] James Fisher was very keen on the parallel series of *New Naturalist* monographs, which had included notable titles such as Buxton's *The Redstart*, Nethersole-Thompson's *The Greenshank*, and his own study of fulmars. Bill had kept extensive notebooks on the woodlark, and I have little doubt that, had circumstances proved fortunate, he would have added another title of distinction to this series.

turtle dove, meadow pipit, kingfisher (be grateful for how faithfully Bill's writing recorded most of these!) So many species lost, and still we witness decline. Read through this book and marvel at how rich a natural environment Bill and Penny Condry knew in post-war Wales. Consider how, both directly by exhortation and implicitly in the celebration of natural beauty throughout his work, Bill urged us into appreciation and defence of the land and all that lives upon it.

> We moved [to Glygyrog Ddu] in March, 1950, on a day when green woodpeckers were bursting with laughter, wailing buzzards plunged and climbed about the sky, pied wagtails chased along the roof-ridge, the year's first wheatear stood brilliant on a sunlit rock and, like a talisman, a woodlark sang his perfect notes standing on our gate post... we were young... We lived mostly out of doors, making a garden, looking after two hives of bees; and we were as contented as Thoreau by Walden Pond. And like Thoreau in his retreat we had many visitors. They made their way up through the steep oakwoods and some of them brought new friendships which have lasted all the years since.

I am glad and proud to have been able to count this principled, good and gifted man as friend. Books apart, his life, and the way he led it, was his achievement. Thoreau would, surely, have regarded him as a friend. Now you, as a new generation of his readers, have the opportunity to grow into such a friendship with Bill and Penny Condry. They will bring you back to the living heart of the matter, to knowledge and to love of nature. I hope that in reading through this book you will come to the same estimate of Bill that I have done; and that you find delight and joy in his writing, which gives the natural world his attentive, honest praise. And that you too, in your turn, like the 'younger scribe' who visited E.H.T. Bible on the banks of the Dyfi, will be ready to make every effort you can to preserve the land, and support the causes that he held most dear. This book has been a project long-harboured, its compilation a labour of love. I offer it to you, his new readers, with these hopes.

Ariege, May 30 – June 4 2015

A NOTE ON THE TEXTS:

In selecting these I have worked on the principle that the last text revised in an author's lifetime is authoritative. The dates given in brackets after each excerpt therefore refer to date of publication of these, and not necessarily to date of composition or first publication. It should be remembered, too, that many of Bill's shorter pieces appeared in *The Manchester Guardian*, *The Guardian* and *Guardian Weekly* at a time when their sub-editorial practices were notoriously quixotic (and its copy-takers – remember those? – often hard of hearing, to put it kindly). It was entirely necessary, therefore, to use where possible the versions Bill had had the chance to revise and correct. To find the books and periodicals – most of them out of print and increasingly hard to obtain – from which these are taken, simply cross-check dates with those of publication of titles in the bibliography. Some of these titles I have not extracted from (*The World of a Mountain*, *Woodlands*, The National Trust *Wales*). No dismissal is intended by this – it was merely that they did not contain excerptable material relevant to my purpose here. All footnotes and italicized passages between excerpts are by the editor.

PART ONE

Exploring Westwards

KINDNESS ON THE WAY TO PUMLUMON

What a debt we youngsters of the thirties owed to the Youth Hostels Association (founded 1930)! Without those cheap and simple hostels we could never have got round the countryside so easily by foot and cycle. We stayed at many a hostel from Shrewsbury to the coast of Cardigan Bay but our favourite was always one near Llanidloes at the hamlet of Y Fan which in those days was known universally as 'Van', a place famous in the annals as the site of one of the richest lead mines in Wales.

Here in the late 1930s, years after the mine had closed, the youth hostel occupied what had been the mine-manager's house. What made it so dear to us hostellers was the warden, Elizabeth Jones, a golden-hearted Welsh lady famous far and wide for the way she mothered us all (in sharp contrast with one or two other female wardens elsewhere who were notorious termagants). Elizabeth Jones, a native of Abersoch near Pwllheli, had come to Van because her late husband, a miner, had found work there. She clearly loved being a warden and if she broke the hostel rules, as she did most of the time, she could always plead she did not understand them because her grasp of English was not very strong. So she ignored the rules, we ignored the rules and everyone was happy, except the officials who occasionally turned up on tours of inspection and who sometimes expressed their horror at the lax way the place was run. But what could they do? Even they could see that nothing would ever change Mrs Jones who couldn't read or remember the regulations, yet was an outstandingly successful warden.

Exploring the Plynlimon (Pumlumon) country from Van hostel (I was usually with Harold Wright or Ray Perry) we soon got to know the many old lead mines whose ruins year after year were nesting places for kestrels, barn owls, stock doves, redstarts and pied and grey wagtails. Once we found a huge, completely inaccessible raven's nest balanced improbably on top of a high wall. Then as time went on we felt curious about the whole long saga of lead-mining. In the villages we inquired round for ex-miners but found they had mostly gone underground for ever, long before their time, as we could see from the dates on many a gravestone. The lead-mining communities, we learned, had been decimated by tuberculosis and their descendants were still not free of it.

Today some of the lead mines survive as crumbling walls and grey vomits of poisoned earth. But the Van mine, when I knew it in the late 1930s, though its underground workings were all flooded, was virtually intact above ground, its buildings in fair condition. The whole site, where a thousand men had once worked, was wrapped in a ghost town atmosphere and one day I had a truly moving experience. I remember getting a key off somebody, going into what had been the mine-manager's office and finding still on his desk a ledger recording the last consignment of lead ever to leave Van mine in, I think, about 1921. For eighteen years or so that ledger had lain ready on the desk as if the mine had closed for a holiday instead of forever. And there I was reading that final entry and feeling I ought to draw a line across the page and write: 'Here ended the famous Van mine which brought much wealth to a few and great misery to many'.

Sheltering Van youth hostel from the westerly gales there was at that time a long row of tall old Corsican pines which gave a distinctive personality to the house. Through their branches the wind sighed or roared, a lovely sound to listen to from the open windows of the dormitory at night. Tawny owls often perched in them, hooting and shrieking; and now and then there was a rarer voice, the moaning cry of a long-eared owl which was sometimes answered by others farther up the valley. This rare owl we longed to see as well as hear and in its pursuit we went on long walks towards the moorlands of Plynlimon[1] by way of the Clywedog valley which was not yet drowned by the reservoir of today. It was on the whole a treeless district and we guessed that the long-eared owls must be living in the widely scattered squares or lines of conifers planted as windbreaks to shelter the sheep on draughty hillsides. Eventually, after a huge amount of foot-slogging, we learned to spot these owls high up in the trees, their bodies pressed against the trunk and drawn up grotesquely tall and thin to make them seem like a swelling on the bark. We also saw them fly from nests which were not of their making but were the old tenements of carrion crows.

From Van the next youth hostel westwards was thirteen crow-flight miles away at Ponterwyd and we got into the habit of walking there over the top of Plynlimon which for several years became our favourite mountain. We enjoyed reaching the summit cairns where the Bronze Age had buried its notables. From up there we saw that huge panorama south to the Beacons, north to Snowdon, east to where we told ourselves we could make out the Clent Hills, and west across the sea to Bardsey. We paid our respects to the sources of the rivers of which Plynlimon is the famous mother – Wye, Severn and Rheidol.

---

[1] The old, Anglicized version of Pumlumon, and the one generally used by Bill Condry.

We splashed across the marshes and climbed the cliffs, getting to know more and more about ravens, peregrines, wheatears, skylarks, golden plovers and ring ouzels. We swore, though not too seriously, that one day we would write a ten-volume monograph about meadow pipits. For of all the upland birds it was these lively little pipits that we came upon everywhere we went, their tinkling songs falling from the sky to emphasize the quietness of the empty hills. (No low-flying military jets in those happy times.)

In the high peatbogs we searched for flint arrowheads dropped by Bronze Age hunters, for many have been found up there. But all we ever picked up was a modern penny which we pushed down into the peat in the hope that someone would find it a thousand years hence. Sometimes we went down into the moorland valleys where we found lonely shepherds' houses (all had long been abandoned to the barn owls) and many pathetic cottage remains which spoke of days when a scattered community, forced into the uplands by poverty, had struggled for existence in a world of hostile climate and unkind soils.

These old Plynlimon houses, some semi-abandoned, some totally deserted, some already ruinating, became a part of our lives: Blaen Hafren, Hore, Hengwm Annedd, Lluest Newydd, Nant-y-llyn, Maes-nant, Drosgol, Llechwedd Mawr, Lluest-y-rhos, Hyddgen. The few that were still roofed we used occasionally for shelter. Once at semi-ruined Hore I climbed part-way into the space between the bedroom ceiling and the roof and found it full of grown-up young barn owls and their two parents. Seeing my head and shoulders suddenly appear they fluttered about the loft like great white moths until they escaped by scuttling over my bowed head. It was a strange experience to have a whole flock of owls running over my head and down my back to freedom.

One April evening I went off alone to Plynlimon with my

bicycle and my sleeping bag. I followed the rough winding track up the Rheidol river from Ponterwyd to Nant-y-moch which was then the highest inhabited farm in the valley and lived in by two bachelor brothers called James who were reputed to have sold their skulls to a museum (to be collected at a later date!) because these skulls were thought by anthropologists to have a peculiarly primitive shape dating back to the very earliest people known to have lived in these uplands[2]. My visit took place long years before Nant-y-moch house was demolished to make way for the present reservoir and before the very rough track had been turned into the tourist road of today.

I rode or carried my bike as high up the mountain as I could and then went on without it. In those days the most exciting bird in my life was the peregrine and my aim was to sleep as close to a pair of peregrines as I could (without disturbing them) for the pleasure of sharing the dawn with them. It was nearly dark when I reached their crag and there was no sign of them as I unrolled my sleeping bag on a wide ledge about thirty feet directly under the nest.

The next day came in calm, cold and cloudless and I watched the cliff slowly take shape above me. There was complete quietness except for the distant murmur of water amongst rocks. Then from higher up the corrie the piping notes of a ring ouzel came faintly out of the near darkness. It was still dimmit-light when the peregrines awoke; and for the next ten minutes I listened to their dawn duet. This was a softly uttered, tremulous series of beautiful notes which conveyed a sense of suppressed excitement. Or maybe I was the one who was excited, for it was a wonderful sound to hear in that wild place. Then I suppose one of the peregrines must have gone off hunting, for there was silence

---

[2] Perhaps not such a far-fetched idea after all – see the paper on 'The Fine-scale genetic structure of the British population' in *Nature* (19th March, 2015).

again except for the ring ouzel still bringing in the dawn; and the spluttering notes of a wheatear just below me. As I made my way down to collect my bicycle I heard no more of the peregrines. But it had been a dawn to remember more vividly than perhaps any dawn before or since.

Another Plynlimon memory is of a wild autumn night when darkness had overtaken me miles up into the moors. Sheets of heavy rain were sweeping across and volleys of thunder were echoing round the hills. I had had a punishing day and crept exhausted into the long-abandoned but still roofed house at Hengwm Annedd. By a mercy I found on the hearth enough dry jackdaw-provided sticks to make a fire and sat a long time in front of it, happily making toast and wondering about those who had lived or tried to live in that lonely place. Then I slept till daybreak.

I can't leave those pre-war Plynlimon days without a thought about the Clywedog Reservoir that lies along the mountain road between Llanidloes and Machynlleth. Overlooking the reservoir there is a spacious car-park, picnic site and viewpoint above the narrow, winding lake. Yet though spectacular it is not a scene I can admire because as I look down on that deep reservoir I see only the valley it destroyed – a tranquil, totally unspoilt, almost unknown gorge with the lovely Clywedog stream hastening over its rocks and vanishing down through woodlands on its way to join the Severn.

It is not merely this reservoir that I dislike. I see no real beauty in any man-drowned valleys however essential they are to industrialization and to cities far away. I heartily detest Brianne in Carmarthenshire, especially as it has a loathsomeness of conifers around it. For the same reason I never rejoice at Vyrnwy (Llyn Efyrnwy). Nor have I ever loved those waters under which the City of Birmingham drowned the beautiful Elan valley. And I understand something of the feelings of those Welsh patriots who still feel so bitter about the City of Liverpool's reservoir in the Tryweryn valley near Y Bala where a small Welsh community was evicted. If we could get access to all the schemes that lie in planners' desks, how many other valleys would we find earmarked as possible reservoir sites?

(1995)

CHERRY BLOSSOM IN TIME OF THE BREAKING OF NATIONS

One of my happier wartime memories is linked back to my schooldays when as a prize I was given a copy of Housman's *A Shropshire Lad*. I took to Housman immediately and soon I could, and still can, recite from memory many of his lines, especially those referring to places Harold [Wright] and I had cycled to: Knighton, Shrewsbury, Uricon, Wenlock, Wrekin, Bredon, Ludlow, Clee, Buildwas and Wyre; and those 'streams too broad for leaping': Severn, Teme, Clun, Onny and Corve.

Years later, when war was raging, there came a day like a shaft of sunlight in a stormy sky. On a perfect spring morning I took that delightful train that used to chug slowly from the Severn at Bewdley up between 'the wild green hills of Wyre' to Cleobury Mortimer where it came clear of the forest to run through a land of cherry orchards which that day were all in perfection of white blossom. Everyone knows Housman's cherries: 'Loveliest of trees the cherry now is hung with bloom along the bough'; and on that train journey over and down to Tenbury Wells and Woofferton *A Shropshire Lad* came poignantly back into my mind, especially when I saw woodlands being clear-felled for the purposes of war and I found myself reciting:

Give me a land of boughs in leaf
A land of trees that stand:
Where trees are fallen there is grief;
I love no leafless land.

(1995)

UP THE CLYWEDOG

An altogether blue, cloud-sailing, beckoning April morning as I go off to revisit an old haunt – the stretch of country that shelters to the east of Plynlimon. Leaving my car at Llanidloes where two rivers meet, I walk not up the Severn which is the natural and ancient pathway to the west, but up the deep and wooded valley of the Clywedog which, like the Severn, has its source on Plynlimon. Everywhere the delights of the upland spring: shining, green river pools, leafing hazels, sunlight shafting deep and bright into leafless oakwoods, dippers singing on midstream rocks, a glistening white plume of black-headed gulls streaming behind a tractor ploughing down an impossible slope on a far hill.

The valley narrows. Steep, unploughable, rock-broken slopes close in on me. Abruptly the trees become sparse. I come to a long-abandoned lead mine and watch a hen wheatear carrying straws into its ruined walls. A long-tailed tit steers a huge white feather into a blackthorn. I wade the river and clamber steeply to a lofty hill-fort that looks far down the valley. For a while I try to trace its banks and entrenchments; then I sit and rest and look about me and think of time and eternity, two good themes when you have far views of mountains and valleys, the sun is warm on the grass, a singing woodlark circles above you and you are sitting on man-made banks that are still good banks after two thousand years. How many generations have climbed that hill, wondered at the purpose of those banks and speculated about the meaning and brevity of life?

I return to the river and go on up its narrow V-shaped valley to where it makes a sharp bend. I eat my lunch looking into a deep, clear pool under a rock where a great trout swims tamely round and round. Carefully I flick him bits of food but he spits them all out quicker than he takes them. Wishing him long life (but doubting if so unwary a fish would achieve it) I now leave the Clywedog, for it is edging me too far north. I take to a rough, climbing road that looks as if it ends at the grey stone farmhouse I can see ahead of me. But like many Welsh farm roads, this one winds through a dog-yapping yard between the buildings and the house and goes on its way towards the uplands.

The next hill is crowned with a long, narrow wind-break of storm-battered pines whose tops all curve sharply away from the south-west. Chaffinches sing in the mountain wind, a hare runs from under my feet, a kestrel slips quickly out of a pine and away round a curve of the hill. In the tree-tops are several old crows' nests wonderfully surviving the gales of past winters. Wondering if the kestrel is using one of these old nests I make my way through the trees. But the bird that at last flies out of one of them is no sharp-winged, red slip of a kestrel but a long-winged, grey, blundering moth of a bird that drops clumsily almost to the grass, flies along the ground and rises sharply to a perch in the top of a pine thirty yards away. She is a long-eared owl, a rare bird of isolated strips and blocks of conifers in parts of the Welsh uplands.

I follow the line of the trees. The whole billowing length of Plynlimon is now close before me; and below me is the last of the upper Severn valley. How changed all that place is since I first knew it years ago! The hollow below me in those days was a great saucer of wet and rushy moorland which had just been planted with infant conifers. I had walked through the long grass there and by chance a short-eared owl had sprung off her nest at my feet. I still have a vivid memory of her as she rose into the sky, then floated away on long, pale wings, an almost invisible bird against the bleached grass of the hills. Today that whole country is deep in trees. All the landmarks have gone; rocks, roads, even houses, swallowed into a heavy pelage of spruces whose dark horizon now reaches almost to the ridges of Plynlimon.

(1958)

'YOU'LL GET TO THE TOP NEXT TIME...'

Close to the dour slate town of Blaenau at the head of the Vale of Ffestiniog you see a shapely dome called Manod Mawr. An altogether beautiful mountain but for me fraught with such special obstacles that I have never managed to get quite to the top. It is the same with several of these Snowdonia peaks whose lower rocks especially are a rich mixture of sedimentaries and volcanics. They are not high these hills, they face you with not even a hint of a climbing problem. It is just that if you are anything of a naturalist they stop you at the first cliff face you come to along their lower skirts. You begin to see interesting plants bristling along the ledges or poking shyly out of crevices. Perhaps nothing more than roseroot, green spleenwort or hairy rock-cress. But these are significant plants. Choosy. They don't grow on any old rock. They whisper that you may be getting on to some good lime-rich rock and that rarer plants could lie ahead.

Of course the chances are that you will find very little, that you will simply be led on in hope. And on and further on, searching patiently and quite happily at a crawling pace round the mountain's hem instead of making headway towards the summit. So the hours pass and at the end you've probably discovered nothing of any consequence. Never mind. You've been contented in that sweet-smelling place up there in the mountain wind. And you'll get to the top next time...

(*1975*)

ACROSS THE RHINOGYDD

'In this vicinity are found *Asplenium lanceolatum*.' So, with a quaint disregard for grammar, Nicholson's *Cambrian Traveller's Guide* of 1840 reported on the coast of Merioneth. Those were the days when a guidebook hardly dared to ignore the ferns, for fern-collecting was one of the fashionable things to do.

One bright morning along the coast road between Barmouth and Harlech, I remembered Nicholson's words. Did this rare spleenwort still thrive there, I wondered, or had those ruthless collectors cleaned it up as they had cleaned up other rarities? (Try to find holly fern in Snowdonia and you will see what I mean.) My pocket guide to plants told me that lanceolate spleenwort grew 'usually near the sea and with a curious predilection for old mine shafts'. I looked up at the nearby hills and remembered many abandoned mines I had seen on former visits. I took an inviting little road that wound crookedly uphill between walls, and soon I was at the old mines, in a world of gorse and short turf with far views across the bluest of seas.

For an hour or more I fossicked around crumbling walls and spoil heaps and peered into the cold damp entrances of levels. There were many kinds of ferns but not the one I sought for and at last I tired of the search. Further up the slope a ring ouzel began to pipe. Straightening my back to listen, I looked away to the hills and the cause of fern-hunting was lost: the high jagged summits of the Rhinogydd gleaming in the sun were altogether too compelling.

I moved inland across a great grassy slope and passed through an oakwood full of the soft green light that comes only through the leaves of spring. The month was May and many pied flycatchers were singing or already feeding young; I know no more delightful place at that season than a Welsh hillside oakwood, and no more delightful birds than the sweet-voiced, confiding pied flycatchers that are so numerous in these trees along the skirts of the Rhinogydd.

Then I was clear of woodland, and round a swelling hill I looked into a wide, quiet vale that narrowed towards the hills. This valley of the Nantcol is perhaps the best of all approaches to the Rhinogydd for it takes you so directly and easily to where tall rocky ramparts enclose you, those of Rhinog Fawr on your left, of Rhinog Fach on your right. You exchange greenness and fertility for naked stone. There are square miles of shattered grey rocks, many of vast size, sticking up out of the heather; other rocks remain firmly secured to the earth's skeleton – the great shelves, terraces and cliffs that look at each other high above the cwm.

There is a narrow path to lead you up through the Pass of Ardudwy (the curse of the mountain gods on whoever tries to turn it into a motorable road!), but if you want to reach the heights you have to strike off, up through the wonderful tangle of bracken, heather and block scree that makes this the most intractable stretch of country in Wales.

So I took the clambering way up Rhinog, often waist-deep in heather and very gingerly setting one foot before the other for fear of dropping into hidden clefts. At last I was helped by a sheep track, or a goat track, for occasionally you see fine feral goats outlined like ibexes on these rocky skylines. So I came up to the highest bastions of the hills. The bracken had failed far below, the three kinds of heather were triumphant and there was a little bright-green parsley fern, and the sea, which I had lost by descending into Nantcol, now reappeared several miles further off than before. I came to more long-deserted manganese mines, their cool mouths green with long pendulous ferns, their depths delicious with the drip and trickle of water. But only common ferns grow there, and that quickly insinuating little plant, the New Zealand willow herb, now so at home on the mountains.

The broken face of Rhinog Fach was now intimately above me to the east, its feet going out of sight behind a nearer ridge. To that ridge there was an easy way, but as the day was still young I went the plant-seeker's way, the way of broken cliff and sphagnum bog. I was too early in the year for many upland plants. In the fullness of summer this is good country for lesser twayblades growing on the bog moss under the heather; but you have to go pretty well nose to the ground to spot those tiny orchids.

I came circuitously up to the ridge, up into colder air, and looked down a wild chaos of rocks to the silvery waters of the tarn called Llyn Hywel. I remembered what Thomas Pennant had said of this lake in the eighteenth century, that in it dwelt 'a race of trouts with most deformed heads, flatted and toad-shaped' and that he had seen them. If so, he was luckier than I, for as I looked a sudden breeze troubled the lake and its depths became invisible. I sat and thought of similar tales of malformed fish in other lakes and wondered why our ancestors were so fascinated by the idea of fish that were strange, misshapen and one-eyed.

A wild whistling sounded up the slope, *wheeoo, wheeoo, wheeoo*, penetrating, shrill, rather wigeon-like. But this was no cry of a bird but of a mountain shepherd, and I soon saw him outlined on the skyline. Several hundred feet higher still, near the top of Rhinog Fach, his two dogs were racing through the rocks and a long line of sheep was moving down. I went up to where he stood. We spoke of upland things, of sheep and lambing and goats. He liked to see the goats, he said. They did not increase, and there were just enough of them to keep some of the most dangerous ledges clear of plants that might otherwise tempt the less agile sheep to their death. He spoke of the numerous mountain foxes and their ways; and of the animal he called *bele* (Welsh for pine marten). He knew it was said to be there but in 30 years he had never glimpsed one and could only conclude that it was exceeding rare and strictly nocturnal.

A little more climbing and I was on the high saddle that links Rhinog Fach with the high grassy dome called Llethr. Now east Wales was before me: beyond the wide Trawsfynydd moors I looked across to the twin peaks of Arennig, and the Arans further to the right, then the wooded vale of Ganllwyd and Cader Idris in the south. I picked a northward way along the rough eastern flank of Rhinog Fach, and went on west through the mountains by the gap called Bwlch Tyddiad. From there it was easy, for from there the Roman Steps descend and you can run freely down nearly two miles of splendid medieval staircase towards Cwmbychan lake.

Hours later, after more deviations in pursuit of bird and plant, I came down to the main coast road. As I descended the last steep lane my eye registered a fern in the wayside wall. But now I was feeling tired and hollow and I had gone on 40 yards before my mind caught up with my eye. I stopped. Surely there had been something a little different about that fern. I felt compelled to go back and bend and examine. And there it was, one, no two, no, a whole row of glossy green plants of the fern I had sought that morning. I went home rejoicing that after a century and a quarter we can still say with Emilius Nicholson: 'In this vicinity are found *Asplenium lanceolatum*'.

(1965)

JUPITER BRIGHT OVER HEBOG

The sun had gone down into a bank of cloud between Llŷn and Anglesey and it was already dusking before I reached the top of Hebog. The lights were showing in Beddgelert but there was still enough daylight to see Llyn Dinas and Siabod standing high and dim beyond. Snowdon, Crib Goch and Lliwedd were still clear and in front of them Yr Aran, sharper-pointed even than Snowdon. In the valley to the north Llyn y Gadair was a pale gleam in the shadows and I could just make out Llyn y Dywarchen and the great rock that stands up in it. I thought of Giraldus and his party going along the valley in 1188 and turning aside to see the wonder of Dywarchen's floating island, which was a large slab of peat that had detached itself from the margin of the lake. I thought of the astronomer Halley swimming out to this unsubstantial island in 1698 to satisfy himself that it really did float. And I thought of Pennant and all his successors dutifully making their way there too in the following centuries, to see this by then diminishing marvel which has now quite gone. Turning south I watched Cader Idris, then Rhinog, disappear into the night. But now Moelwyn and Cnicht had cleared and were catching a last pale light, enough for me to see something of the way I intended to go next day.

All round the west and north the sky was aflame with the setting sun. Holyhead stood up in blackness and there was peak after little peak all along Llŷn, only their tips visible, poking out of the mist. But Cardigan Bay was clearer: I could see the lights of the houses at Abersoch; the little St. Tudwal's Islands, one beyond the other; and, like a full stop at the end of Llŷn, the hump of Bardsey. I thought of the birdwatchers in the observatory there and hoped they were recording more birds than I was seeing on Hebog. Bardsey light is not visible from Hebog but South Stack and Skerries were flashing in the north-west off Anglesey. Beyond them, beyond all Anglesey and Llŷn, and beyond the sea, lay many undulating miles of the Irish mountains cut out black under a bright crimson belt of sky. I sat so long in the warm dusk at the top of Hebog that it was already dark and starlit as I made my way down the west side; yet it is surprising how much light the pale grass holds and all the way down I could see the difference between dark rushes, light grass and palely gleaming rocks. I unrolled my sleeping bag by a murmuring stream and went to sleep looking at Jupiter bright over Hebog and thinking of the botanist J. Lloyd Williams who, when a young schoolmaster here years ago, found the Killarney fern, Snowdonia's rarest species, along one of the streams on this side of Hebog. It has not been seen since because the precise locality was never recorded; but it probably grows there still in the spray and shade behind some little waterfall[3].

Early next morning I made my way by road to Llanfrothen, for the direct route into the heat of Moelwyn is by the road up Cwm Croesor under the steep south side of Cnicht.

It is a rough road but a straight one that takes you boldly up the valleyside to Croesor quarry. The road is still in use by lorries because although no slate has been worked here since about the 1930s, the mine's spacious underground cathedrals are thought a safe place for storing explosives. I arrived in time to see a little engine and a train of wagons disappear into the mountain, its muffled sound getting less and less until I could hear nothing. I looked at the ferns that have made free use of the lime-mortared walls of the quarry buildings here. There were ten species in a few yards either in the wall or on the bank below it: bladder fern, polypody, hartstongue, common spleenwort, parsley fern,

---

[3] It does indeed. Both Bill and myself were taken to see it by the botanist Dewi Jones of Penygroes in the 1990s, after he had re-discovered it in a very discreet location above Cwm Pennant.

male fern, broad buckler, hard fern, mountain fern and lady fern, and I expect wall rue and rusty back could have been found not far away. High above the quarry the usually dark north-east-looking cliffs of Moelwyn Mawr were bright in the morning sun, but in an hour they would be back in the shadows which they and their plants experience most of the time. The gullies up there have been gouged out of fairly lime-rich rock and have some interesting calcicole plants. But as I had botanized there a few months before, I now turned my back on Moelwyn Mawr and followed the small cliffs round the head of Cwm Croesor. I have never had time to search these cliffs, always being bound elsewhere, but they bristle with rose-root; and as rose-root is often the first step to something good, there may be quite a variety of species on those ledges.

From there it is only a few hundred yards across wet moorland and ice-smoothed rocks to the desolation of abandoned quarries at the head of Cwmorthin. This was a very lonely and beautiful place in the eighteenth century. Out of all the wonderful and wild places Pennant saw in his travels, he singled out Cwmorthin as especially sequestered. The nineteenth century changed all that when man made his violent intrusion. For many years the slate veins were followed deep inside Moelwyn Mawr and Moel yr Hydd. Enormous tips of slate-waste were spewed out onto the slopes below the mine-levels. Everywhere were men, railways, engines, buildings, dams, reservoirs and turning machinery.

Now it is all long finished. I looked down to where, below and beyond the tips, long roofless buildings and shattered single walls stood silent in the soft autumn sunlight. I walked down to the ruins. It was like discovering the remains of a lost civilization. My shoes clattered loudly on broken slate. Two choughs rose from a building and scolded me from the hillside with high, churring, nasal cries, their black feathers glossy in the bright light. I peered into the dripping darkness of a level-entrance, standing awhile in the cold draught from the mine, for slate quarries are dismally cold inside. On the ground among the broken slates grew parsley fern, quantities of the tiny New Zealand willow herb and, inevitable relic of man's occupation, stinging nettles. I clattered out of the ruins along more enormous tips to look down into Cwmorthin, a colossal gash of a valley with scars and cliffs high up on both sides. I could see two abandoned houses, a derelict chapel, a desolate lake and the empty quarry road winding out of sight down towards Tanygrisiau. And I was alone in all that world of mountain, valley and past human labour; myself, two choughs, a handful of shrill-voiced pipits and the quiet sheep of the hills.

(1966)

THREE VERSIONS OF THE END

1: Shepherd of the Hills

To go and see Jenkins is to go back a century. You let the winding track lift you up amid wind and rocks and heather and from there you look back to the lowlands as to a foreign country. You round a last bend in the lane and there is the lonely farmhouse under the snowy slopes of the mountain. And here, greeting you in the lane, stands a primitive figure. On his head an ancient hat once worn by his mother when in her eighties she worked on top of the hay loads. Round his shoulders a sack pinned at his breast by a four-inch nail. Under the sack a policeman's tunic bought for a few pence at Machynlleth mart.

Jenkins is ageing now but still very strong. His face is furrowed by long exposure. His eyes have grown smaller. His lips are chapped by frost. His character has gone hard as the rocks. He lives alone now in the cold, comfortless house, though he is reputedly wealthy. So he always has lived and all his people. And so he will go on living. 'Not softly in hot-houses down there,' he says, looking with contempt to the valley. No, he will live hardily, mostly out-of-doors with the sheep; doctoring himself, if ever he has to, by his own herbs. So, he claims, he will still be well and active when the years have gathered thickly about him. I believe he will.

2: Consider the Lilies

An old man lived in a cottage on a bend of the winding hill. He had a garden which he loved, and no wonder for it grew Madonna lilies as few gardens will. They spread wildly into every corner of that garden and in summer they filled it from hedge to hedge with their fragrant white trumpets. Once he gave us a few bulbs but in our garden they failed. We always intended going back to ask for more, but passing one day we noticed the cottage was empty. The old chap would grow no more lilies. We went away hoping the place would fall into the hands of someone who would care for the lilies. Instead, the authorities seized the chance of demolishing the cottage in order to take the bend out of the road. They would claim they are getting rid of a dangerous corner. But I wonder if we are really any better off?

I know we are not allowed to say in a voice louder than a whisper that speed is a major cause of accidents. So when the traffic comes down the hill faster than ever we shall be expected to applaud and say this is progress. But all I can see is that we have exchanged a garden beautiful with lilies for a dull roadside bank. And drivers can now go racing into the next bend even more recklessly than they could before.

3: A House far from Anywhere

A house near here is called, aptly enough, Plas y Mynydd (The Mountain House). It stands at a lakeside in a remote hollow of the moorland, 1,300 feet above sea-level. It is somewhat sheltered on the west by trees but it has no protection against the east winds that come at it from the ridges of Pumlumon. It is a lonely house. Wide empty hills stretch all about, and for neighbours you must go three miles north, four miles south, two miles west or seven miles east. And if you went off south-east you would walk all day before you saw smoke in a chimney.

Not that this Plas y Mynydd has always been so neighbourless. When it was built there were little occupied crofts (*tyddynod*) scattered about the hills. All these are gone except for a few crumbling walls and are only names in the memory of far off village folk who got them from their parents and grandparents.

The *tyddynod* were poorly built and once abandoned they quickly rotted in the moorland rains. But Plas y Mynydd was bigger and stronger and has been occupied until recently. But now its time, too, is up. Already its back wall has fallen to the grass and very soon there will be nothing more than a grassy mound for the passer-by to wonder at. And there will be no house at all in all those miles of hills.

(1958-1962)

PART TWO

Seven Early Nature Essays

FLYCATCHER OF THE WESTERN WOODS

The ancient and beautiful hillside oakwoods of Wales: whether they clothe the lower flanks of the mountains, or cling along the plunging sides of narrow valleys, or hang over gorges, these woods of sessile oak have a character and a fauna which set them apart from all other present-day British woodlands. For these damp, undergrowth-free, often rocky, always windswept woods are the haunt of three rare creatures: polecat, pine marten and kite. To the botanist they offer not so many flowering plants as more primitive forms of vegetation: lichens, liverworts, mosses and ferns in delightful profusion. To the birdwatcher they offer in spring not the full chorus of birdsong audible in a lowland wood where undergrowth is abundant, but the songs of lesser singers not commonly to be heard together elsewhere: the delicate songs of wood warbler, redstart and pied flycatcher.

The cock pied flycatcher, with his two or three sweetly repeated notes, is almost inseparable from these western valleys. At the flowering season of the wood-sorrel and the golden saxifrage, he belongs more than any other bird to the world of straight, thin oaks tiered steeply above one another on the mossy wet slopes. Occasionally pairs will nest away from woods in scattered roadside trees, or even on the outskirts of villages, or in lowland gardens. But ninety-five out of a hundred in Wales nest in oakwoods, often where their songs come indistinctly through the noise of streams in rocky places.

The period of full song is short. The cock of one late-arriving pair had been singing for 10 days only when his song began to dwindle, about May 26, with the laying of eggs. But, if brief, the song is persistent. A very tame cock, which last year adopted a nest-box on our bedroom window-sill, sang his few notes with endless repetition from dawn till evening a few feet from our windows, especially during the two or three days before the hen arrived and while she was building. In most parts of these woods pied flycatchers are common enough to stimulate each other into rival song, and often three or four at a time are within hearing.

An April or early May cock pied flycatcher makes full use of his conspicuous black-and-white plumage to call attention to himself. His incessant song is often uttered from an obvious bare twig, high up for all to see. At human intrusion he will frequently fly down and sing or scold from a few feet away. He is the most aggressive small bird I know. Right from the first hour of his arrival in a territory already long occupied by resident birds, he starts a programme of deliberate and persistent assertion. From a strategic perch he swoops like a shrike, not nearly so much on passing insects as upon other birds. Robin, chaffinch, hedge sparrow, all are driven off with a flurry of pied wings, the pursuit being brief and ended suddenly.

It is the hole-nesters, however, which he recognizes as his special rivals; tits and nuthatches are his favourite victims. Standing intent on his high twig, his tail slowly working up and down (it has a thin white line down each side for an added touch of display), he dashes down wildly on one bird after another, routing several in a few seconds. Or he has a strange way of more gently parachuting upon them like a courting blue tit or a flight-singing wood warbler. In either event his intention is clear: it is not physical attack, but assertion through display, for the whole affair goes with much tail-spreading and wing-fanning. The two white spots on his forehead add to his ferocious look. He is a true cousin of the butcher-bird.

His plumage is deceptive: he is often neither truly black nor white. Close to, the black lacks depth and often appears brown, especially on the spread wing. Catching sunlight, his back will appear ruddy-brown, as does a willow tit's cap. But individuals vary much from one to another. Sometimes the primaries are quite brown in any light, and in some birds even the tail feathers, the most consistently black feature, appear dark brown in bright light. The breast is not really white, but silver-grey and silky in texture.

After aggressiveness, curiosity is the male's outstanding attribute. Without any visible hint of hostility, he will follow a prospecting nuthatch in and out of hole after hole, tree after tree. This nuthatch-pied flycatcher association occurs every spring in woods where both species are common, lasting for just those few unsettled days after the flycatchers' arrival. Cock pied flycatchers will sometimes follow enquiringly after people, visit their gardens, and most readily adopt their nesting-boxes. But mainly their inquisitiveness is directed towards the activities of other birds. I watched one cock pied flycatcher standing quietly twelve inches from a chaffinch and listening to it singing for nearly half an hour without moving. When the chaffinch flew, the flycatcher followed close behind. Another came and perched on a mid-stream stone to watch a blue tit bathing. Another divided his attention about equally between myself and a pair of coal tits I was watching at their nest.

To describe the hen pied flycatcher, after the male, is like turning to another species. Bird photographers like the male's contrasting plumage, but there are in the hen subtle beauties and delicate markings which make her an even more attractive, because more challenging, subject. Her ways match her looks. Where the male is bold and assertive, she is shy and easily missed. Now and then she will drive away other birds, but I have not found her at all inquisitive. At first sight, especially on the wing, she is rather warbler-like, grey-brown of back, silvery-breasted. But see one working along a hedge with a willow warbler, and the comparative stolidness of the pied flycatcher becomes apparent. A warbler restlessly weaves through the twigs, stretching sharply and slimly forward for insects, or fluttering delicately after flies.

A pied flycatcher will also search for caterpillars, but more often waits, dives out, snapping its bill loudly, and then carries on to another perch, rarely returning like a spotted flycatcher. Standing still, the female has often the look of a hen chaffinch. She does all the nest-building, mainly using coarse dry grass, quite long pieces, and a few dead leaves, all gathered within a few yards, if possible. The cock occasionally takes in a grass, but only as a formal gesture of courtship. Mainly he sings in front of the hole, sometimes following her into the nest with an excited sizzling note, and coming out again immediately and waiting for her. In most of the nests I have seen there have been six or seven eggs, rarely eight, very rarely nine.

Intrude upon pied flycatchers when the young are growing up, and both parents will fly from perch to perch close around you, calling out their mild alarm note, a single, half-suppressed *pwit*. The cock, being less directly concerned with the nest itself and more intent upon the keeping of territory, is often more excited than the hen by human intrusion, but less ready than her to visit the nest. As soon as the spotted, robin-like young are on the wing the whole family immediately disappears, presumably to follow a wandering life high in the leafy tree-tops of full summer. One week a valley may seem full of flycatchers. Next week we find none at all.

(1954)

A FLASH OF RED

House sparrows are not so inevitable about human dwellings as people think. I have lived in three cottages in different parts of the Welsh hills and never seen a sparrow under their eaves. But there were redstarts at all three, nesting in the walls or not many yards off, and you cannot have redstarts about your cottage all day, singing on your chimney or chasing each other across the garden, without getting very fond of these loveliest of summer birds.

If the songs of willow warbler and tree pipit are eagerly listened for as a sign of spring's return to the hills, very welcome too is the bright flash of red tail feathers along a wall which is often one's first glimpse of a redstart. What unwonted colours the first cock redstart brings to the still sombre April woods! Black cheeks and throat, white forehead, light-grey crown and back, reddish breast and fiery rump and tail: this sudden bright vision reminds us of how starved of vivid colours are our northern eyes most of the year. By the end of April redstarts are abundant in their Welsh breeding haunts; and the nature of these haunts surprised me when I first came to Wales from the English Midlands. For there, in the district where redstarts were most plentiful, I knew them as birds of dry, sandy parkland, scattered with pine and birch, and their nests were usually in holes in trees, well away from humanity. But here in Wales they are frequently upland birds, haunting hanging woods, sheep-farm buildings, field-walls and the walls of cottages whether inhabited or not: they seem to prefer to nest in artificial sites and are often close neighbours of man.

Their special haunts here are the wooded slopes along mountain streams: cool, wet places green with ferns and mossy rocks, where the male bird's song is hard to hear in the noise of white-splashing water. Yet even there, where they seem remotest from man and where the gnarled and rotten trees offer many a good hole, the redstarts prefer to lodge their nests in a man-made site: a boundary wall, a mill-ruin, a lead-mine relic, the shell of a slate-shed. If none of these is available they will use the woods for feeding and roosting, but nest in a wall some distance away.

To me there is a strange quality of wildness in the redstart's song, in that brief, tremulous opening phrase. What follows varies much from bird to bird: it may be a rattle or a hoarse squeak, but sometimes a long plaintive phrase of indefinable beauty. Of all spring's delights one of the greatest is to hear the dawn song of several cock redstarts singing loud and close to each other in the hillside oaks. Listen on a May morning from the hour when the dawn-light touches the higher slopes. Above the trees a nightjar reels his last song, tawny owls cease their hooting, the first wheatear scratches out a few notes from among the dark rocks. Then, quite suddenly, inside the wood, redstarts and robins come one after another into song and for perhaps thirty minutes have the still morning to themselves. The quick, vehemently repeated phrases of the redstarts and the slower, richer music of the robins come more purely to the ear at that hour than at any other.

Boldness and shyness are curiously merged in the redstart. We have had pairs build in our cottage walls, a few yards from the door, with people constantly about. This suggests that they are inclined to be familiar, like robins; but they are not. They nested in our wall because the hole there was a deep, dark one not to be improved upon in their area and because they had used it in previous years when the cottage was empty. So, despite our presence, not because of it, they used it again, overcoming their fear of us. But they remained shy, silent, and evasive as long as they could. The hen came to the nest always from round the back, slipping so quickly into the hole that we were not even sure she had built until one day we looked and found six blue eggs in the nest. The cock, too, kept away, and usually sang from a hedge a hundred yards off. Only when we were very quiet indoors would he venture into the garden to sing from the apple tree close to our window. His song at four yards' range was lovely to wake to in the morning. One day – the first morning he arrived – he perched on the open window and looked into the bedroom, no doubt wondering if this 'cave' had any possible nesting sites in its recesses. I am sure that redstarts, like pied flycatchers, could be attracted more about houses in the hill country by the provision of nesting-boxes, for they will use them fairly readily. One pair I heard of built in the toolbox of a hay-elevator that had been left out all winter. Another pair nested in a pile of wood-shavings on a carpenter's bench.

It was with some astonishment that our farmer neighbour, passing by one day on his round of the sheep, beheld at the end of our cottage a crude platform on tall poles on which we were erecting a square tent of sackcloth for the observation and photography of the redstarts. For now the eggs had hatched and both parents had changed their demeanour abruptly. Now they became bold, indifferent to intrusion: their alarmed *poo-it chic-chic* became a constant sound above the cottage. Then it was a joy to see them landing together on the grey roof-slates, beaks full of flies and caterpillars, their orange tails atremble, and a few seconds later disappearing with a final splash of red into the hole in the masonry. We could compare them then as they waited on the low roof, eyeing us anxiously. Perhaps, after all, the hen, in her quiet plumage, is the lovelier of the two: her large eye showed more lustrous against her light feathers, her soft-grey wings went beautifully with the bright orange tail. But the cock, unlike many cock birds when feeding young, was much the bolder. He would fly out in front of our faces, cross to the hedge, quickly grab a beakful of green or brown grubs and return straight past us into the hole. Only the presence of the timid hen made him also hesitant. She went no farther than he for food, making a speciality of grasshoppers caught on the bank behind the cottage.

Throughout the last day that the young were in the nest the cock called as if with deep anxiety. But I do not think this really betokened anxiety. It was like the incessant *wee-tac* of whinchats at the same season, an unconscious development of voice which at the appropriate hour serves to call off the young. Meanwhile he sang often, though now almost solely the vibrant opening phrase. The young seemed to leave the nest rather prematurely, for, instead of flying away, they fluttered down to the wood-pile, where they remained all day and roosted. Next day they were strong enough to go and the cock now used a new note to call them off, a husky *chat-chat* which the young repeated exactly. So off they went into the hawthorn thicket, five of them, light-spotted, dark-brown little creatures, young robins except for their bright tails. We saw them about for a few days and then no more. None of our redstarts have had second broods.

(*1954*)

THE SURPRISING SPARROWHAWK

A sudden smashing sound, a tinkling of broken glass and a pigeon-sized bird lying stunned on the window-sill: such has been more than one countryman's introduction to the sparrowhawk, for hawks have not the understanding of the peculiar qualities of glass which many small garden birds have. On such an occasion it would be well to look closely at this bird while we have the chance, for in a few minutes it will be up and away. Note the slim bullet-shape for speed; the long heavy tail for sharp cornering; the wings strong for power yet rather short for slipping neatly between trunks and through branches; the eyes which look forwards and yet which look sideways and backwards also; the very sharp down-curved beak for meat-tearing; above all look at the thin but steel-strong yellow legs and feet taloned for killing. Now the hawk recovers consciousness. Its eyes open. One of them is bruised and blood-filled and will take time to heal. The other is large, round, yellow, black-pupilled and has that fixed, staring quality peculiar to the eyes of birds of prey. Take up the hawk – you'll be surprised how light it is – go outside with it and let it feel the breeze. One moment it will be dazed and limp in your palm and in the next it will have burst out of your hands and flown round the nearest corner almost too quickly to see.

In those few minutes you will have seen a side of the sparrowhawk's character which places it apart from all others, even from other British birds of prey. For in the pursuit of prey sparrowhawks are the embodiment of intentness, tautness of nerve and recklessness. With perfect singleness of purpose they select an individual from a flock of small scattering birds and follow headlong its every twist and turn until either they catch it, or it drops into cover, or until some man-made obstacle to which hawks are not by nature adapted to avoid – a window, a greenhouse or a wire-netting fence – brings disaster.

The tense, nervous sparrowhawk, so unpredictable. What other bird of prey could suddenly sweep round the corner of your house, perch on your gate and stare at you in your garden at a range of six feet? Yet this has happened at our cottage, which is adjacent to a wood beloved of hawks. How few we notice even where they are common, so careful are they when not hunting to keep out of man's way, to fly on the other side of the hedge or to keep below a bank. How often these silent birds must slip close behind our backs unnoticed, or even pass unseen before our eyes, so dark are they and so low do they fly along the dark ground. In the woods we would seldom know of their presence were it not for the peculiar shrill chorus which tits set up – especially long-tailed tits – whenever a sparrowhawk flies close. In more open country the hawks become more obvious. Where I live in mid-Wales nearly every wooded valley has its several pairs and they, hunting singly, frequently pass up the dingles of tributary streams, cross the bare shoulders of the lower mountains in quest of small moorland birds and glide down another dingle back to their valley. Or they leave the valley for far skirmishes across the lowland fields; or over the fresh marshes to the estuaries where they hunt not the open mudflats but rather along the lines of embankments and gutters; or they follow the shoreline to veer suddenly up over the cliffs or skim aside through sand-dunes: going everywhere at the same steady high speed with rapidly beating wings or stiff-winged glides usually only a few feet above the ground. They do not sight their prey from afar like a peregrine, or from overhead like a kestrel. They rely entirely on surprise, confusing their prey by the unexpectedness of their arrival. If they strike and miss they have lost the advantage of surprise and make no second attempt. The usual prey of a male sparrowhawk is birds of finch or thrush size but the bigger female kills many woodpigeons and magpies in the woods, and on the shore take waders up to at least the size of oystercatchers. Locally sparrowhawks seem to specialize in hunting for a particular species: one I observed seemed to kill nothing but great tits; another, chaffinches; a third decimated a jay population.

If one's view of a sparrowhawk is dissatisfyingly short there are occasions when their flight can be observed at length – when they are soaring. I have seen this every month from November to April but mostly in late March and early April. On calm, fine days particularly, the male, sometimes the female, and occasionally both, will circle on outstretched wings and widely fanned tail, the primaries slightly parted at the tips, over the nesting wood or an adjacent hill, sometimes spiralling up till you need a field-glass to see them. These courtship flights are worth watching throughout for they may end with an exciting steep plunge by both birds together down into the trees below.

Though so faithful to the oakwoods of the Welsh valleys it is remarkable how infrequently the sparrowhawks actually build their nest in an oak. The sessile oaks, growing close together, are but thinly leaved and then only at the crown. The hawks prefer thicker cover and if there is a dense old spruce growing amid the oaks there they are most likely to build. Failing that the hawks like nothing better than a plantation of tall larches for nesting in. But though they like cover I do not remember seeing a nest in an ivied tree. Occasionally their nests are but slight and precarious: one I saw was in a thin holly and so badly supported that it tipped day by day at an ever steeper angle until the eggs rolled out into the gorge below. I have heard of sparrowhawks breeding on cliff-ledges in north Wales but the nearest I have seen to such a site was a nest four feet from the ground in a dwarfed, windswept larchwood high on a Montgomeryshire hillside.

At the nest the female sparrowhawk is almost the opposite of wary. What infinite precautions we took, in building our first hide by a hawk's nest, to add a fragment at a time at intervals of several days. And what a surprise we eventually got when we found that this bird, so difficult to approach in the field, was boldness itself at the nest, a boldness quite ludicrous when, wanting the hawk to change to a position more suitable for photography we found, after making experimental low sounds, that no matter how much we increased the noise the hawk stayed rigid at the nest. My strangest experience with a wild bird is that of sitting in a tree-top hide shouting my loudest at a hawk ten feet away and getting no reaction beyond an inquisitive cocking of the head. But shake the canvas wall of the hide ever so slightly and she is gone like a bullet. A spell of watching at a sparrowhawk's nest is a wonderful experience. If the young are still small and downy it is not long before the female returns to the nest. There will be a short spell of calling close by – a shrill *ki ki ki ki*, lower pitched than the kestrel's similar note, followed by dead silence as the bird listens. Then a thin whistle of wing and with startling suddenness there is the big hen at the nest. Her white breast is well barred; her back is a dark reddish-brown which in certain lights looks slatey. She has a pale line over her eye. (This is a bold streak in some hens, lightly pencilled in others.) It is hard to persuade oneself that her staring eye is not looking right through the hide. She holds a plucked, unidentifiable bird firmly in her talons and from this she energetically tears morsels with her bill and distributes them to her twittering, excited young ones, eating the bones and the bigger pieces herself. She walks round the nest and then settles on her young to brood them, though until they quieten down she is tossed about like a ship on a rough sea. The nest is kept clean right to the end, food not being allowed to accumulate at the nest as it is with buzzards and kites. The male hawk is usually as timid as his mate is bold. At most nests his visits are very rare; and if he comes at all he is likely to drop his prey into the nest in flight and vanish immediately, which is why good still photographs of male sparrowhawks are scarce. Male sparrowhawks vary a lot: while all are blue-grey on their backs, some have whitish, some bright-pink breasts. A bird of the latter type is such a brilliant creature with the sun lighting up his colours that I have always wanted to see more of him at the nest than I have. The male announces his arrival with food by a repeated, buzzard-like *kee-o kee-o* uttered from a nearby tree and then, normally, the hen goes to him for it. The food-cry of the young hawks, after they are past the twittering stage, is a cat-like mewing which is the nearest they can get to the adults' buzzard-call and which they will keep up in chorus while being fed and even afterwards. The result is a volume of sound audible downwind for a quarter-mile, a dangerous advertisement of the nest site.

Some of my happiest birdwatching memories are of hours spent in hides by the nests of hawks, harriers and buzzards. Only then can you observe these vigilant birds off their guard for long periods and get to know something of their personalities and the way they react to the trivial events that make up their daily lives through the months of the breeding season. In April there is the care which the female sparrowhawk puts into selecting and assembling just the right thin sticks for the nest and just the right bits of bark for the lining; in May and June the thirty-three or so days of motionless sitting on the eggs, oblivious of the flies constantly walking over her plumage, as indifferent to small birds feeding in the branches about her as they are to her; and after midsummer the weeks of caring for the young in the nest. A hen sparrowhawk occupied with the little incidents of nest-life is a delightful subject. One I watched used to stare for long periods at her young after feeding them, occasionally picking up a stick in her beak and with deliberation carrying it round to the far side of the nest only to return it to its former position a little later. Another accidentally dropped her prey from the nest. She listened carefully as it fell through the twigs to the ground, walked to the nest-edge and looked down for some moments and then fluttered down like a dove to recover it. Perhaps what I have learnt chiefly from my long watching of sparrowhawks is how much more there is to their character than the bent for killing; in short, how unhawk-like they are most of the time.

(1955)

BLACKCOCK AT DAWN

Out into the dewy dawn of this April morning to see the display of the blackcock. Years ago this would have involved a long and perhaps fruitless journey into remote mountain country, but today, with forestry plantations spreading everywhere, the blackcock has become easily accessible, for no bird is more intimately connected with coniferous forestry. So now I have only to go a mile from home up onto the nearest hills to hear the strange bubbling of the blackcock any time of the day, but especially morning and evening.

The last owls called as I walked through the deep wet tussocks of purple moor-grass up to the rocks I had chosen as a watching place. It was getting dimly light and the wind was cold. Quietly I settled in the shadows with my back against a rock and waited. Though I have heard the blackcock a great many times the first musical bubbling that breaks the silence of dawn is still as good a sound to me as if I heard it for the first time. It is a wild and primitive call that takes you right out of the twentieth or any other century, straight back to the earliest dawns of life. The rocky outcrop that hid me was just outside the forest fence, commanding a view of a grassy arena that sloped down to the trees. Presently I heard the first blackcock calling. A long silence. Then he came flying from the shadowy trees into the half-light outside the fence. There he stood and gobbled and curtseyed and displayed to nothing more responsive than a sheep. But in a few minutes a second blackcock appeared from somewhere, soon followed by two others and immediately the whole play was on. What a strange performance it is, all these stylized dawn rituals, all these leapings into the air, these struttings and cavortings, these bowings and tail-raisings, these displays of scarlet wattles and of white tail-feathers against black ones. We can sit at home and see close-up films of it all on television and hear the wonderful noises that go with it. And both vision and sound may well be clearer than we can experience in the field. But it does not live as it lives in the greyness of dawn.

(*1956*)

CORMORANTS' INLAND CITADEL

To get to Bird Rock (Craig y Deryn) near Tywyn, in Merioneth, could not be easier. You can go by bus if you want. You get out under the Rock, the bus roars off and quickly vanishes round the narrow lane that skirts a knee of the rock, and you are left in a quiet, green, flat-bottomed valley with mountains and woods all round, an opening seawards to the west and the billowing outlines of Cader Idris to the east. You look up at the face above you, and there, crossing and recrossing the sky, so high and so dwarfed by their surroundings they look like jackdaws, are the cormorants. If it is a still day your ear will catch the gruntings and growlings with which the birds greet one another as they land on the ledges. But they are very far above you and the viewpoint is not a satisfying one.

It is the hill-walker who enjoys the best approach, across country from the south. You climb up through woods, and wind round undulating brackeny hills where wheatears play hide and seek among the screes and the air is sweet with lark song. At last you top a rise and there, dramatically, is the sudden deep rift of the Dysynni valley. And there too, if the wind is right, you first catch the smell. You may still be 200 yards from the brink of the precipice, but if the wind is north a reek comes to you that for a moment bewilders. Smells are linked wonderfully closely in our memories with places, and this one gives you an instantaneous flash-back to sea-cliffs and the beat of the ocean below and the voices of seabird colonies. Then you return to the present, to the lichen-scabbed rocks, the moor-grass blowing in the wind, the encircling Merioneth mountains, the pastoral vale. But though the sea-image fades, the unmistakable smell of seabirds persists.

You clamber cautiously across a scree to the edge, go on to your hands and knees when you feel the wind tear up at you, and peer over. And there a few feet below on the white-washed ledges, their nests almost touching, are groups of sitting cormorants. As your head appears, they writhe their snake-like necks as they appraise you from various angles. Farther along the cliff other cormorants which have not yet spotted you hold themselves upright and unmoving, like great black models of birds that have been stood along the ledges. One holds his wings half-open; another stands on one leg, balanced on a big webbed foot. Your gaze travels down the face past a lower group of cormorants, past a crowd of jackdaws fluttering in and out of a fissure, past cliff-slopes pink with campion, down to a bright green field an eighth of a mile below, a field scattered with pairs of white blobs in two sizes: each pair a ewe and a lamb.

Such, then, is these cormorants' unusual view of the world. They look down to no tossing ocean, but a pattern of fields and farms set among woods and sheepwalks. They have no shoreline to descend to for seaweed for their nests; instead they flutter up to the slopes above and waddle about the grass, gathering gorse-sticks, rushes and grass. There is no welcoming sea for the young to flop into at the end of their maiden flights. In fact, not a drop of water is visible from their ledges except the thin waving ribbon of the Dysynni stream glinting over its shallows on the far side of the valley. Only the shine of the sea, six miles away, reminds them of their true home. There they must travel for food unless they prefer to fish the estuary or go up to the mountain lakes.

The intrusion of your silhouette onto their rocky skyline is only a short-lived shock for the birds. If you keep still or are gentle about your movements, they soon forget you and return to their cormorantine ruminations or whatever goes on in their minds as they sit there day and night awaiting the emergence of skinny young from the three or four chalky eggs. Soon their mates arrive, swinging into the cliff on half-closed wings, their primaries almost screaming with vibration. They alight amid a deep-voiced chorus something like *errug, errug, errug* – primal sounds in keeping with birds that powerfully evoke the primitive and suggest the pterodactyl. Then there is silence. The incubating ones become restful again. One of the newcomers retches and vomits a fish on to the nest edge, but nobody wants it yet. Another hangs his wide wings and turns into the wind. For a long while there is no movement whatsoever. These silent, still creatures grouped on their ledge might be a tableau in a museum depicting life groping from the reptiles towards the birds.

Then a wave of feeling travels through the colony. There is talking in high tones, falsetto croaks of contentment which rise to a crescendo of tremulous exclamations. And one after another the birds not on nest-duty dive outwards. The north wind, squarely hitting the face of the rock, sheers upwards, taking each bird with it. On long, shapely wings they ride the updraught together, and circle and play, dive and climb; and two go spiralling up and up and up until they are specks against the clouds. Nothing reptilian about them now. Their uprising is majestic, inspiring. Their descent is spectacular. They come down in a breathtaking corkscrew plunge and roar past to their ledge with a sound as if all their feathers were tearing. In a few moments, the ritual of greeting is over, they are still and silent in their places, emotion forgotten. The hours pass, threaded with the same rhythm of peace and boisterousness. As the sun curves away into the north-west it begins to shine on their nesting ledges, illuminating one bird after another in a golden light. And now you see the cormorants in their true colours: not black as they looked before, but brown and purple, green and blue. Now you not only see their white faces and thigh-patches, but notice also that some still retain on their heads a few filament-like white plumes they developed in the late winter. Only the smell is the same.

This is only a small colony as cormorant communities go, a mere 25 or 30 pairs. But it is historic; though how historic does not seem ever to have received the attention of serious researchers. That it goes back at least a few centuries is a matter of common agreement. But how one would like to be able to distil the truth out of the welter of conflicting local opinion concerning the cormorants' history over the last 60 or 70 years! For while some say there are as many in the colony as ever, others are quite emphatic about an enormous decrease and can recall that in their childhood days 'thousands of cormorants nested on both faces of the rock'; that is not only on the north side but also on the much less precipitous west side. I expect that, as usual in such conflicts of opinion, the truth lies somewhere between, that there never were thousands, but that there was at some recent time a decrease. If so, what date is more likely than about a century ago, until which time there was an important herring and mackerel fishery on this coast? If these fish decreased, might not the cormorants also have diminished as a result?

(*1957*)

SPRING IN THE HIGH WOODS

James Thomson's notion of spring: 'Come, gentle spring! Ethereal mildness, come' is as we all know in our fitful climate only a convention of poets. I suppose it arose because poetry in his day had long been saturated by influences from Greece and Italy, where spring is a more certain season. We know spring as the opposite of gentle; if it is really mild one day, the wind is pretty sure to go round into the north the next and blow really cold. As a Scotsman, Thomson ought to have known better.

But even in Britain there are two sorts of spring: the prolonged, less unkind spring of the plain and the late-arriving, icy-fingered spring of the mountains. The people of the Welsh uplands have an expressive word, *hirlwm*, which means 'long bleakness' and which refers to those endless weeks that drag between midwinter and the time when the grass begins to grow again in mountain pastures.

Hirlwm is the word that comes to my mind when I think of spring creeping into the high woods that stretch black along the wintry hillsides, and do not even yellow until after the valley woods are deep in leaves. What a glad time that is when you can make a mid-May scramble up through the mossy rocks, up into the oaks, and see the unfurling leaves turning from yellow to palest green, and see the long, thin male catkins shaking in the breeze. In such a wood you are not confronted with bare trunks merely, but live for a while in close intimacy with high branches, buds and leaves. You have tree-tops all about you, even below you, and chaffinches are shouting into your ears. You clamber on to a rock the size of a cottage and can examine the flowering twigs without so much as reaching for them.

They are never great trees, these contorted, crag-grasping oaks of the old rocks of Celtic Britain. No 'wooden walls' ever came from them, only fuel for furnaces, bark for tannin, stakes for fencing. I know that Cowper wrote:

> Sage beneath a hoary oak
> Sat the Druid, hoary chief

But that was no mountain oak but one of the great pedunculate oaks of the lowlands, the sort that Shakespeare knew in Arden. But it was as a mountain tree that Sir Walter Scott knew the oak:

> Aloft, the ash and warrior oak
> Cast anchor in the rifted rock.

Yes, that is just how they grow. Many an acorn has sprouted in the heart of a cleft rock and produced an oak that for want of root-hold has had to anchor itself by spreading its trunk across a face of rock to grip its edges as a man does in climbing.

Other trees flourish among the oaks, notably birch and thorn and ash. Of these the ashes are much the last to leaf, and you can pick them out clearly in the woods in late spring by their still bare, whitish branches sticking out like antlers above the leafing oaks, their thick, bold twigs curving against the sky. In summer you can know the ashes from afar by their different green: often a belt of grey-green among the bright-green oaks and lying in a straight line down a woodside from top to bottom. Not planted so by man as you might at first suppose, but because some stream flows or some dampness seeps down the woodside there. For ash loves the damper places provided the moisture is neither excessive nor stagnant; not because it is a great drinker but because it loves the richer soil that gathers along runnels and streamsides.

Who does not like to feel the smooth hardness of an ash-stick, or to see in winter the stiff silvery twigs with their pairs of black buds and the big, swollen bud at the tip? In the high woods it may be June before these buds throw open their black doors, to release dense purple clusters of primitive, petal-less blossoms that stand so bushy and stiff along the twigs that from a distance the tree seems already in leaf. How quickly they sprout, these flowers of ash, and how soon they fade and fall. Only a few days does the woodpigeon have to find them and gorge on them before they are gone and leaves are sprouting in their stead.

'The ash', said Virgil, 'is loveliest in the woods.' Perhaps he was thinking of how pleasant it is, when you have been under the deep shade of other trees, to find when you arrive under an ash how the feathery, mobile leaves filter the sun's light into the woods and chequer the ground with dappled shadows.

And under the trees? In most parts of the high woods you will find flowers neither abundant nor varied. Thin, acid soils are the domain of heather, bilberry and moss. In seeking spring flowers in such woodland you may well let the ash trees be your guide. For they, as I said, find the richest, or least poor, spots in the wood and it is at their feet, in the damper areas, that you will find the flowers: yellow and green mats of golden saxifrage hanging over dripping rocks; violets, wild strawberry, primroses, sanicles, ground ivy and others that riot in the lowland woods but which, up here, have to be sought for plant by plant. Tennyson made a well-observed point, perhaps better than he knew, in the line:

> by ashen roots the violets blow.

In the same situation he might have chanced upon another plant of humble stature, so humble that its very name, *Adoxa*, means 'of no account'. This little musky moschatel was long hounded from one family to another by botanists unable to trace her true affinities. Once classed as an ivy, she was for a while promoted to close kinship with honeysuckle, guelder-rose, elder and wayfaring-tree. But now science has despaired of discovering her next-of-kin and has left her all alone, sole member of a unique family. So there is food for thought for you some soft April day when you see the first fragile square stems and pale triple leaflets of moschatel pushing delicately through the litter of last year's oak-leaves: by what infinity of chance and change through evolutionary time has this small plant come down to us, so bereft of relations? Were they of even less account in the struggle for survival than moschatel herself, and so perished?

How cheering it is to find that this flower of no account is after all something unique in the world. What other plant unfolds, from a yellow pinhead bud, a cube of four green clock-faces with a fifth looking skywards? Then there is the plant's respectable world range. Never think of moschatel, if you know it only in soft southern woods and hedges, as a half-hardy cringer in the shelter of giant neighbours. For if ever you are lucky enough to see the Arctic flora you will find our little moschatel braving it out there on the tundra, springing up in the wake of the melting snow. And in Britain you may find it far up the flanks of our mountains: which brings me back to the high woods, especially those on limy soils where ash is abundant.

There comes to my mind a remote Welsh valley on a perfect day in May. I had followed a stream up through woods of ash and oak, botanizing casually and thinking I ought to meet moschatel in such a rich place. But if it was there it eluded me, and I came clear of the trees at last. I was now faced with a long scree topped by a crag. Here I forgot my plant-hunting at the sight of a tiercel-peregrine – patrolling back and forth on a slow gliding beat above me. The crag looked a promising nesting place, and sure enough as I toiled up the scree the falcon came flickering off a ledge, to chatter with deep, angered notes as she hurled herself about the sky. But as is usual with peregrines, the nest was not to be reached: at the top of the scree I found my way blocked by 20 feet of sheer, slimy rock. So I looked about for plants instead.

But it was not until I squatted to eat my lunch that I saw beside me, in the shadow of a boulder where it could never have seen the sun, a small patch of moschatel that looked down a thousand feet onto the woods where I had sought it.

Though spring may come late to the upland woods there is this compensation: that in some May drought in the lowlands, when all the green gaiety of the spring has dried up into brownness and seed, you can go to the wet gullies of the high woods and find the year still new there, and rejoice again in the delicate crimple of opening primrose leaves and find wood sorrel and windflower still fresh and fragrant in a green, unthirsty world. Then, when the oak-rollers and geometers have decimated the foliage of the lowland oaks and the hot woods are unpleasant with the rain of caterpillar-droppings, you can climb to the hill-woods and find the oak leaves clean and almost untouched. For there in the cool upper air insect life is far less abundant. It is as if the high woods are swept clean by the mountain winds.

(1958)

REDPOLLS AMONG THE SPRUCES

Whatever the rights and wrongs of large-scale afforestation, there is no doubt that the excluding of sheep and other grazers from large areas of moor and mountain and the planting of trees in their stead is an experiment of marvellous interest to the naturalist.

Nature never wastes a chance like this. Not only do grasses and such plants as heather and bilberry rejoice in this release from the dreadful incisors of the flocks and herds, but countless insects, spiders and other small creatures also respond to this ecological revolution. And attracted by them and the wealth of lush grass and seeds come a multitude of small mammals, followed inevitably by larger, predatory mammals and birds of prey. Meanwhile thousands of little conifers grow up and in their cover breed a host of small bush-loving birds – warblers, finches, hedge sparrows, robins, yellowhammers and so on – species which are normally alien to mountain habitats. Of these small species one of the most interesting and least noticed is the lesser redpoll, a little finch known to be increasing in Wales where it has become one of the most successful colonizers of the upland conifers and now breeds in most forests where trees are at the right stage.

The right stage is vital. When a forest is planted there is an immediate move-in of whinchats and tree pipits. They are nesters in the long grass and enjoy the tiny conifers as perches. In the next few years the trees pass through a gooseberry-bush stage, thickening into one another to form a low, impenetrable jungle. By this time the whinchats and tree pipits have abandoned the site but undergrowth-lovers such as hedge sparrows, bullfinches and warblers have come in. Then up shoot the trees to ten, twelve, fourteen feet. It is at these heights that they are attractive to redpolls.

The best redpoll locality I have known was a moorland valley in Wales which some twenty years before had been planted mainly with Norway and Sitka spruce all over its flat marshy bed at about 1,000 feet and up its steep sides to about 1,300 feet above sea level. Here there nested some twelve to fifteen pairs of redpolls. But it is wise to be cautious in estimating redpoll numbers in such a breeding haunt, for the birds seem to be everywhere at once as they fly about high over the trees, constantly crossing the valley from slope to slope, ranging the whole stretch of the forest, exploring the tributary valleys and even wandering up over the rim of the forest on to the open hills above.

Redpolls have no regards for that division of an area into territories which dominates the lives of most other land birds at nesting time. In favourable weather they are never long in advertising themselves by their song-flight, which may be performed by single birds or by several together. They begin by perching in a group, each on the tip of adjacent firs, singing or calling. Then all burst steeply into the air with a hurried chatter of short notes. Rising to about fifty feet and keeping close together, they fly with a quickly undulating, almost hopping flight which in a few minutes may bring them back in a circle above their starting point, to which they pitch steeply down together. Or they drop to the trees perhaps a hundred yards, perhaps half a mile, away.

The song is simple. It is rather a toneless trill, *trrrrr*, which alternates rapidly with the typical low flight-note which is usually written as *uch-uh-uch*. Both sounds carry far and in spring or summer a male redpoll never seems to fly without uttering one or the other. In full song he has a third characteristic note: a ringing but tinny *tew tew tew tew*. Their liveliness formerly made redpolls extremely popular cage birds, but I cannot think that anyone who has seen their wild free flight over the breeding ground could want to see a redpoll, any more than a lark, in a cage. These song-flights begin very early in the morning. Listening to the dawn chorus in mid-May in an upland conifer forest, I found that redpolls began sixth in order of singing (being preceded by whinchat, song-thrush, cuckoo, ring ouzel and willow warbler), but that their song was by far the most sustained over the whole day, though even redpolls have occasional hours of silence. Only on very windy days are they mainly silent, especially if there is cold and rain with the wind.

The nests I have seen in conifer plantations have varied from between two feet six inches to ten feet above the ground. They have nearly all been built against the stem of the tree and resting on two or three fairly level thin branches; but I have seen a few out on flat sprays a foot from the stem. All have been in thickets of unthinned Sitka spruce, not inside the most impenetrable clumps but on the fringe of such where the trees, although growing close enough to touch each other, nevertheless allow you to push your way between them. A few nests have been alongside rides. Some of them have been well hidden, but most of them, placed just above eye level in the more open portion of the tree, have not been so difficult to spot as you might at first fear when you are faced with the prospect of searching through acres of closely planted spruces for the nest of a bird whose behaviour may give you little clue as to the whereabouts of the nest.

Once found the nest is easily identified by the smallness of the inside cup, even though the outside may be fairly bulky. A typical conifer-built nest begins with a loose base of tiny, dead spruce twigs. From that foundation it is built up mainly of dry moss, with an interweaving of hair, bits of dead fern, thin straws, wool, rootlets and similar material as available. The lining may have a feather or two in it or a little wool but is commonly a substantial pad of willow down.

An incubating redpoll is often quite indifferent to near intrusion by human beings. One hen remained upon her eggs while I put up a hide only six feet from her, during which operation I frequently brushed against the nesting tree and tied strings to it to support the hide. When I saw how tame my first redpolls were at the nest I supposed that photographing them would be simplicity itself. It was not so. For even when incubating, when other species are very still and watchful, the hen redpoll cannot rest. She is constantly shuffling, yawning, turning about, nibbling at the rim of the nest or deeply into the nest or turning to look up at passing birds, especially crows and hawks. If another redpoll flies over, the sitting hen will sometimes quiver her wings and call softly. So that delightful as it is to watch these lively birds you can spoil a lot of film in trying to catch their movements.

Whenever I see this eager colonization of the conifer forests by all these different creatures I am reminded of the Latin refrain of a song we learnt at school: *Ubi bene ibi patria*. This might be translated by our forestry redpolls as: 'We shall be quite happy to settle in this neck of the woods for ever provided the trees remain just as they are'.

But alas! The redpoll-stage of conifers does not endure. Where the trees are growing well it may last four or five years only, and then the trunks get tall and slender, the bushiness so dear to most birds is gone for ever and the forest reaches those strangely silent years of its maturity which W.H. Hudson likened to 'the twilight and still atmosphere of a cathedral interior'. Then though there are more large birds than before almost the only small birds are the needle-voiced goldcrests and the occasionally drifting parties of mixed tits. By then the warblers, finches and redpolls will have gone to seek friendlier shelter in new plantations.

(*1958*)

PART THREE

Friends and Mentors

THREE APPROACHES TO THOREAU

1: A Hundred Years of Walden

I like what old Walt Whitman once said about Thoreau: '... my prejudices, if I may call them that, are all with Emerson; but Thoreau was a surprising fellow – he is not easily grasped – is elusive: yet he is one of the native forces – stands for a fact, for a movement, an upheaval... he looms up bigger and bigger: his dying does not seem to have hurt him a bit: every year has added to his fame. One thing about Thoreau keeps him very near to me: I refer to his lawless-ness – his dissent – his going his absolute own road let hell blaze all it chooses'.

Thoreau made merry with society in deadly earnest. In order to think he did not retire to a library to pore over dry-as-dust systems. Instead he went and borrowed a friend's axe and built himself a shanty by a pond, where he could grow rows and rows of beans. And as he worked he chuckled to himself at the odd ideas about life which came to him out there in the robust air with the smell of the healthy earth about him. And when he sat down to write in the evening all those odd thoughts came tumbling out to make the merry masterpiece called *Walden: or Life in the Woods*, published in 1854. The book was re-published from time to time for the remainder of the century, enjoying a modest following of enthusiasts especially this side of the Atlantic. In Ireland, W.B.

Yeats recalled how his father's reading of *Walden* to him inspired him from boyhood with a yearning to have a Walden of his own, and in after years, remembering this desire, he wrote 'Innisfree', whose 'nine bean rows' are in reminiscence of Walden.

In England, where George Eliot had years before reviewed *Walden* kindly in the *Westminster Gazette,* Robert Louis Stevenson saw fit in 1880 to assail the book in an ill-humoured essay whose sentiments he afterwards recanted, admitting that Thoreau was one of the inspirations of his life and writing. Perhaps this recantation was symptomatic of the changing times. Britain's cities were mushrooming into enormous agglomerations of slums and factories; and access to the countryside, except expensively by rail, was yearly becoming more difficult. A new interest in the land and nature arose the more people felt cut off from them. There came a great surge towards simple living, the country-cottage, the open air. Such a movement had to have its literature and its prophets: *Walden*'s day had arrived.

It was the early socialists who took up *Walden*, in the days when they revered Shelley and Carlyle far more than Marx and Engels. Few of these enthusiasts understood, or wanted to understand, much about political theory. Some were content to say with Thoreau that the best government was that which governed least. Many strove towards a now almost forgotten type of socialism, which as Mr. E.M. Forster puts it in his essay on Carpenter, was to be 'non-industrialised, unorganised and rooted in the soil'.

Edward Carpenter, who had an enormous influence on the life and thought of his times, embodied that age perfectly. Inspired by Whitman's *Leaves of Grass*, Carpenter's great prose-poem *Towards Democracy* let much fresh air into Victorian drawing-rooms. Inheriting £500 a year, Carpenter might have settled to a comfortable literary life. Instead, determined to get back to the land, through toil and the simple life, he went into market gardening, which he soon found was not so simple... Eventually, *Walden* fell into his hands with its message of real simplification which went far beyond anything he had imagined. Of *Walden* he wrote: 'Its ideal of life spent with Nature on the very ground-plane of simplicity... has shattered the conventional views of thousands of people. It helped, I must confess, to make me uncomfortable for some years'.

It was Carpenter who described the Victorian Age as marking 'the lowest ebb of modern civilised society'. So it is a natural step from Carpenter to that greatest of all English Thoreauvians, Henry Salt. Salt and his brother-in-law, J.L. Joynes, were young masters at Eton, which institution they shocked by adopting vegetarianism (after Shelley) and socialism, and by protesting against that then favourite Eton pursuit, the coursing of hares. Quitting the luxuries of Eton as Carpenter renounced the status of clergyman, Salt, too, went in for the simple life in a country cottage, there to write, among other works, his studies of Shelley, Thoreau and Jefferies, and (again like Carpenter) to be visited in his rustic retreat by many of his distinguished contemporaries. His influence on the socialist, anarchist and humanitarian movement was great. Among his friends were Gandhi (whom he introduced to Thoreau's *Civil Disobedience* with important results), Ramsay MacDonald, Shaw, Carpenter, Olive Schreiner, Kropotkin, Havelock Ellis, W.H. Hudson, Cunninghame Grahame, John Galsworthy, G.K. Chesterton, Edward Garnett and William Morris. He was a leader of the onslaught which in those days took place against vivisection, blood sports, 'murderous millinery', prison conditions, the game laws, slaughter-house conditions, corporal punishment, bad diet, the oppression of native races, and so on. Salt worshipped Thoreau, or as Mr. Henry Williamson once put it: 'Salt *was*

Thoreau'. Salt was a naturalist, too, in the Thoreau tradition. Shaw said that Salt 'never went out of doors without binoculars to watch the birds'.

William Archer, who as the Ibsen champion helped to bring about a revolution in English drama, was another Thoreau enthusiast. He, too, took to country life and lived from 1890 to 1895 at a cottage near Ockham in Surrey which he called 'Walden', and from which he went for long walks with Shaw, Pinero and A.B. Walkley. Shaw, in his preface to Stephen Winsten's *Salt and his Circle*, wrote: 'It was Salt who introduced William Archer to me. Both of them were Thoreau specialists. It was through this introduction that I started writing plays.' Though Shaw never read Thoreau, he heard so much of him from Archer and Salt that even he was heard to quote Thoreau on occasions.

Influential in a quiet way, Henry Salt was not a man to make headlines. Quite the opposite was Robert Blatchford who also slept with *Walden* under his pillow, and of whom Chesterton said: 'Very few intellectual swords have left such a mark on our time, have cut so deep or remained so clean.' With a single book Blatchford achieved a staggering notoriety. *Merrie England* (1893) sold two million copies (mostly at a penny each) by rising at the psychological moment on the wave of social and intellectual discontent that swept through the Nineties. Blatchford was to the fore in the open-air movement as well. His ideas reached ever wider audiences through his popular paper *The Clarion*. There sprang up *Clarion* discussion groups, *Clarion* theatre-groups, and through *Clarion* cycling-clubs town-bound young workers on their new 'safety-bicycles' sought the open countryside at weekends. Blatchford began *Merrie England* with the injunction that if his readers first read *Walden* they would more easily understand his book, and thousands read and took to heart Thoreau's message.

The turn of the century was an exciting time when alongside America's *Walden* one could breathe in even more daring new ideas from Europe in the works of Nietzsche, Kropotkin, Bakunin and Tolstoy; and when little magazines vied with each other to put across their various revolutionary messages. There was *The Eagle and the Serpent*, nineteen issues of which were published in London between 1898 and 1902 and which 'Dedicated to the Philosophy of Life Enunciated by Nietzsche, Emerson, Stirner, Thoreau and Goethe, Labours for the Recognition of New Ideals in Politics and Sociology, in Ethics and Philosophy, in Literature and Art'. In Derby there was published *The Candlestick*, whose editor, W.L. Hare, went to prison in 1902 for refusing to pay taxes to support the Boer War; in this act he was inspired by Thoreau's example, who, as he relates in *Walden*, spent a night in jail for refusing to pay the taxes imposed by a government which sent escaped slaves back into slavery. To go to prison for a principle was an act typical of the age, and found an echo a little later in the martyrdoms of the suffragette movement, and the pacifist movement of the first World War.

But 1914-1918 changed everything, suddenly completing the triumph of science and mechanics. Before then few cars stirred the dust of country roads. Many villages were as remote as they had been in the eighteenth century. Rural Old England was still much as the New England of *Walden*: the townsman's dream of a Thoreau-style rustic retreat still seemed possible. But in the intensely organised and urbanised society of the post-war years, the ideal of the simple life waned. That the popularity of *Walden* did not wane with it was a measure of the book's depth. There was and is an enduring core of readers who love *Walden*, not as a book of clever and quotable ideas, but as the superbly expressed utterance of a man not concerned with 'isms' but with the search for individual integrity.

Among modern writers there have been many who, like H.M. Tomlinson, have loved *Walden*. But none perhaps have been quite as captivated as H.W. Nevinson, who directed his long-lasting energies to the support of the oppressed on so many fronts such as Greece, Turkey, Ireland, South Africa, India and Russia, as well as England. Visiting America in 1920, Nevinson went to see those 'quiet relics of Concord: the houses of Hawthorne and Emerson'. Then he walked out to Walden Pond: 'There I sat for long, for there was the place I had wished to visit more than any other in America. It was there that my friend Thoreau had lived, and there in loneliness had conceived the little book which to me is the most beautiful product that ever sprang from American soil, as he himself was the most beautiful and courageous nature'.

Now in this centenary year we can ask: will *Walden* remain readable for another hundred years? I think it will. As long as a love of the open-air, of natural beauty, of intellectual freedom and of the dignity of the individual endures, *Walden* will be cherished.

Perhaps the prophecy made by W.H. Hudson in 1917 on the occasion of the centenary of Thoreau's birth will prove right. Hudson wrote: 'I have failed to find, in all the books and articles on Thoreau which I have read, a satisfying and adequate statement or exposition of the man and his true place in the world of mind and spirit. The reason for my failure, it might be said, is that I have put him too high, that my enthusiasm has spoilt my judgment... Nevertheless, I will stick to my belief that when the bicentenary comes round and is celebrated by our descendants; when... are forgotten all those who anatomized Thoreau in order to trace his affinities and give him true classification – now as Gilbert White, now as a lesser Ralph Waldo Emerson, now as a Richard Jefferies, now as somebody else, he will be regarded simply as himself, as Thoreau, one without master or mate, who was ready to follow his own genius whithersoever it might lead him… and who was in the foremost ranks of the prophets.'

(1955)

2: *Men of Straw*

Thoreau digresses at every turn of the river, and hauls us off in unexpected pursuit not of cougar, wolverine or even porcupine, but of poetry or Yoga or the theory of history. We come upon these digressions, as Lowell said, 'like snags, jolting us head foremost out of our places as we are rowing placidly up stream or drifting down. Mr. Thoreau becomes so absorbed in these discussions, that he seems, as it were, to catch a crab, and disappears uncomfortably from his seat at the bow-oar.' Fortunately, he recovers adroitly and we continue our riverine way, forgetting the intellectual backwaters as Thoreau resumes those subjects which are really his own: the natural history of his native waters, the sounds, scents and visual delights of a boating-holiday amid beautiful surroundings.

Halting for a nightly bivouac, and having transferred our stores from boat to tent, lit the fire and supped, we sit under the lantern in the author's tent and hear him 'read the Gazetteer' in order to learn the latitude and longitude not only of our camp along the river-bank but of our situation in the universe itself. Or we row down-river in pursuit of an errant melon: 'We set one of our largest melons to cool in the still waters among alders at the mouth of the creek; but when our tent was pitched and ready, and we went to get it, it had floated out into the stream and was nowhere to be seen. So taking the boat in the twilight, we went in pursuit of this property, and at length, after long straining of the eyes, its green disc was discovered far down the river, gently floating seaward with many twigs and leaves from the mountain that evening, and so perfectly balanced that it had not keeled at all, and no water had run in at the tap which had been taken out to hasten its cooling.'

A Week on the Concord and Merrimack Rivers was many years a-growing. The actual river-trip was in 1839; the bulk of the book was written piecemeal from journals at Walden in 1846; it was altered and enlarged until just before it was published in 1849; it thus provides a ten years' vista of its author's mind and temperament. Its genial mood reflects the optimism and self-assurance he had gained in the leisured solitude of Walden life. There he had known ecstatic hours and sublime visions; had learnt to know himself and trust himself; had been satisfied that his nature, though at odds with human institutions, was in tune with life at a deeper, truer level. 'Waves of serener life' had passed over him, 'like flashes of sunlight over the fields in cloudy weather'. To give himself time to work on this book at Walden, he had planted fewer beans the second spring and a greater crop of 'sincerity, truth, simplicity, faith, innocence'. He was nearing the height of his literary power and fixed in his independent way of life. As he watched the easy flow of words across his page he saw his projected career as a writer more clearly before him than he was ever to see it again. *A Week on the Concord* is the work of a contented man and reflects a genuine state of inward strength, calm and goodwill. It is the work of a man more than commonly affected by the beauty of the world and nowhere is his power of description better displayed than when he writes of his beloved native stream: 'Gradually the village murmur subsided, and we seemed to be embarked on the placid current of our dreams, floating from past to future as silently as one awakes to fresh morning or evening thoughts. We glided noiselessly down the stream, occasionally driving a pickerel or a bream from the covert of the pads, and the smaller bittern now and then sailed away on sluggish wings from some recess in the shore, or the larger lifted itself out of the long grass at our approach and carried its precious legs away to deposit them in a place of safety. The tortoises also rapidly dropped into the water, as our boat ruffled the surface amid the willows, breaking the reflection of the trees. The banks had passed the height of their beauty, and some of the brighter flowers showed by their faded tints that the season was verging towards the afternoon of the year... But we missed the white water-lily, which is the queen of river flowers, its reign being over for this season. He makes his voyage too late, perhaps, by a true water-clock, who delays so long. Many of this species inhabit our Concord water. I have passed down the river before sunrise on a summer morning between fields of lilies still shut in sleep; and when, at length, the flakes of sunlight from over the bank fell on the surface of the water, whole fields of white blossom seemed to flash open before me, as I floated along, like the unfolding of a banner, so sensible is this flower to the influence of the sun's rays.'

Yet the tranquil mood of the book occasionally breaks down into something less patient, giving a foretaste of the trenchant style of many passages in *Walden*. For that 'singular yearning towards all wildness' which was to be the keynote of *Walden* could never be muffled when Thoreau felt his rights to individuality and free-thought challenged by traditional religious or moral codes. From the God of the Hebrews, Thoreau had turned to the worship of Pan, whom, in Walden Woods, he had found still reigning 'in his pristine glory, with his ruddy face, his flowing beard, and his shaggy body, his pipe and his crook'. To Pan-worship he joined a great reverence for the philosophy of India which he felt had a breadth and depth of vision denied to western thought: 'Beside the vast and cosmogonal philosophy of the Bhagvad-Geeta, even our Shakespeare seems sometimes youthfully green and practical merely.' In this rejection of formalism, authority and tradition, Thoreau followed Emerson, who had left the Church because it worshipped 'in the dead forms of our forefathers' and because he thought a 'Socratic paganism better than an effete, superannuated Christianity'. 'If I should ask the Minister of Middlesex', wrote Thoreau, to let me speak in his pulpit on a Sunday he would object, because I do not *pray* as he does, or because I am not *ordained*. What under the sun are these things?'

It was in the same glowing spirit of revolt that Thoreau, early in 1848, in his room at Emerson's, wrote the first version of his famous outburst on civil disobedience, which, since it inspired Mahatma Ghandi, can claim to be one of the fountain-heads of the passive resistance movement in India and elsewhere. It first took the form of a lecture called *The Rights and Duties of the Individual in Relation to Government* which Thoreau read before the Concord Lyceum. That unfailing ally of 'the newness', Elizabeth Peabody, published it in Boston in May 1849, in a Transcendentalist anthology called *Aesthetic Papers*. It is now universally referred to as *Civil Disobedience*, and it is still much read and quoted by those who would like to see force resisted by other than force.

In *Walden* Thoreau relates how one summer's evening, on his way back to the pond from Concord, where he had been having a shoe mended, he was arrested and put into the village jail for not having paid his poll-tax. He spent the night in a cell and was released after breakfast the following morning, somebody, presumably one of the family, having paid his tax for him, much to his vexation. A trifling enough incident, yet one which set Thoreau thinking. He had a mind which worked down into the implications beneath quite trivial events, seeking to define the principles involved. Living alone had led him to consider at length his relationship with society, but it was not until that society had pawed him physically and he had faced the cold realities of a cell, that he fully comprehended the immensity of power which governments wield over individuals. He was forced at last to get his ideas sorted out clearly and firmly.

He did not object to paying taxes levied expressly for social purposes such as road-building or education, but he and many other liberal-minded men resented the poll-tax as the instrument of government aiming at repression and imperialist expansion. For although slavery was confined to the southern states, Massachusetts and the north were bound by the Fugitive Slave Law which made it a severely punishable offence to harbour escaped slaves or assist them on their way north to Canada. The law required that captured slaves had to be returned to their southern owners. But in the north the anti-slavery movement was making rapid growth. The Thoreau home was only one among many where reforms of all sorts were being passionately advocated. Alcott had gone to jail in 1843 for refusing to pay poll-tax, and his example encouraged others, including Thoreau. Hating slavery, these rebels also hated the expansionist tendencies lately manifested by the American government in its war against Mexico. In *Civil Disobedience*, Thoreau makes a multiple protest against slavery, armies, war, government, politicians and legislators, speaking out for individual conscience in conflict with unjust government, which, he feared, meant every government that ever was.

He wrote: 'A common and natural result of an undue respect for law is that you may see a file of soldiers, colonel, captain, corporal, privates, powder-monkeys, and all, marching in admirable order over hill and dale to the wars, against their wills, ay, against their common sense and consciences... Now what are they? Men at all? Or small movable forts and magazines, at the service of some unscrupulous man in power?...' And since you never know when the state and your conscience are going to clash next, forcing you to move on, he advised: 'You must always live within yourself and depend on yourself, always tucked up and ready for a start.' Thoreau reacted against unjust laws as the sensitive plant shrinks from the touch of human fingers: 'I was not born to be forced – I will breathe after my own fashion. If a plant cannot live according to its nature, it dies, and so a man.' In these words lies the whole strength of his essay on civil disobedience. It is Thoreau at his controversial best. He neither preaches, rants nor thunders, but speaks like an oracle against the sheep-like way in which society allows itself to be governed by men of straw.

(1954)

3: 'There is but one Thoreau'

To Thoreau, as to [Gilbert] White, the popularisers of nature have owed much. In Britain, by 1900, W.H. Hudson was following the tradition of writing about nature exactly, beautifully, but unsentimentally. In America, the nature writer John Burroughs spoke for many when, towards the end of his days, he wrote: 'There is but one Thoreau, and we should devoutly thank the gods of New England for the precious gift. I wish I had a little of the Thoreau quality – that high moral and high stoical tone that I haven't got that makes his work nearer the classical standards.'

But for whatever reason different readers admire him, Thoreau will be remembered by most as the advocate of living close to nature. No one has ever put the case better than he did in *Walden*: 'Our village life would stagnate if it were not for the unexplored forests and meadows which surround it. We need the tonic of wildness – to wade sometimes in marshes where the bittern and the meadow-hen lurk, and hear the booming of the snipe, to smell the whispering sedge where only some wilder and more solitary fowl builds her nest, and the mink crawls with its belly close to the ground. At the same time that we are earnest to explore and learn all things, we require that all things be mysterious and unexplorable, that land and sea be infinitely wild, unsurveyed, and unfathomed by us because unfathomable. We can never have enough of nature.'

(1954)

'NASTY BIRDS'

In these parts, as I recall with pleasure, we used to have a character with an unorthodox attitude to nature. Being a wealthy landowner he could afford to indulge his particular eccentricity, which was bird-protection of a very special kind. We all know that our legislators have decided for us which birds are nice and which are nasty, some indeed so nasty that not even bird-protection societies will usually raise a finger in their defence. It was this second group, the out-and-out vermin, that our eccentric landowner chose to protect.

All the detested crow tribe found sanctuary in his woods (and what he said to the pests officer who came to reduce the rookery may not be printable but it was effective). And sparrowhawks and woodpigeons nested peacefully in his coverts, along with a whole eisteddfod of rabbits, badgers, polecats, foxes, stoats and weasels.

Which was satisfactory so far as it went. But the fate of one bird worried him: the cormorant, then so persecuted by angling interests. For cormorants, being waterbirds, naturally never sought the shelter of his waterless estate. There was only one thing to do: to acquire the rights of a stretch of cliff complete with nesting cormorants and make it a bird sanctuary. Which, after long negotiations, he succeeded in doing. Now, some years after his death, his cragful of cormorants still thrives, a lasting monument, be it hoped, to a friend of birds that are not quite nice.

(1993)

'THIS ENRAPTURED MAN'

I owe a debt to dear old Evan Roberts of Capel Curig (1909-1991). So do we all, all of us who have found delight in the mountain plants of Snowdonia, for over many years he was the fountain of all knowledge on the subject. Evan, leaving school at fourteen, spent thirty-three years as a slate-quarry worker high on Moel Siabod, but at the same time he taught himself about plants with such success that he eventually earned his living as a Nature Conservancy botanist and, later still, was given an honorary M.Sc. by the University of Wales. Always eager to help others he became a botanical guru for many of us. A day out with Evan was always memorable, not least for the infectious excitement with which he pointed out the plants of his beloved Eryri.

I have two especially treasured memories of being out with this enraptured man. The first was when he introduced me to the flora of Ogwen. We walked up the rocky path towards Cwm Idwal, then veered left to clamber steeply to the (in those days) seclusion of Cwm Bochlwyd. From there he led us along the ridge called the Gribin and on ever higher to the crags of Cwm Cneifio. For the first time in Britain, I saw moss campion, mountain avens, alpine meadow-rue, alpine bistort, alpine saw-wort and the unique Snowdon lily. I have been a Snowdonia plant enthusiast ever since.

My other outstanding day with Evan Roberts came many years later on the Great Orme, that bold and shapely chunk of limestone that stands into the sea at Llandudno and, though so long a playground for thousands of people, is still splendidly rich in wildflowers. I picked Evan up at Capel Curig but it was not until we reached the Orme and began to look for plants that I realized he had by now almost completely lost his sight. Was that a handicap for him? Hardly at all. He knew his way about the Orme perfectly and it was fascinating to see him go down on his hands and knees and identify each species by touch: spring cinquefoil, vernal squill, common rockrose, hoary rockrose, kidney vetch and so on. From birth Evan Roberts had been blind in one eye; but with his one good eye he was to find far more plants than most of us manage with two.

In his last years he became completely blind. Yet one day when I called at his house I was told he had gone botanizing in the Alps! There, I learned later, he achieved a lifetime ambition. With one of his sons to guide him he saw (or rather touched) the alpine forget-me-not (*Eritrichium nanum*) whose brilliant blue flowers have earned it the title: 'King of the Alps'. King of Eryri would not have been a bad title for Evan Roberts.

(1995)

THE MERRY GENIUS OF GEORGE BORROW

Silver-haired, six feet two and broad with it, he comes striding along one of the rough hill tracks of mid-nineteenth century Wales. It is a November afternoon and getting dark because mist has enveloped the mountains. Down the last steep hill the road has a dangerous drop below it and he has to feel his way cautiously. By the time he gets into a valley that marks the border between Carmarthenshire and Glamorgan it is raining hard and he is soaked to the skin. It is quite dark when he reaches the coal-mining village he calls 'Gutter Vawr' (Y Gwter Fawr) now known as Brynaman. Someone guides him to the village inn.

He books a room and then goes into the kitchen which has a good fire in the grate and is crowded with colliers and carters all smoking, drinking, singing and shouting.

Let George Borrow relate what happens next: 'My entrance seemed at once to bring everything to a dead stop: the smokers ceased to smoke, the hand that was conveying the glass or mug was arrested in air, the hurly burly ceased and every eye was turned upon me with a strange enquiring stare.' This theatrical entry and the lively exchanges which follow are quintessential Borrow. If it seems like a scene from a novel this is because Borrow was undoubtedly one of nature's great story-tellers; and though *Wild Wales* is certainly not a novel there are many times when it comes very close to being one. Or perhaps a piece of theatre. To turn this book into a play would be easy when page after page contains such sparkling dialogue.

Make no mistake about it, *Wild Wales* is very far from being yet another sober and factual chronicle of a walk through Wales to add to the many that preceded it. It is the unique work of a master craftsman out to produce a highly original piece of creative writing. Alas, it proved far too original for many of the reading public of the 1860s. Looking for a conventional tour through the Welsh countryside with descriptions of mountains, valleys, towns, villages, castles, abbeys and gentlemen's seats, the average mid-Victorian reader was totally unprepared for this ostentatious, boisterous, tale-weaving and ever exaggerating individual, who, although he was an English gentleman, found English middle-class gentility and fashionable life abhorrent, who persistently hob-nobbed with the lower classes and had a genuine affection for down and outs, tinkers, gypsies and many others who lived outside the stockade.

Right from the first edition (1862) the title page of *Wild Wales* carried Taliesin's plaintive prophecy:

63

> Their Lord they shall praise,
> Their language they shall keep,
> Their land they shall lose
> Except Wild Wales.

Also from the start the full title was *Wild Wales, its people, language and scenery*. Note the order of these items. Borrow keeps to it consistently. His primary emphasis is on the people and their language. The scenery, even when he takes us up Snowdon or Plynlimon, is hardly more than a splendid stage setting for his own frolics and thoughts.

In calling his book *Wild Wales* he really means it. And he looks for the wildness of Wales not only in the scenery but also in the people. He wants to meet those who are least contaminated by modernization and English influences. So his moment of greatest delight comes in the hills above Dinas Mawddwy in Merioneth where he finds people saying '*Dim Saesneg*' (No English). 'I was now indeed in Wales among the real Welsh,' he rejoices. Again, between Machynlleth and Ponterwyd, he is very happy when 'a buxom laughing girl' asks him in Welsh: 'What would we do with English here?' He particularly admires Welsh for its long duration. This ancient language ('a tongue older than Greek,' as he puts it) was for him at the heart of the wildness of Wales.

Borrow's long holiday in Wales in the summer and autumn of 1854 began conventionally enough. With Mary his wife and his step-daughter Henrietta, he came by train from their little estate in Norfolk via Birmingham to Chester. But there Borrow's natural unconventionality took over. Leaving his companions to go on to Llangollen, Borrow quit the train at Chester. For this, his first crossing of Offa's Dyke, was going to be a sacred moment in the life of a man with a long devotion to Wales and who believed that 'the Welsh are equal in genius, intellect and learning to any people under the sun.' That he had never been to Wales before was because for thirty years he had been totally preoccupied elsewhere, much of his time being spent in Russia, Spain and other countries. So having got to Chester he felt he had to walk into Wales. For how could he enjoy the full flavour of crossing such a holy frontier if he were to be rushed across it in a train?

Why was this native of Norfolk so in love with all things Welsh? This is one of several mysteries surrounding the life of George Borrow. It was in his late teens in Norwich that he learnt Welsh. Mostly he taught himself by intensively studying, for three years, Milton's *Paradise Lost* alongside a Welsh translation of it. (What a way to learn a language!) For help with spoken Welsh he took weekly lessons for a year from a Welsh-speaking groom named Lluyd who came from the Devil's Bridge area and who happened to be working in Norwich. Borrow was clearly a linguist to his finger-tips. With total ease, while still a youth, he soaked up twelve foreign tongues including German, Italian, Danish, Arabic and Armenian; and later he made translations from over thirty languages. It was a gift he had developed in boyhood. 'God help the child,' said his father, 'I sent him to school to learn Greek and he picked up Irish!' His father, an army man, was at the time stationed in Ireland, and Borrow liked the Irish ever afterwards.

He never learned to pronounce Welsh very well. But then, his primary ambition had always been to be able to read the Welsh poets rather than to speak the language. Listening to him in north Wales people took him for a south Walian. In south Wales they thought he came from the north. Still, he managed to make himself more or less understood wherever he went, which was not a bad achievement for a Norfolkman who had never been to Wales before and had probably not brushed up his Welsh for thirty years.

He caused amazement everywhere. And how he loved doing so! It is part of the fun of his book, this delight he got from seeing the astonishment on people's faces when they heard an English gentleman speaking Welsh. After all, not even many Welsh gentlemen spoke Welsh in those days when Welsh was officially frowned upon. Borrow also got much satisfaction out of holding forth to Welsh people about their own culture, not only about their poets but also about their history and great Welshmen like Owain Glyndŵr, Edward Lhuyd and Lewis Morris. But if he impressed the Welsh peasants they also impressed him, delighting him with their knowledge of their bards. 'What a difference,' he remarks, 'between a Welshman and an Englishman of the lower class. What would a Suffolk miller's swain have said if I had repeated to him verses out of *Beowulf* or even Chaucer?'

Which chapters are the best of *Wild Wales*? No doubt many readers will prefer the hilarious encounters in the taverns with Borrow scoring points right and left in his arguments, a jug of ale in his hand. Others will prefer the chance meetings along the highways or the mountain tracks, especially those with the 'real Welsh' or the 'wild Irish'. The ascent of Snowdon is well reported. As he goes up the Llanberis path arm in arm with young Henrietta, he sings a Welsh stanza at the top of his voice. (What their guide thought about it all is not recorded.) When they reach the top there are great panoramas to be described and coffee and ale to be drunk in the summit cabin. Inevitably on this very special occasion he has to stand on Snowdon's topmost rocks and declaim some Welsh poetry. Whereupon to Borrow's great amusement, a Welshman standing near asks him if he is a Breton!

When he goes off on his own to Anglesey it is because 'there never was such a place for poets', and here the parish he was most eager to get to was Llanfair Mathafarn Eithaf near the northeast coast. For there had lived the poet, Goronwy Owen, 'who died poor, leaving nothing behind him but his immortality.' The whole episode of this pilgrimage, a ten-mile walk in blistering heat, in search of memories of Goronwy Owen, is one of the most moving in the book.

Borrow is never more joyful than when he is swinging along at full speed with things happening fast and the scenery ever changing. We too can be joyous as we fall in beside him, especially along such wonderful roads as the one that leads us from the pass of Bwlch y Groes down into the valley of the upper Dyfi, a district as wild and unspoilt now as it was in Borrow's day. A few miles south we can try to keep up with this long-shanked walker as he faces the wilderness beyond Machynlleth. There he discusses the way with one of the locals. 'Well,' says Borrow, 'I suppose you would advise me to go by the hills?' (This being by far the nearest way to Devil's Bridge.) 'Certainly, sir,' he is told, 'that is if you wish to break your neck, or to sink in a bog, or to lose your way, or perhaps if night comes on, to meet the *Gwr Drwg* [the Evil One] himself taking a stroll. But to talk soberly. The way over the hills is an awful road, and indeed for the greater part is no road at all.' Of course, that is the road our hero chooses; and his account of the journey is masterly.

So too is his story of the climbing of Plynlimon which he approaches from Devil's Bridge, picking up a guide at the Dyffryn Castell hotel. It is one of those rare sunny days with which November occasionally blesses the mountains after a wet and windy night. Yet on this lovely day, as Borrow reminds us, one of the bloodiest conflicts of the Crimean War, the Battle of Inkerman, was being fought. There are several other references in *Wild Wales* to that far-away war with its heavy losses and great sufferings. They serve to give a touch of realism to a narrative which at times seems to be taking us into a world rather like Tolkien's.

It is with our author in top form that we ascend 'the grand Plynlimon'. But he immediately hurts the guide's feelings by remarking: 'It does not look much of a hill;' to which the guide's indignant retort is: 'I question whether there is a higher hill in the world. God bless Pumlummon Mawr!' Together they reach the summit cairns and inspect the sources of the rivers Rheidol, Severn and Wye, with Borrow drinking ceremoniously at all three. On the summit he bursts into song, singing his own translation of a poem by Lewis Glyn Cothi. By sunset they are back at the Dyffryn Castell hotel and Borrow goes off on the final three miles to Devil's Bridge. 'The evening was calm and beautifully cool with a slight tendency to frost. I walked long with a bounding and elastic step and never remember to have felt more happy and cheerful.'

Wild Wales is in fact a happy and cheerful book. Borrow, his biographers tell us, had been in a state of depression in recent years. Whatever the truth of that we can be sure that the clouds had unravelled by the summer of 1854 and that walking through Wales he was in great spirits all the way from Chester to Chepstow as he filled his notebooks with lightning sketches and caricatures of the people he met, or with deft word-pictures of soaring mountains, brawling rivers and leafy vales. There is plenty of light and shade in the book. If at any time the road may seem to be getting dull we can be sure there will be laughter round the next bend as yet another wayfarer is adroitly buttonholed and subjected to Borrow's almost third-degree type of interrogation whereby he winkles life-stories out of total strangers.

Many of these stories have their funny side but some are

poignant. Between Newport and Chepstow he meets an itinerant, bare-footed Manchester-Irish girl. Here is one of the most vivid and touching interviews in the book. At that time Wales seems to have been still full of Irish wanderers, refugees from the potato famine of a few years earlier; and Borrow was as fascinated by them as he was by the 'real Welsh'. That he was such a Celtophile could perhaps be because his father was a Cornishman?

Borrow's life-long prejudices were many and he deliberately brings them in wherever he can to raise the temperature of his confrontations with people for the sake of dramatic effect. As a strong Church of England man he never misses a chance of tilting at Roman Catholics on the one hand and chapel-goers on the other. But we need not take him too seriously. In fact he obviously had a soft spot for the Irish Catholics at Holyhead in that hilarious incident when thirty of them, mistaking him for a priest, insisted on kneeling before him while he blessed them 'in holy Latin'. As he explains: 'I gave them the best Latin blessing I could remember out of two or three I had got by memory out of an old Popish book of devotion which I bought in my boyhood at a stall.' Likewise with the chapel-goers: though he knocks at Methodists in general he is not blind to the virtues of Welsh Methodists: 'The worthiest creature I ever knew was a Welsh Methodist,' he admits. And when he gets to the village of Quakers Yard, half-way between Merthyr Tydfil and Caerphilly, he has nothing but praise for the Quakers.

Much has been written about Borrow and appraisal of his life and work will no doubt continue, especially as there is now an enthusiastic George Borrow Society. In the past there have been a few studies heavy with psychology and sociology. How misdirected they are! Authors of such books do not like colourful characters such as Borrow. He lives outside their world, beyond their grasp. They devote tedious pages to picking him to bits as if his writings were intended to be as serious and solemn as theirs. One critic even attacked *Wild Wales* for ignoring the social and political problems of nineteenth century Wales! What, in Heaven's name, do such critics think Borrow came to Wales for? They should remember what his wife wrote about him in a letter from Llangollen: 'He keeps a daily journal of all that goes on so that he can make a most amusing book.' Surely a writer in such a holiday mood should not be expected to give us his thoughts on parliamentary reform or the plight of the agricultural labourer.

Wild Wales has gone through various editions and will see more as time goes on. Why has it lasted so well? Its attractive style has to be part of the answer. It is blessed with simplicity, directness and candour: and these are enduring qualities. In addition there is a wind off the heath blowing through the book, a breeze that has strong appeal these days as the out-door movement continues to grow and country walking gets ever more popular. Then there is the companionable author himself, this agreeably eccentric, larger-than-life, jovial man whose laughter rings all through the book. As when he, a Norfolk gentleman, walks up the road from Maentwrog to Ffestiniog singing old Welsh war songs inciting the Welsh to exterminate the English, or when he manages to buy whiskey at a temperance house.

When we look back, at the end of *Wild Wales*, we realise that it is not so much a book about Wales and the Welsh as it is about George Borrow, a man of intriguing personality, boundless energy and unfailing vivacity, who has enjoyed every minute of the way, right up to the last evening when he celebrates the fulfilment of his odyssey by drinking wine and singing Welsh songs in a hotel in Chepstow. Then he gets into an overnight train, is in London by four o'clock in the morning and the whole strange episode of *Wild Wales* is over. As the train rattles through the night does he wonder which elements of his journey he will remember with greatest pleasure? Will they be the earthy contacts with those people which fill most of the book? Or will they be those rarer moments when he goes floating off on clouds of Romance, as if the Wales he really yearns for is some unattainable realm of medieval mythology, as when he is alone on the Berwyn moors? 'Here I turned and looked at the hills I had come across. There they stood, darkly blue, a rain cloud, like ink, hanging over their summits. Oh, the wild hills of Wales, the land of old renown and of wonder, the land of Arthur and Merlin.'

(1995)

EVAN PRICE EVANS

1: Mab y Mynydd

On 30 March this year [1996], we celebrated a man who was inspired all his life by a mountain. He was Evan Price Evans of Meirionnydd; and a gathering of people – many of them botanists – witnessed the setting of a plaque in his memory on the former primary school at Corris Uchaf, a couple of miles south of Cadair Idris[4]. Here, Evans served for a time as what was then known as a pupil teacher. Cadair Idris was the mountain that captivated him, as it raises its miles of beckoning precipices high above the Mawddach estuary in the north and the Tal-y-llyn valley in the south; it has long been the most cherished mountain in southern Snowdonia.

Evan Price Evans was born in 1880, at Aberllefenni, a small slate-quarrying village four miles south-east of the mountain. It is in a district honeycombed by quarries, now nearly all long

---

[4] As with his use of 'Plynlimon' for Pumlumon, Bill would naturally have used the older accepted version of 'Cader Idris', though, as here, the new orthodoxies came generally albeit inconsistently to prevail late in his life. I have not chosen to standardize them.

disused, where men have been winning slate for generations. Price Evans' father was one of those men, a quarry foreman with a keen eye for veins of perfect slate.

After village schools, Price Evans went to Tywyn Grammar School and decided to become a teacher, making himself useful for a period at the little school in Corris Uchaf. His formal teacher-training was at the Normal College, Bangor, after which he returned to Tywyn Grammar School as a teacher. It was here that he met his future wife, Dorothy Bass, who was there on holiday.

Price Evans's main subject was geography, and it was not long before he was taking the boys out of doors on surveys which combined the geography and natural history of the Dysynni valley – from the coast at Tywyn upriver for six miles as far as that unique inland breeding place for cormorants, Craig yr Aderyn (Bird Rock). So, at the very beginning of the century, he was pioneering what, many decades later, became popularly known as environmental studies. It is likely that he had already been fired by the early writings of A.G. Tansley, who founded the botanical journal, *New Phytologist* in 1902, and whose book *Types of British Vegetation* (1911) was to be a landmark in ecological studies. In later years, Price Evans and Tansley were close friends, as well as fellow members of the British Ecological Society, founded by Tansley and others in 1913.

After about six years in Tywyn, Price Evans moved to a post at Ryhope Grammar School in County Durham, where he was able to base his teaching on ecological studies carried out by his pupils in a small wooded ravine called Ryhope Dene, a place of rich and varied soils and plants. A few years in County Durham and then he transferred to Cheshire, where he taught at the Boteler Grammar School, Warrington, for the rest of his working life, ending as headmaster.

But, throughout those years in Durham and in Cheshire, the rocks, soils and plants of Cadair Idris were never far from his thoughts; and every July for 40 years, as soon as term ended, he and his wife were off to spend weeks on end at a farm under Cadair Idris called Bryn Rhug, their three sons with them until the lads grew up. Those wonderful holidays gave Price Evans the leisure he needed to fulfil what had become his life's dream, of getting to grips with a subject no one had yet seriously tackled – the ecology of the Welsh mountains.

His first classic study of Cadair Idris appeared in 1932, in the *Journal of Ecology*, the second following in 1945, both papers skillfully intertwining geology with botany. No one had then interpreted the ecology of a British mountain better than Price Evans revealed that of Cadair Idris.

The plaque commemorating his life and pioneering work is set on a wall of the Corris Uchaf school (now an outdoor pursuits centre), where he made his first efforts at teaching. The site has a marvellous view across the Tal-y-llyn valley to the craggy outlines of Cadair Idris three miles north-west. The plaque reads:

> Evan Price Evans – 1880-1959
> Geographer Botanist Ecologist
> Who was born in Aberllefenni
> And once taught in this school.
> For forty years he studied the
> Rocks and plants of Cadair Idris
>
> ————————————————
>
> Mab y Mynydd

The Welsh words at the end mean 'a son of the mountain'. Price Evans would have enjoyed that description of himself.

Thirty or so words on a plaque can only hint at the achievements of a lifetime. Price Evans wrote much else besides his studies of Cadair Idris. In *School Science Review*, June 1920, he wrote a memorable article on 'Local Ecology as the basis of School Botany'. There were also his papers in the *Journal of Ecology* on Carrington Moss (May 1923) and Warburton Moss (August 1928), two peatbogs near the Lancashire-Cheshire border. He contributed valuable papers on Welsh upland ecology in the annual reports of the Montgomeryshire Field Society for 1950, 1952 and 1953. And, with A.G. Tansley, he wrote a very useful guide for teachers, *Plant Ecology and the School* (1946), in which he summarized his pioneering work on Ryhope Dene.

There was also his work for conservation. For several years, in the 1950s, he served on the first Wales Committee of the Nature Conservancy, advising on the establishing of pioneer national nature reserves, such as Cwm Idwal, Newborough Warren and Cadair Idris. And it was at his insistence that Merionethshire's first conservation body was created in 1953, as a branch of what is now the North Wales Wildlife Trust.

Those of us who knew Price Evans were impressed, above all, by his unquenchable enthusiasm and by the enthralling way he always spoke about his beloved mountain. There is a charming word-picture of him in his early seventies, in a book by Dorothea Eastwood called *Valleys of Springs*. In the summer of 1951 she was with Mary Richards, a leading Merionethshire botanist, on the occasion of a visit by the Montgomeryshire Field Society to Cwm Cau, a corrie high on Cadair Idris. It began to rain heavily and half the party, not dressed for the weather, had retreated off the mountain. 'Mrs. Richards and I,' reports Dorothea Eastwood, 'were fortunate in the possession of mackintoshes, thick shoes and the consoling presence of a real expert, a delightful, massive, white-haired old gentleman who knows all so far to be known of the geology and plant ecology of Cader. He discoursed as we climbed, on rocks and soils... and on Cader's first eruption from the sea when its peaks were 23,000 feet high and its rocks fiery.'

Days out on Cadair with Price Evans were often misty or downright wet. And that is how we most vividly remember him, leaning against a rock-face and telling us, with the voice of some prophet of old, about the mosses, ferns and saxifrages all round us – and never seeming to notice the chilling winds that buffeted us nor the cold raindrops bouncing off his bald cranium – truly, *mab y mynydd.*

(1996)

2: *'The Upper Basic rocks of Cader Idris while London's traffic roared all around us.'*

In his retirement he was in demand as a leader of field meetings, shepherding us forth in sunshine or in rain, lecturing us in the sweetest way in the world about why plants grow here but not there, or there but not here. Both Hugh Chater and Price Evans, as ecologists, taught us and so many others not only to look at plants but also to think about them and their place in the world.

Guided by Price Evans we began to grasp something of the ecology of Cader Idris and why some cliffs were curtained with green vegetation while others were gaunt and naked precipices with not a leaf of any plant in sight. We ventured along slippery ledges farther than was really safe; peered into caves for rare ferns; slithered, almost tobogganed, down endless screes; sloshed across marshes and waded into lakes in search of water plants. Price Evans enjoyed recounting how one day, while botanizing on Cader Idris, he came upon a geologist who explained that he was trying to trace a certain band of igneous rock across the mountain's north face. To this geologist's total amazement Price Evans felt in his pocket and brought out a map with the said band of rock marked on it for several miles. He then had to show this laborious tapper of the rocks how the outcrop he was seeking was child's play for a botanist to follow because it was rich enough in lime to attract lime-loving plants that are quite absent from the rest of this acid-soiled mountain. All that was needed was the ability to identify the little fern called green spleenwort and one or two calcicole mosses; or a few alpine wildflowers such as purple saxifrage, mossy saxifrage, lesser meadow-rue or mountain sorrel. For the record, the geologist in the story was Arthur Hubert Cox who was to become the author of a classic paper on the geology of Cader Idris in 1925.

Hugh Chater used to tell a story to illustrate Price Evans's devotion to his favourite mountain. He happened to bump into Price Evans in a London street (they were both heading for a Nature Conservancy Council meeting). 'Having exchanged greetings', said Chater, 'it took Price Evans just two minutes to get on to the subject of the Upper Basic rocks of Cader Idris while London's traffic roared all around us.'

If Price Evans had a favourite Cader Idris plant it was *Genista pilosa*, a dwarf shrub with yellow pea flowers. In English it is hairy greenweed though there can be nothing at all weedy about a plant which has probably faced Cader's weather for a vast reach of time. Curiously rare in Britain it has had a patchy history on Cader Idris, its only British mountain locality. It was found up there before 1800 but was then lost sight of so completely that it was dismissed in the nineteenth century as an error. It was not refound until 1901 and then seems to have been lost again till Price Evans came upon it in 1927. Since then botanists have kept a regular eye on *Genista pilosa* and have now shown it to be more widespread on the Cader range than had been thought. For two reasons it is an elusive plant: when not in bloom it is far from eye-catching, and when its flowers do appear they are very soon over. Strangely, though it steadfastly faces awesome frosts not only on Cader but also on the Continent, it is best known in Britain on the coasts of Pembrokeshire and Cornwall where you might well suppose it to be a tenderling in need of a frost-free seaside climate.

(1995)

MARY RICHARDS CAERYNWCH & FRIENDS

1: 'A lady whose enthusiasm was prodigious and infectious'
Into our lives in 1953 came another friend who was to lead us even further into the realm of green plants. Mary Richards of Dolgellau was a lady whose enthusiasm was prodigious and infectious. Ty'nllidiart, her cottage that looked across to the great cliffs of Cader Idris four miles away, was an open house for botanists from all over the country, especially Kew Herbarium where she had several friends. She loved to take her visitors up Cader to show them the alpine plants, and even in her old age most of them got tired before she did. Going out so often with Mary Richards we learnt much about the flora of the botanically rich country around Dolgellau. And about birds, mammals, insects and everything else.

2: From young Mary Stokes to young Mrs. Richards
North of Dolserau the land rises up to the Nannau estate and two shapely hills, Foel Cynwch and Foel Offrwm, both crowned by the remains of Iron Age hill-forts. Nearby are the far-seeing Precipice Walk; the fishy lake, Llyn Cynwch; a former deer-park; and the tree-surrounded pool, Pwll y Gele. This superb estate was a playground for Mary Stokes because of the close links between the Vaughans of Nannau and the Edwardses of Dolserau. Further north the land goes on climbing to Rhobell Fawr from whose rocky summit there is a magnificent panorama not only of Cader Idris but also of the whole exciting profile

of the Rhinog range. From her childhood Mary loved the Rhinogydd and in later life often spoke of youthful adventures exploring Cwm Mynach, the Clogau gold mines (which she knew as a nesting place of choughs) and the manganese mines of the uplands. At Bont-ddu her family were friendly with the Beales of Bryntirion who enthusiastically combined field sports (they had a grouse moor on the Rhinogydd) with an interest in natural history. The Beales also lived in Birmingham where Charles Gabriel Beale was a distinguished alderman. At the City Museum and Art Gallery there is the Beale Memorial Collection of nesting groups of British birds created in his honour in 1913.

Between the Rhinogydd and Cader Idris lies a scenic masterpiece – the estuary of the Mawddach which Mary Richards loved for its fishing, its birdwatching, its plant-life; and for the sailing the family had long enjoyed at Barmouth. And alongside the estuary there were the woodlands at Abergwynant and the peatbog at Arthog – all good country for naturalists. But of all this region within easy reach of Dolgellau, it was probably the coast that appealed to her most strongly in those happy days before the present ugly sprawls of permanent caravans had arrived. Along the coast her favourite spot in the 1920s and 1930s was Mochras (Shell Island) and the nearby dunes, now Morfa Dyffryn National Nature Reserve. Here she often came with the family or with naturalist friends like James and Mrs. Backhouse of Arthog. In spring and summer she enjoyed the spectacular displays of wild orchids in the damp dune hollows; and the burnet roses with their showy white flowers and shiny black hips. The Mochras area is no longer what it was in her day. She knew it as a breeding place for many redshanks, oystercatchers, ringed plovers, shelducks, black-headed gulls, skylarks and wheatears. Today the ground is far drier, the summer pools she was familiar with have mostly gone, there is infinitely more disturbance by people and adjacent to it there is today a military airfield. In her later years, if she went to the coast, she preferred the botanically rich, less disturbed dunelands of Morfa Harlech, five miles north.

While the children were young in the 1920s, Mary relived her own childhood, encouraging them in nature study just as Fraulein Wahl [Mary's German governess and botanical and literary mentor from the age of twelve] had inspired her in the 1890s. They did all the things children had been brought up to do since nature studies began in Victorian times. They sprouted oaks from acorns, reared newts and frogs from tadpoles and produced butterflies and moths from caterpillars. They kept sticklebacks in an aquarium and watched them guarding their nests and bringing forth their young. They had a whole zoo of other creatures: guinea pigs, hedgehogs, water snails, water spiders and the larvae of caddis flies and dragonflies. They learned about predation from seeing how, in the aquarium, the larvae of the great water beetle could kill lampreys and elvers.

They noted the wildflowers in their seasons, beginning with celandines, dog's mercury, pussy willows and hazel catkins. Along the Clywedog stream below the garden they found mosses in abundance, sheets of Wilson's filmy fern and, on the trunks of waterside oaks, the large and beautiful leafy lichen, tree lungwort. From the shore they brought home seaweeds and pressed them. In autumn they collected fungi, some mushroom-shaped, some finger-like, some strangely formed like the brown Jews-ears they found on dead elder branches. They laid the caps of toadstools on sheets of paper and marvelled at the patterns of spores they found next morning. In the family log there are hints of more serious lessons in botany, as on 20 August 1927, when 'between Gwanas Drive and the lodge' at Caerynwch, they picked a large bunch of wildflowers. These they then listed systematically: rose family, borage family, figwort family, thyme family and so on, 75 species in all. But Mary made a point of never forcing botany down their throats.

3: The bottoms up brigade

1928 was also the year when Mary [Richards] made an interesting new friend. John Henry Salter, one of the best all-round naturalists of his day, had long resided at Aberystwyth where (1891-1905) he had been first Professor of Botany at the University College. He was, as he described himself, 'a naturalist of the old style, knowing something of all branches and not being an authority on any… My ideas are mid-Victorian.' He expressed no admiration at all for politicians, but he liked Prime Minister Neville Chamberlain much better on learning that he was an expert on moths. Though devoted to the flora of Cardiganshire, Salter had long been interested in the plants of Cader Idris; and in September, 1928, he wrote to Mary Richards, whom he had never met, inquiring about several Cader species.

His letter was one of old-world formality beginning: 'Dear Madam'. He wanted to know about rarities like alpine saw-wort, bog orchid and oblong woodsia; and then: 'But the plant I especially want to inquire about is *Genista pilosa*. Following directions received from Mr. D.A. Jones, I made a careful search of Cwm Gau Graig a week ago but failed to meet with it'. Hairy greenweed (*Genista pilosa*) is probably Cader's most distinguished plant. To most botanists it is known as a rarity of the mild coasts of Pembrokeshire and Cornwall. So it is very strange to find it flourishing on the heights of Cader where winters can be so harsh.

So it came about that the hairy greenweed drew together two botanists in a friendship that was to last till Salter's death in 1942. Occasionally he was invited to lunch at Caerynwch which he reached by train to Dolgellau (he never had a car) and then two miles on foot up to the house by way of the Torrent Walk. But though arriving for lunch he always brought his own food so as not to deviate from a lifetime of strict vegetarianism. His friendship with Mary Richards was, on the face of it, an improbable one. He was a Quaker and a pacifist; she was High Church and a soldier's wife. He was no lover of hunting and she revelled in it. Yet they always greatly respected each other and had many a happy day together in the pursuit of natural history, often with their mutual friends, James Backhouse of Arthog and E.H.T. Bible of Aberdyfi. For Mary's children, their mother's friendship with these staid, middle-aged to elderly naturalists was a source of amusement. 'Mummy's young men', they christened them. They also called them 'the bottoms up brigade', a name suggested by a frequent posture of botanists.

4: A skeleton (1930)

Two days later they were watching ravens again, this time on Cader where they spotted a nest in the cliffs above Llyn Aran 'just above where I found the skeleton', says Mary's diary in a reference to an incident a few years earlier when she had been in Cwm Aran with her friend Florence Bristow, and Florence's husband, the orthopaedic surgeon Walter Bristow, of St. Thomas's Hospital, London. While the Bristows rested by the lake, Mary went scrambling up the rocks in search of plants but what she found was a heap of bones. Picking one up she brought it down to show to Walter who said: 'By God, Mary, it's a human arm-bone!' 'I know,' replied Mary, 'the rest is up there.' The identity of the skeleton still remains a mystery but it is presumably that of some luckless hill-walker who had fallen off Mynydd Moel[5].

---

[5] Kilvert's diary has a similar story to tell from this side of Cader – clearly a place to exercise great prudence.

5: Squire's night out

In October there was a curious dog incident. The day was so glorious that Mary could not resist the call of Cader. With her went her spaniel, Squire, and she enjoyed perfect views from the top. On the way home she was given tea by the Pughs of Penrhyngwyn, one of the Caerynwch estate farms. Squire meanwhile was shut up in a stable but during tea he escaped and, not knowing where Mary was, ran away towards Cader. By dark he had not shown up and Mary went home without him. She was also without her rucksack which, she now remembered, she had left on the top of Cader. Next morning in a gale of rain, farmer Pugh, who held a Royal Humane Society medal for mountain rescues, went up Cader. There on the summit was Mary's rucksack and Squire quite fiercely guarding it.

6: A garden in the bush

We found Mary Richards living five miles north-east of Abercorn along a sandy road through the bush. Her house, Ndundu, set back about a quarter of a mile from the road, looks down through the trees to Lake Chila in the distance. It is a garden entirely surrounded by the wild trees of the bush except that the house itself is set against a background of tall eucalyptus trees, so typical a feature of country houses all over the district. The popularity of these Australian trees is not surprising for they grow quickly into lofty elegance, add perfume to the air and their timber is excellent. But what did most to bring them into favour in Central Africa, where they were introduced last century, was their reputation for keeping malaria at bay. This was in the days before the mosquito had been convicted as a carrier and when the disease was attributed to a poisonous miasma floating in the atmosphere and so was called 'mala aria', the Italian for bad air.

Ndundu has a lovely garden. In a flamboyant setting of

poinsettias, bougainvilleas, jacarandas and bottlebrush trees, there are beds bright with salvias, lilies, gladioli, geraniums, zinnias and roses. We were surprised to see the roses of our British gardens growing splendidly in the tropics, for there are hardly any wild roses there.

From her botanical trips Mary Richards has brought back numerous tree orchids for the garden. Nothing could be easier than the cultivation of these curious plants, the only material required being a piece of string and a rough-barked tree. You simply tie the orchid to a branch and the plant does the rest, firmly anchoring itself by sending its roots down into fissures in the bark where enough humus accumulates to satisfy its water requirements. The brachystegia trees round the garden are ideal for this purpose and most of them are draped with the fleshy leaves and the hanging clusters of delicate white flowers of the various kinds of tree orchids. The orchids do the tree no harm: they live quite independently and are not in any way parasites. But the speciality of Ndundu is the aloe bed. Central Africa is rich in aloes and Mary Richards has collected them from far and wide for science and for her garden. Aloes belong to the lily family but do not look as if they do. They have spiny, fleshy leaves in a basal rosette and look much more like cacti than lilies. Only when the flowering spikes shoot up and the hanging flowers open their bells do they look more like the conventional idea of a lily. One aloe in a garden, a small species with orange flowers, was a plant of special distinction for it is known to science as *Aloe richardsiae*, named in Mary Richards' honour after she discovered it in the wilds of south Tanzania where it was growing, as she said, 'as thick as bluebells in an English wood'. This aloe is only one of a growing number of plants named after her because she was their first discoverer. Another is a grass, *Richardsiella cruciformis*. The vast number of beautifully pressed plants she has sent to Kew and other herbaria constitute one of the largest collections ever made in Central Africa and have greatly helped in the writing of such works as the recent *Flora Zambesiaca*.

7: Octogenarian African plant-collector

At Abercorn in November, Mary was delighted to see Vesey[6] (he still had his house there) and to be invited to spend Christmas with him at Momela. Another good item of news came when John Owen, head of the Tanzania game department, turned up at Abercorn on holiday and suggested that she should go and collect in the Ruaha National Park. To be one of the first to botanize in that slice of wilderness was an opportunity not to be missed and she agreed to collect there after Christmas. Meanwhile she was getting letters from the family suggesting she ought to leave Africa because of the crisis caused by Rhodesia's Unilateral Declaration of Independence. Mary's comment was: 'The English papers are alarmist. Here all is normal.' So on 3 December off she went with Sam and Mhilu on the long journey to Arusha which they reached in four days. She collected around Momela for a fortnight, then she and Vesey were off to Lake Manyara to meet Iain Douglas-Hamilton, a young Oxford zoology graduate who, at John Owen's suggestion, had come to study Manyara's large elephant population. Ten years later he was to write his classic book: *Among the Elephants*. By Lake Manyara they came upon large numbers of buffaloes, impalas and elephants and saw rufous-tailed weavers at their large, untidy, hanging nests.

Back at Momela on the eve of Christmas, 1965, they watched elephants 'till it was so dark we could just distinguish the gleam

---

[6] Desmond Vesey-Fitzgerald (1909-1974) – educated at Wye College, he worked from 1949 to 1974 as Senior Scientific Officer at the Anti-Locust Research Centre, Abercorn, Northern Rhodesia and from 1964 to his death was ecologist and conservationist in the National Parks of Tanzania.

of their tusks. The top of Kilimanjaro came out of the cloud, white with snow. A very still evening. The hippos below us gave an occasional splash. A skein of sacred ibis flew over. Cormorants came to roost in an acacia below us. On the further shore some egrets were roosting in another acacia. Faint small bursts of song from small birds going to bed. Then silence and one star came out beyond a yellow sunset and deep, dark clouds.' Two days after Christmas they walked up to Mount Meru's great caldera, their camping gear carried in large panniers by six donkeys. So Mary spent her first night on this mountain that was destined to dominate much of the rest of her life. From the caldera rim they looked back at the Momela lakes; and when they looked up at Meru they saw 'a beautiful lammergeyer with wedge-shaped tail soaring among the clouds.' Then, risking the danger of rhinos, they went down into the Podocarpus forest in the caldera, finding many unknown plants.

On 6 January, 1966, she was off with Sam and Mhilu to begin collecting in the Ruahu; but it did not take her long to realize what an awesome commitment she had let herself in for in that very new and very wild National Park. For, as well as lack of roads – something she was well used to – there were other difficulties. Elephants, for instance. They were not only abundant but also dangerous because they had been much harassed by hunters. So they had to be given the right of the road at all times, which meant long, frustrating delays while waiting for them to move on. But the elephants had their uses: they made paths through the thickets; and in one place they had knocked down two species of *Commiphora* trees, so enabling Mary to obtain their fruits. Worse than elephants was the weather. It was extremely hot and so dry that few flowers were showing. 'It is a maddening place,' wrote Mary, 'and tsetse flies are in clouds.' Fortunately, although they often bit her, they left no after effects. The Ruaha vegetation was of a type she was not at all used to: 'The trees and shrubs are quite different from anything we have met before. I wish Peter Greenway could come here for a day!' When Sam went down with malaria she had to do all the pressing on her own: 'I worked all day… I was very weary. This morning a large herd of buffaloes came down the hill just where we were collecting yesterday. They say they are very wild and charge cars and people.' After six weeks of heat, drought, hostile animals, flies and hay fever, she was quite glad to leave the Ruaha and make her way home to Abercorn which she reached on 23 February, having collected fewer specimens than she had hoped.

(1998)

PART FOUR

The Naturalist Afield

DOLPHINS

The other day, sitting on rocks by the Welsh sea, I was startled by a shrill repeated whistling. It came from the sea, not, it seemed, from a distance but from close at hand. Quickly I searched for animal or bird. There was nothing. The sunlit green waves surged in and broke in whiteness up the rocks but there was nothing alive there. Anyway, no bird has a long, shrill whistle like that, not even the dunlin. I thought of otters but their whistle is quite different.

The whistling went on, shriller, louder. I could tell myself quite certainly now that it came from the water immediately below me. I stared and stared and got more and more excited seeing nothing. Then, quite suddenly, an apparition of delight, a dolphin and then another, then a whole eruption of dolphins came boiling up out of the depths and rolled and played a few yards from me; silently now for their whistling was, I think, submarine only.

I have often had porpoises surface pretty close to me, but to have dolphins so near and dolphins whistling was new. Then I was astonished to see one of these great beaked creatures not once but several times leap up from the water, white belly upwards, and fall heavily upside down on to the back of the dolphin next to it. So they leapt and sported as they made gradually away up the coast. Then quite abruptly there was not a sign of them.

(1993)

PERSPECTIVES ON SQUIRRELS AND STOATS

1: Exit the Red Squirrel

I can hardly believe it, because my memories are still so vivid, but come this summer it will be all of 20 years since I last saw red squirrels hereabouts. I remember also what an agony it was to see the lovely red ones disappearing and the not so lovely grey ones taking their place. The first greys were seen here in late December, 1952. Not the nicest of Christmas presents, we thought. But for as much as seven years they remained quite shy and scarce.

Then they began to increase and quite suddenly, in 1961, everybody was reporting them in woods and gardens along the roads, even on the promenade at Aberystwyth. This it seems was the pattern in many districts as these Americans spread through the land, stealthily consolidating their position for several years, then quite abruptly changing their life-style and becoming the bold and obvious creatures we know today.

A note I made on 16 June, 1963, reads very sadly now: 'Today I saw a red squirrel in the pine wood. It is the third this week so maybe they are increasing.' So much for the optimism of a fine summer morning. The reality was that I never saw or heard of another from that day on. After ten years of struggle the red squirrel had finally given up a place it had occupied perhaps since the post-glacial forests first crept across Britain. But, if mother nature can produce one quirk maybe she can manage another. She may have ousted the red squirrel today but in another twenty years who knows?

2: Opportunist squirrel

Salt marshes, those wide areas of mud and grassland especially characteristic of estuaries and low-lying coasts, are famous for birds but what about their mammals? At first sight they hardly look promising for mammals for although the ground is honeycombed with lovely holes and tunnels these are all frequently flooded by the tides.

So on the saltings we find no hole-dwellers such as rodents or rabbits, moles or shrews. But the opportunists come, those who can cover plenty of ground in a short time and have the wit to retreat before quickly advancing waters. Foxes particularly, judging by their footprints in the snow, must often venture across the saltings on winter nights in pursuit of roosting water birds. And sometimes we see mammals out there by day, especially hares. Once a stoat came swimming across the river. Though mobbed by yodeling redshanks and dived at by outraged shelducks, he hunted calmly over the grassland in broadest daylight, no doubt hoping to collect some unsuspecting bird.

But the most unexpected animal I ever saw on the saltings was a grey squirrel. Flushed by a spaniel from long grass far out in the estuary, the squirrel looked round for a tree to climb, but seeing none in sight, rushed up the dog-owner's body as the next best thing and stood on the astonished man's head. So resourceful a species deserves success, don't you think?

3: Stoats on the Bird-table

Until this week I had never been much of a stoat-watcher, but suddenly I have become quite an addict. It all began when we saw a stoat running across our garden (stoats always seem to run rather than walk), and what a striking animal it was! Instead of having the usual reddish-brown back, it was a very pale pink. Its shoulders were conspicuously white and so was its long tail, except for the black tip. It came again next day and amazed us by climbing up the bird-table to eat peanuts with such ease of manner that it might have done this every day of its life. On the third day we had another surprise when a different stoat, one in normal brown pelage, came and helped itself to the peanuts. Since then both stoats have returned to the bird-table but never together.

The question that naturally arises is why should we have a bird-table for thirty years without ever seeing a stoat on it, and now, suddenly, have two as regular visitors? The answer may lie in those peanuts. For they were given to us by a friend of ours who had mixed them in various meat and poultry fats. So presumably when these carnivorous stoats are crunching those tasty nuts they think they are eating the bones of animals. Perhaps I ought to add that no one need fear that a stoat turning white or partly white in winter is a portent of hard weather. In fact, the records show that a few stoats may turn white even in the south of England in any year, regardless of the weather.

4: Stoat gymnastics

Recently I mentioned a pair of stoats that were visiting our bird-table. Since then we have seen them regularly and have been able to learn something about their food preferences. By long tradition stoats are invariably portrayed as bloodthirsty. But, from what I have seen lately, I would say that they will sample pretty well everything, and are very happy to settle for meat and two vegetables at lunch-time, which is when they always appear at our bird-table.

Yesterday there was a very strange episode. One of the stoats appeared to go quite berserk, dashing all over the lawn at a tremendous rate in a series of wild zig-zags. Then he executed a succession of forward gambols at the same breakneck speed.

Things got even wilder when he leapt high into the air several times, landing flat on his back but he immediately raced on again.

I soon realized that I was witnessing the famous dancing of the stoat, a stunt by which rabbits and birds are supposed to be so fascinated that they venture very close out of curiosity. The crafty stoat, so the tale goes, then suddenly leaps and seizes the victim from among the circle of bewitched spectators.

I have always put this story firmly among those about shaggy dogs and now that I have seen the act for myself I am even more sceptical. For no rabbits or birds arrived as witnesses and I would have sworn that the stoat, far from playing a clever part, was in reality having some sort of a fit. So I prefer to believe that stoats suffer from a strange nervous disorder that causes these outlandish performances.

(1993)

On the squirrels, Anglesey remained a stronghold of the reds despite their mainland decline. Bill's hopes for their return to the latter, albeit thirty years beyond the time he suggested, have proved well-founded, a few colonists having made their way across Afon Menai and established themselves in Bangor University's botanical gardens at Treborth. His comments about the fitting stoat show what a good and keenly observant naturalist he was. The behaviour is now generally accepted as attributable at least in part to nematode infestation of the stoat's synuses by the roundworm Skrjabingylus nasicola. *For an informed account of this phenomenon, see Paul Evans,* Field Notes from the Edge *(Rider Books, 2015), pp. 109-115. [Ed.]*

CO-HABITANTS

Farm houses and buildings are nesting places for a few specialised birds. Even on the higher farms, well above the level of breeding sparrows and starlings, you will often find swallows and house martins, the swallows commonly in cowsheds, the martins under the eaves. Both are colonial but four or five pairs of either are as many as you are likely to find at any farm. Elsewhere you may happen on larger communities of house martins, like those sheltering under the generous eaves of the Hafod Arms Hotel, Devil's Bridge, where in some years there have been scores of nests all crowded together.

There can be very few farmyards in Wales without a pair of breeding pied wagtails. Some have wagtails all winter as well but the upland farms normally lose them in autumn and do not see them again until April. Farmyards lucky enough to be near a stream often have the beautiful grey wagtail. Spotted flycatchers are also frequent farmyard birds and so are redstarts. But while everyone notices wagtails and flycatchers, few are aware of redstarts though the male's tremulous song may be repeated hour after hour in spring from a branch above the farmyard. Often the nest is in a hole in a nearby wall but the birds slip in and out so furtively they must frequently bring off a brood quite unnoticed.

For a hundred years or more Welsh farmers and shepherds have been deserting upland houses for a softer life in the valleys. Once abandoned these houses were soon taken over by the birds. It only needed one slate to fall off and the roof would be full of jackdaws. Then a window would shake open and there would be barn owls in the bedrooms. In open country offering no alternative nesting places these owls were particularly dependent on empty houses. But sooner or later wind, rain, frost and force of gravity brings every abandoned house to a pile of ruin and nettles and the birds depart. In forty years of hill walking I have seen many old dwellings decay. Some have become totally ruined, others have been restored as holiday cottages; but in either event the barn owls are left homeless and I conclude that there must be fewer of them breeding in the uplands now than in the first half of the century.

Often such high-placed houses had a group of sycamores planted near them as shelter, for few trees are as sturdy against gales. Rowans too were planted by the garden gate to keep away evil spirits. These little clumps of trees, outliving the houses they once sheltered, are oases in the bleakness of the uplands and become a focus of life for insects which in turn attract various birds. There may be whinchats and reed buntings in nearby patches of rushes; wheatears, pied wagtails or spotted flycatchers in the walls; and a nest of crow, raven or buzzard in the sycamores. Then in autumn come ring ouzels to fatten up on rowan berries before going off on migration. Wandering mistle thrushes find them too.

(1981)

ON HARES

1: Hare Madness, 1960

Though the woods here are teeming with wild beasts I admit you don't often see them. Not that this is very surprising, for very few of them exceed an ounce in weight (dormice, woodmice, voles and shrews) and most are nocturnal. So if you go to the woods by day only, you'd never have reason to suspect the multitudes of very small animals asleep just under your feet. And with the carnivores of our woods also being mainly night-active, we're not left with much to see by day except squirrels, rabbits and hares, for we have no deer. But red squirrels, even here, are getting scarcer; the newly come grey squirrels are exceedingly furtive; and the rabbits are still fairly uncommon.

So for day-time that really only leaves us the hare, the quite unpredictable, altogether delightful hare, and even he snoozes a lot of the daylight away. But not this morning. For as I scribble this, sitting in the wood with my back against an oak, there are four lovely big hares, as red as foxes in the bright sun, chasing wildly through the trees on what is evidently a roughly circular course; for every few minutes they all four come galloping by in Indian file with a reckless disregard for the row they are making on the dead leaves. They take no notice of me at all though they pass within yards of me every time. Mad as April hares in fact.

2: Leverets in our kitchen

Some weeks ago two baby leverets, rescued from the ploughshare, were given to us to rear. They were wonderful little creatures. Though so recently born they were well furred, alert, open-eyed, ready to face the world. Each fitted snugly into the palm of a hand and their food was a sip of milk at intervals. But how quickly young animals grow! In a few days their teeth could give us a sharp nip and they were nibbling lettuce leaves. We called them Big and Small, so different were they in size. Their characters were curiously different, too. Big was shy and backward; Small was friendlier and was the first to learn to lap milk and eat lettuce.

Now they are almost hares, very strong, hard-kicking, hard-scratching hares. No longer is it easy to pick them up and fondle them. Not that we have wished to tame them, for they must go back to the wild with the best chances of survival. Their appetite is now great, yet selective. They eat grass and the leaves and flowers of dandelions, but not docks or daisies. They accept cabbage but much prefer purple-sprouting broccoli and lettuce. They could not have been easier to rear: all along their feeding has never been the slightest problem. The only problems lie ahead: to find somewhere to release them and, even harder, to bring ourselves to part with such lovable, gentle-eyed, long-whiskered, softly-furred beauties.

(1993)

Wheatears and meadow pipits

A bird that in the nesting season often shares big bouldery screes with the wren but is certainly no cave-dweller is the wheatear. But though wheatears are numerous and breed from sea-level to the mountain-tops they are not everywhere in the mountains. Even on ground between 800 and 2,000 feet, which is their stronghold, there are innumerable small gaps in their distribution in Snowdonia. They tend to be grouped in local, loosely-knit communities. Where you find one breeding pair you are likely to find several others near by. It is the same with whinchats, ring ouzels, curlews, sandpipers, dunlins, golden plovers and perhaps most species except the super-abundant.

Wheatears belong most characteristically to stretches of close turf scattered with boulders: short turf because they can run and dart quickly over it after insects; boulders because they need them as vantage points and singing posts. Clearly the mountain sheep, keeping large areas of grassland closely nibbled, is an essential ally of the wheatear. The same could be said of the mountain wind that keeps the summits almost bare of vegetation, for the wheatear is one of the very few birds that can find a living up there, using the summit cairns for sheltering, nesting and perching. But summit-dwelling wheatears are not common. Where wheatears are commonest is perhaps along the wall-margined sides of moorland tracks near the highest occupied farms, tracks that are in frequent use by farm animals whose droppings attract a concentration of insects. There the wheatear will sometimes nest in the walls but more often in a hole in the ground under a rock.

The first wheatear of spring can be a delightful surprise. It is mid-March and in the mountains still quite wintry. Neither larks nor pipits have yet moved up from the valleys and the world is looking pretty lifeless when, perhaps from behind a snowdrift, a cock wheatear unexpectedly appears, looking very alert and bright in his breeding plumage. From now on all through the spring the hovering courtship displays and plungings of the cock wheatears and their squeaky, scratchy songs will be a welcome touch of life among the grey rocks. After mid-June the young will be out, flitting about screes and roadsides, conspicuous with their very white tails. In a good summer a second brood follows the first and by September the wheatear families can be very plentiful. But by then all wheatears can look rather alike in the field because most of the males at that season have moulted their breeding dress and turned brown as the females and the young.

When carrying food the adult wheatears usually stand and watch warily as you approach. But even more distrustful [than wheatears] are the meadow pipits. They are extremely reluctant to take food to their young if you brazenly try to watch them back to the nest. They will play out the patience game standing on a rock or tussock with worms curling in their bills for longer than most people care to wait. They are double-brooded and their song goes on undiminished into late July and fragmentarily into August even after the flocks are beginning to form. Every summer I am grateful that the pipits' nesting time is so prolonged, for some of the great mountain grass-slopes would be very quiet and lifeless in July without the pipits and their families flitting and calling everywhere and many still courting and in full song. Some of these pipit songs are very fine. Perhaps they sound a bit thin in the lowlands in May if you hear them against a chorus of thrushes, blackbirds, tree pipits, robins and warblers. But up in the mountains, especially on a fine summer evening when all is still and the hills are cut out black against a yellowing sky, then the falling songs of the pipits seem particularly beautiful. It has often seemed to me that the song and the accompanying flight, finishing in a long glide over the grass, is more prolonged and richer in the evening than at any other time.

From June onwards young pipits are everywhere. As they become independent they spread all over the hills until no matter where you walk they fly up before you. They develop the curious habit at this season of taking long siestas in little hollows they shape in the grass. In these bowers they evidently crouch for long periods, judging by the quantity of droppings that accumulate there. Many is the time, seeing a pipit burst from the centre of a tuft of grass, that I have thought to have discovered a nest only to find one of these siesta couches, which are of course very crude compared with the true nest, for a meadow pipit's nest is perfectly cupped and nearly always lined with very delicate, light-coloured straws, against which the chocolate-coloured eggs make an attractive contrast.

In a summer's walk across the hills it is usual to chance upon one or two pipits' nests by nearly treading on the sitting bird. In this way I have found as many as six in a few hours yet at other times, deliberately searching for nests, I have failed completely. Only once have I found a meadow pipit's nest by spotting the bird in the nest. I was bending down to examine a moss on a rock and saw her large dark eye first before I connected it in my mind with a bird. It is rare that one gets within two feet of the nervous pipit but this one was brooding callow young, which is when the bird sits tightest. I was struck by the very great beauty at close range of a bird that looks so sombre at a distance. The delicate pencilling on her crown, the suggestion of an eye-stripe, the bolder streaking down her back, the steady shining eye, the thin, sensitive beak: these went well with the soft green sphagnum moss surrounding the nest and the silver and purple lichens on the rock beside. Much of the beauty of the mountain birds and their surroundings is made up of such quiet colours.

Most abundant of the upland birds, the meadow pipits inhabit not only grassland but also heather, bracken, rushes and the wettest bogs. But they are abundant only from spring to early autumn. By winter only a few are left which somehow manage to survive on the high ground provided the weather is not abnormally severe. What an insect-eater such as a pipit lives on in the open mountains I cannot imagine, unless it turns seed-eater for a while. By mid-March the returning pipits begin to approach the uplands but at first remain in flocks – sometimes a hundred or two together – round the lower skirts of the moors, not moving up until the end of March or early in April when the temperatures rise to spring-like levels. At that season the flocks are very restless and excitable and there is a lot of calling and chasing. Once in the hills the flocks quickly break up and do not re-assemble until late summer.

(1966)

KILLARNEY FERN

I have just been searching for one of Britain's rarest ferns. It is called the Killarney fern and is said to have been found fifty years ago in one of our local ravines but has not been seen since. You may think it outrageously optimistic to expect to find a plant after so long an interval, but botanists are nothing if not optimistic. The ravine I searched is a magnificent cleft cut into a steep mountainside and shaded from top to bottom by woodland. It climbs for several hundred feet and is full of the thunder of waterfalls, one above the other. The air is permanently damp with spray and sunlight rarely penetrates. In other words it looked just the place for the Killarney fern to be happy in.

As I scrambled about the gorge I first got my feet soaked through slipping off a rock into the stream, and then I got my head wet while trying to look behind a waterfall. I saw many kinds of fern and a marvellous assortment of mosses – but not a sign of the Killarney fern. I comfort myself that in several hours I had covered only one-third of the gorge, so I must return one day and continue the search. In such unsuccessful ventures I also find solace in that lovely modern Greek poem about getting to the island of Ithaca. It is a very long way to Ithaca and there is nothing much to see when at last you get there. But what matters is the quest. As the poem concludes: 'Ithaca has given you the beautiful voyage. Without her you would never have taken the road.'[7]

A NEW BIRD FOR EUROPE

The keen students of bird migration who, spring and autumn, man Britain's bird observatories are a race of optimists who hope for everlasting anticyclones centred north of Europe so that the resultant light easterly winds will divert hordes of continental migrants west across the North Sea to Britain. And since September is the month with the greatest likelihood of anticyclonic days, which then average more than ten, that is the time when ornithological hopes run highest. All the same, September can also produce deep depressions over the North Atlantic, and these bring high winds and rains raging across Britain from the west to confound all hope of birds being

---

[7] The concluding quotation is from Constantine Cavafy's memorable 1911 poem *Ithaca*, the last stanzas of which might serve as motto for Bill's own life-quest:
Always keep Ithaca in your mind. /To arrive there is your ultimate goal. / But do not hurry the voyage at all. /It is better to let it last for many years; / and to anchor at the island when you are old, /rich with all you have gained on the way, /not expecting that Ithaca will offer you riches.
Ithaca has given you the beautiful voyage. /Without her you would have never set out on the road. /She has nothing more to give you.
And if you find her poor, Ithaca has not deceived you. /Wise as you have become, with so much experience,/you must already have understood what Ithacas mean.

blown here from the Continent. So it was in the second week of September, 1957: there were days of very strong winds which increased until by the 11th high seas were pounding the whole western side of Britain. It was on that day that a strange bird arrived on Bardsey off the north Wales coast – a bird so unusual that none of the experts at the island's observatory could at first name it or say what family it belonged to, even after it had been caught and could be examined in the hand.

The first who saw it flying along a hedge said it was like a big greenfinch, but was as yellow as a golden oriole. This was not a bad field description, but in the hand the bird resembled neither greenfinch nor oriole, nor any bird that could be found in the *Field-guide to the Birds of Britain and Europe*. So resort was had to the *Field-guide to the Birds of the Eastern United States*, and it was among the admirable colour-plates of that work that a likeness of Bardsey's strange visitor was found. The bird was evidently a summer tanager, one of the American family of fruit and insect eaters related to the finches. Tanagers, though not found in any other continent, are represented in tropical America by some 200 species, of which only four migrate from the tropics to breed in the United States. One of these is the summer tanager.

We can imagine flocks of small birds, including various tanagers, passing down the eastern seaboard of the United States. As a vast depression deepened south of Iceland an eastbound gale begins to whip across the Atlantic. The birds are whipped out to sea like leaves. Perhaps many perish, some struggle back to land and one, a summer tanager, is hurtled tail to wind over 3,000 miles to the coast of Wales. Supposing it flies at 30 m.p.h. before a wind of 40 m.p.h., giving a total speed of 70 m.p.h., about 45 hours would be needed for the crossing.

We might ask whether a small land bird could fly for 45 hours without rest or food. It seems unreasonable to suppose this impossible. But in any case there are ships to rest on, though not for long because hunger would soon impel the bird on. It is known that migrant birds habitually lose much weight on long sea crossings. That this tanager increased its weight by half while on Bardsey shows how starved it was when it reached the island.

The male tanager is rosy red in spring, turning yellow in autumn, and the female is greenish yellow. As the Bardsey bird was yellow, but with flecks of red in two places, it was evidently a male in a transitional stage of plumage. Catching the sun from a hedge-top, he looked a bright all-over yellow. But this was the result of colour suffusion because at very close range only the upper breast and the sides of the neck were a clear yellow; the head was yellow-brown, the back greenish and the wings and tail brown. The heavy, sharp bill was a striking feature, and in it a tanager could hold and chew a big blackberry with ease. And chew is just the word for what the bird did. Of many blackberries I saw him pick he never swallowed one. Slowly he masticated the fruit, swallowed the juice by visible throat movements and rejected the pith and seeds, taking up to five minutes to deal with each berry. The result was that under his favourite feeding perches small piles of chewed blackberries accumulated. Only once did I see him take any other food; this was when he deftly flew out of the hedge to take a passing insect in the air.

Standing alertly, he looked rather like a flycatcher or shrike, and once or twice, listening to a noise which slightly alarmed him, he erected well-developed crest feathers all over his head and half-cocked his tail. His flight was rapid and direct, reminiscent of redwings dashing out of winter hedges. Normally he flew low along bank or hedge and when disturbed preferred to fly into the nearest cover rather than go high and put distance between himself and danger. It was interesting to see how this stranger immediately took up a beat or territory for his stay on the island.

Though Bardsey has many bramble hedges, the tanager selected a favourite one and spent most of his time there, returning to it despite being often disturbed.

Getting photographs of the tanager after he had been on the island for a week and was daily getting livelier and more wary took a long time. For detail I wanted to picture the bird in the hand and that meant catching him, which took several hours. For a natural portrait I wanted the bird in the field and that meant building a hide by a likely perch and waiting for him to come at his leisure.

So I sat a couple of hours on the slope of Bardsey Mountain observing the tanager feeding along the hedge below and noted the places where he most commonly perched to masticate his berries. Of these favoured perches I chose two: a stick of dead bramble poking out of a bush and a strand of barbed wire across a gap in the hedge. Opposite these points a friend and I built a crude hide of gorse – crude but effective, for a few mornings later the tanager, though mildly suspicious of these intrusions, did at last settle on both of these perches, and so was photographed.

(*1957*)

TWO VIEWS OF THE FOX

1: 'A dog idealized and made beautiful'
Often in the past few weeks we have heard a fox barking in the wood near our house and one morning two were seen playing together outside the wood. When disturbed they ran across the field with that unhurried gait that foxes have and before slipping into the wood both of them paused and looked back over their shoulders. Then even our fox-detesting farmer-neighbour was moved to utter a few admiring comments. For they looked extremely good, the two of them standing there so richly red and so vividly alive in the morning sun. W.H. Hudson relates

how when he once got a close view of an early morning fox he was struck by the superiority of the appearance of the wild fox over the domestic dog. For him at that moment the fox seemed 'a dog idealized and made beautiful.'

No wonder the fox is so popular as an animal for the chase. For the animals most hunted for sport are commonly the most beautiful and graceful, such as deer and hares and foxes, as if to kill what is especially beautiful adds a spice to killing. In the wilder parts of Wales there is little tradition of fox-hunting as a sport. Here the fox has always been treated as vermin. Yet despite a long and determined persecution the fox proves ever resilient. Thousands are annually destroyed. Yet their number grows not less. It is as if each year they spring by spontaneous regeneration from the mountain rocks.

2: A fox on Gower's cliffs

One day last week I found myself on those limestone cliffs of south Wales whose caves are reckoned to have been the haunts of our very earliest forebears. Regretting not having come at low tide when the caves are accessible, I fell to examining the nearby inland cliffs. And there a hundred and fifty feet above me I espied an opening. Suppose this were an unexplored cave, I thought. What might I not find in it? But I had to climb up here first. The first hundred feet were simple. Then a harder twenty-five feet up to a ledge. But the final twenty-five feet, demanding a risky squirm round a bulge, defeated me. Then, as I stared up at the entrance, I got a surprise that nearly unbalanced me off my ledge. A face slowly appeared round a rock and eyes looked down into mine. A few dream-like seconds passed before this half-shadowed face resolved itself into that of a fox. I waited to see what he would do next. Surely he would slink back into the cave? Nothing of the sort. He was coming out and prepared to wait till I had shifted. We stared unblinkingly at each other for several minutes. Then I surrendered and scrambled down from the ledge. Whereupon the fox nonchalantly leapt to where I had been sitting and raced beautifully away up the face and was gone in a few seconds.

(1993)

BURROWING HALCYON

Not often is a kingfisher caught off its guard. So yesterday I was surprised to be able to creep up on one as it dug out a nest-hole in the bank of a stream. My success was pure fluke. I was not even looking for kingfishers but just happened to be standing beside a stream-side alder when I heard one whistling nearby. I looked up-stream and down and was puzzled to see nothing though the calling continued loudly. But eventually I noticed a trickle of sand dropping into the water from a hole in the opposite bank and realized that a kingfisher was tunnelling there. It had never occurred to me that these birds may shriek even when digging their nests. I now lay on the ground to observe for half an hour, though all I saw most of the time was just a hole in a bank. But every three or four minutes I was rewarded by the most brilliant display of colour I have ever seen on a bird. For at pretty regular intervals the kingfisher came shooting out of the hole, fluttered round for a second practically under my nose and then dived back out of sight. Once inside it continued to shriek. Too excited about everything to be able to keep quiet, I suppose. But isn't it pretty reckless of kingfishers to advertise their nests so blatantly?

(1993)

STRANGE LIFESTYLE OF THE WOODCOCK

The cold weather this week has brought us that bird of mystery, the woodcock. This nonconformist member of the wader tribe lies all day so invisible on the woodland floor that I have never yet spotted one before it has spotted me and gone swerving away through the trees. Woodcock are emphatically loners. You may flush many in an hour or two but nearly always one at a time and it is only in the severest weather that I have ever known them to gather into what was almost a flock. My memory goes back to the great snows of early 1947, when blizzards drove countless woodcock from more eastern districts into what they hoped would be the milder west. In the event, it was snowier here than anywhere else and the woodcock were soon starving and weak. In desperation they found their way in hundreds to the rough slopes above the sea cliffs where the ground was less frozen. But even there many perished.

Each year when spring comes the woodcock are early to nest but sadly very few breed in this part of Wales. Here and there, however, we can watch the curious evening flight of the males who make slow circuits around the woods, alternately croaking and squeaking. They have another strange habit. When danger threatens, an adult woodcock can pick up its young between its legs and airlift it to safety. I confess that for years I doubted if it were possible; then one season I saw the trick performed twice within a few days. I felt duly chastened and now I try to keep a more open mind about the countless old wives' tales of natural history.

(1993)

TWO ADDER TALES (AND SOME GRASS SNAKES)

Every spring in our garden we have a small invasion of grass snakes. Some of them may be as much as four feet long and when you meet these outsize individuals, harmless though you know them to be, it is difficult to avoid a quick tremor of alarm, so fundamental is our fear of all serpents. Snakes are said to be deaf to many sounds that we can detect, otherwise I'm sure they would rejoice to hear the lawnmower making the first cut of the year. For it's the lawn mowings piled up on the compost heap week after week that makes the garden so popular with grass snakes. In July the females will disappear inside the heap, lay their piles of white eggs and then depart, leaving the heap of rotting compost to do the hatching. Mercifully, that poisonous snake the adder does not lay eggs and so has no interest in compost heaps. So although we have a few adders as neighbours they mostly keep outside the fence. One that did try to get in got itself caught in the mesh of the rabbit wire surrounding the garden and I was summoned to deal with it. Gingerly I approached with my wire cutters but the adder showed no fear as I cut it free and carried it back to the wild in a cardboard box. I wish I could relate how I intrepidly picked it up by the tail the way experienced snake handlers do it. But this is a trick I have never yet seen done and until I have I doubt I'll be brave enough for what sounds like a delicate operation.

(*1993*)

On 4th April I saw the year's first adder asleep in the sun on a patch of dry raised ground in the heart of a reed-bed. It took me back to an early spring day thirty years ago when I met with three adders just out of hibernation in exactly that place – a suntrap sheltered from every cold wind. Two were males, beautifully patterned in silver and black. Between them, and very different because reddish-brown, was a female. I tiptoed towards this somnolent group as lightly as one can tiptoe in gumboots. At three yards distance one of the males raised his head, flickered his tongue and poured himself silently into the reeds. At two yards the other male did the same. But the female proved to be totally approachable. She lay in a coil with her head raised just off the ground and held rigidly immobile with no flickering of the tongue. She seemed more like a wood carving than a living snake. Gingerly I bent over her and after long hesitation, because I am no snake charmer, I dared to touch the top of her head very lightly. She did not react in any way. Then very softly I stroked her head. Still no sign that she was aware of my presence. Just as lightly I caressed her throat. She remained entirely indifferent. It was not until I stroked her back all the way from head to tail that she decided it was time for her to go, which she did slowly as if in a dream, leaving me grateful to have experienced such a rare encounter in the wild.

(1999)

HARRIERS

1: Hen Harrier

Of all the birds that fly over the winter estuary none is finer than the male hen harrier. But I think the picture in the books do him little justice. They make him look too subdued, too blue-grey, not striking enough. For in the sunshine he is white and conspicuous, with boldly contrasting black wing tips, an altogether fascinating bird as he comes on long-winged and leisurely flight low across the saltings. Often he drops into ditches and creeks, quickly rising again for he rarely seems to catch anything. Crowds of curlews and wigeon rise in anxiety as he passes but their fears seem groundless for his preferred prey is usually much smaller fowl.

There is a female hen harrier here also, so different in her dark-brown plumage as to seem a quite different species. But though I see one or the other nearly every day I never see them together, for harriers in winter are strictly individualists. Sometimes they fly close to me, turning to look at me with total indifference, without either fear or even curiosity. Then on they go, rising high over woods and hills to marshes miles away, as if they were off on far migrations. Yet I know they will return. In two or three hours, or maybe not till tomorrow, they will come to hunt here again and cause another flutter of panic among the birds of the estuary.

(1993)

2: Montagu's Harriers

There are few more attractive birds of prey than Montagu's harriers. Lightly they float over marshes and heathlands, the female a rich dark-brown in strange contrast with males that are pale as herring gulls. But they are sadly rare in Britain now, these harriers. A couple of decades ago you could have said their future was almost promising. After a long bad spell there seemed hope that they might make a come back for they were breeding in quite a few counties. But then came a rapid decline. On a favourite marsh of mine in west Wales I watched a pair for the last time in 1963. From a nearby hill I saw them playing gracefully on the upper air in courtship display. Many weeks later there was the joy of seeing them and two young ones on the wing. But they have never nested there since. Yet, such is human optimism, I have visited the marsh every spring in the hope that the harriers will return. Which brings me writing this in the bright May sunlight with sedge warblers and reed buntings singing all round me. But there are still no harriers. Nor I fear will there ever be again until something is done to stop the destruction of these lovely birds when on migration in the Mediterranean region where they are said to be shot down by trigger-happy sportsmen interested in them only for target practice.

(1993)

Bill's comments about the male hen harrier are spot on – it's the most striking and beautiful of all British raptors; and still one of the most persecuted. 'Sportsmen' and their lackeys still shoot them in Scotland, on the High Peak moorland of Derbyshire, and even, infamously, on the Sandringham estate in Norfolk where a young royal and a banker friend brought one down in front of a reputable witness, and no legal action was taken against them. It does make our indignation against the slaughter of migrants passing over Malta seem hypocritical when we cannot adequately police conservation matters in our own backyard, especially where 'the very best people' are concerned. No doubt under the U.K.'s new (2015) Conservative administration, the leader of which is a committed bloodsports enthusiast who has promised a free vote to repeal the ban on hunting with hounds, the situation will worsen and our rare and beautiful species will be ever more threatened.

THRENODY FOR THE WOODLARK

There was a time (but it is years ago now) when I seriously thought I would write a book about the woodlark. For in those days this was a bird I met with nearly every time I went out of doors and the more I heard and saw of it, the more interested I became. I first heard a woodlark in my youth one sparkling day on the Clent Hills in Worcestershire. I thought it the finest song I had ever listened to; and though I have heard many other birds since then, it is still the song of the woodlark that delights me most.

In the Midlands woodlarks were scarce, and I had no chance of getting at all familiar with them until years later when I married and came to live in Wales. My wife and I lived for a time in a little upland cottage close to Plynlimon where, at 1,000 ft, the woodlark's song came to us across rushy moorland along with the bleating of snipe and the yodelling of curlews. But at that altitude woodlarks were uncommon and it was not till we moved down to a village near the sea that we found them everywhere, all over the coastal hills and valleys right out to the breezy cliffs.

In the spring we often discovered their nests, but only after patient watching. Most we found hidden in bracken on the slopes, though some were in fields of young corn and occasionally, as befits a bird with such a name, the nests were in woods. Never large woods, only small copses and thickets. The woodlarks were very often near houses. There were plenty of them, for instance, on the outskirts of Aberystwyth where I often heard them in the grounds of the National Library. The most suburban nest-site I saw, as well as the most remarkable, was in a shallow box containing experimental grass, one of many similar boxes placed on the ground in rows close to greenhouses of the College Botanic Garden, with people passing to and fro all day. The wonder was not only that a 'field' 2 ft by 1 ft was a sufficient nesting place but that the birds could also remember which was their box among so many exactly the same size and shape.

March was the woodlarks' great month. Day after day I went out on clear frosty mornings to watch and listen. I had only to go through a gate at the end of our garden, climb the nearby hill and there I was alone in the still and frigid air with the woodlarks singing, chasing, mating and building their nests. I wrote everything down and my notebooks grew fat. But those were restless days, and soon we moved, this time northwards. Not many miles but it meant a change of county by crossing the Dyfi estuary to Merioneth. To a woodlark enthusiast this looked a depressing move because the *Handbook of British Birds* (first edition) was quite uncompromising on the breeding distribution of the woodlark in Wales: 'Not in Merioneth', it said. As definite as that. But the *Handbook* had been written in 1938 and our move to Merioneth was twelve years later. By which time the woodlark had also moved north and put the handbook out of date.

So it was that, around our cottage on the hills above Aberdyfi, we had more woodlarks than ever before. Or rather they were closer. What a joy it was to find them as a garden bird. They sang above us all day, either circling in the air or standing on the roof. We were completely isolated, above oakwoods that dropped steeply to the estuary: all around us was bracken, gorse, grass and rock – perfect woodlark country. And our little cottage and garden seemed to serve as a focus for all the activities of this woodlark community. When I should have been at other tasks I spent long hours adding more and more notes on their courtship, their squabbling, their nests, eggs and young. Their lives filled my days as their songs filled my ears. I now look back on that spring with the woodlarks on a beautiful Merioneth hill as a real idyll; and one never to be repeated, for again we moved – back south across the shining estuary to Cardiganshire.

The years passed. But the woodlarks never lost their delight for us. My hopes of writing a book about them remained. I sketched out its main topic: the woodlark's world distribution, for example: how it was almost purely a bird of Europe. And how its place in Britain was decidedly in the south, suggesting a species that was only half-hardy. Other chapters were planned, and meanwhile I went on making notes, taking photographs. I felt in no hurry. The woodlarks would always be there, and the longer I studied them the more I would learn.

I had reckoned without the accidents of nature, the ups and downs of birds' fortunes, those cycles of widening and shrinking that we would find affecting the numbers of all species of animals and plants if only our records could go back far enough. The winter of 1962-3 arrived, one of the very coldest and snowiest, when birds died in multitudes. Among the resident species in our district those that suffered most included long-tailed tit, mistle thrush, wren, kingfisher, green woodpecker, barn owl – and woodlark.

It was a sad spring that followed, with so many favourite birds quite absent or rare. But we had no long-term worries. We had lived through other such bad spells and felt confident that, as before, even the most affected birds would recover in a few seasons. And so it proved for all of them except one – the woodlark. After four years, by which time other species were getting back to normal, I had neither seen nor heard a woodlark. Then in the fifth year – delicious moment – I did hear one. There it was, the old cheerful tune carolling down from the sky. The woodlark, it seemed, was going to make a comeback after all.

Not so. That solitary singer was there for one spring, then another, then no more. And now ten years have passed since the great frost, and the woodlark has virtually disappeared not merely from this part of Cardiganshire but is described as hard to find in many of its former habitats in southern England and Wales. Like wryneck and red-backed shrike it is retreating to the Continent. And who can prophesy when it will return?

But why should the woodlark have gone like this and so suddenly? Was the winter of 1962-3 so much more terrible than previous arctic spells? What about 1947 for instance? That year brought dreadful weather from late January to March, yet the woodlark survived. So perhaps the truth is, as some observers claim, that the woodlark was already declining in many districts and that the 1962-3 winter merely pushed it further down the slope.

So I bid the woodlark farewell. My diaries lie gathering dust and my book will never be written, which I daresay will be no loss to the world, only a source of regret to me when I think how I would have enjoyed writing in praise of so admirable a bird. To me the countryside would be poorer for the loss of any kind of bird, even crow, starling or sparrow. But to have lost the woodlark of all birds, is melancholy indeed.

(1973)

ROLLICKING RAVENS

For us it is now the raven season. For though we see these splendid birds on and off all the year it is now they appear in numbers. Strange in many ways, ravens are out of tune with the rest of nature, being always a season ahead. Early winter is their pairing time and by late winter they are building their great stick nests on rocks and trees. So in December we see them chasing each other wildly about the sky amid great croakings, barkings and gruntings. Life can never be dull as long as ravens are about.

As pets they are famous entertainers and they are just as good in the wild, often making funny noises or up to something interesting. This morning I watched one coming over in a long, slow glide. Without warning he turned over on his back, uttered a loud, deep *pruk-pruk*, then righted himself. This he repeated every fifteen seconds, the notes always being uttered when he was upside down.

Once he seemed so lost in the joy of flying upside down that he glided on for a dozen yards in that strange position. Finally, he flew slowly away making a noise like a stone dropped in a bucket every few seconds. Then he called in a ridiculous falsetto voice, pulled a few corks out of bottles, turned over three times in rapid succession and vanished by a sudden plunge into an oak-wood.

(1993)

THE MIGRANT SWANS

This week the wild swans came. I saw them far away in the early dusk, a pure white line across the mud of the darkening estuary. Here, every year without fail, in the first days of March, these Bewick's swans from Ireland come dropping in like old friends. But only for a couple of hours or so. They have spring in their blood and they know the ice is about to melt on their breeding grounds in Russia. As we live in an age of bird-counts I felt obliged to put a figure on my swans. Very slowly I walked towards them across the saltmarsh until the white streak began to break up into individual birds. Now I could hear their voices. They were chatting privately among themselves, a continuous gentle conversation that filled the twilight with musical croonings and honkings. How long have they been making this annual spring journey we shall never know. But what is certain is that we live in drainage-mad days, that huge wetlands have been reclaimed in the last two centuries and that for swans the world is still rapidly shrinking. There is a very long tradition of man's dislike of the wilderness. And not so long ago a distinguished historian described the reclamation of the marshes as 'beneficial to everyone'. Such blinkered attitudes are still widespread. For even in these days when millions are entranced by nature programmes on television, very few people really know, care or understand about the needs of swans and other creatures of the wild.

(1984)

MARTS SWEET AND FOUL

In almost any parish in Wales, if you plod your way through the churchwardens' accounts of the eighteenth or early nineteenth centuries, you will find, amid a mass of badly spelt English and Welsh, reference after reference to monies paid out for the destruction of unpopular animals. 'To Dai Jones pd. Fourpence for kill fulbart' (a polecat). 'To Evans, miller, 3s 6d. for cild old fockis Bitch and four Youngers.' *'Am ladd cath goed'* [For killing a wood cat] 3s 4d. So they go remorselessly on, these chronicles of endless war between man and hostile nature.

A wonderful source, you might suppose, these parochial archives, for the history of our wild fauna. But you would be only partly correct. The truth is that there are hideous difficulties of interpretation, especially because two languages are involved. Take the wild cat. In the records it may be explicitly 'wild cat' or *'cath wyllt'*. But more often it is just 'cat' or *'cath'*. Occasionally it is 'mountain cat' or *'cath fynydd'*. Very often it is 'wood cat' or *'cath goed'*. All quite satisfactory until we realize that any of these names were also used locally for martens, polecats and heaven knows what else. Do not forget that 'puss' was in common use for a hare. So was *'cath eithin'* ('a furze cat'). This complete universality of 'cat' stems from the fact that in one form or another it has existed since ancient times in Greek, Latin, Celtic, Teutonic and Slavonic languages and in its long history has been applied to many animals.

So archivists have to accept that 'wild cat' and all its variants in the old records are rather useless words leaving us forever more in doubt about how long *Felis sylvestris*, the true wild cat, went on surviving in Wales. What would help would be a good range of dated and genuinely Welsh wild cat specimens in museums. But these are lacking: and all is speculation and assumption.

It is safer to talk about pine martens (formerly 'marten cats'). At least we have genuine Welsh specimens preserved and the language has a better word than merely *cath*. It is *bele* (pronounced something like 'bellay') and when the parish scribes wrote *bele* there is no doubt they often meant a marten. Other Welsh words for marten are less reliable, *carlwm*, for instance. Of my two Welsh dictionaries, one defines *carlwm* as a marten, the other says it is a stoat. J. Walters's dictionary of 1794 even tells us that a marten is '*rhyw wiwair*' which means ' a sort of squirrel'!

Despite the problem of semantics we can be sure that martens were fairly common in Wales until towards the end of [the nineteenth] century. They were an accepted, if unwelcome, part of everyday rural life in many districts, and even an object of the chase. Yet in [the twentieth century], which has on the whole favoured the survival of predators in Wales, the marten has become exceedingly rare. This is especially strange when you compare its fortunes with those of its relative, the *ffwlbart* or polecat. By the end of [the nineteenth century] these two seem to have been equally uncommon here. But since then the marten (or sweetmart) has gone further downhill while the polecat (or foulmart) has prospered almost beyond belief.

It has all happened since World War I. Till then the Welsh gamekeepers kept the ranks of martens and polecats very thin indeed. Then after 1914 gamekeeping virtually ceased and in many districts was never resumed after 1918 on anything like the pre-war scale. Most predators were soon thriving abundantly. But not the pine marten. Why? There is or used to be a theory that once a species is reduced to a really low level it may reach a point of no return no matter how much its environment improves. A strange, unproven idea but there may be something in it.

Whatever the reason, the polecat, though it disappeared from the whole of England and Scotland, survived in Wales. Today it flourishes not only in its old strongholds of Ceredigion and south Merioneth but has spread even into the extremities: the Llŷn Peninsula, the south-west of Pembrokeshire, north-east Wales and down the English border. It has even advanced east out of Wales, especially into Shropshire, Herefordshire and other counties.

So when you come to Wales can you expect to see polecats wherever you go? Far from it, for the polecat is rather a loner and is almost as nocturnal as a badger, much as it would like to be out by day, as occasionally it is. I have seen one in my garden, nosing its way into an outbuilding, obviously sniffing out rodents, and passing within six feet of me with outrageous carelessness. But normally polecats hide by day in the deepest cover. How then can I claim they are so common. Thank the traffic for that. Polecat corpses are now frequent enough on roads in many parts of Wales to assure us that they are present in good numbers, and often close to human habitation. Remember that 'polecat' in Norman times was 'poule-cat', the cat that played havoc with pullets. He was a hanger round farms and cottages and so he still is, never happier than when he can hollow out a winter den in a haybarn.

But the polecat belongs to the wild as well – sea cliffs (but not islands), sand dunes, moorlands, peatbogs and all types of woodland, both broad-leaved and conifers. How many there are in the mountains nobody knows, but it is a fair guess that cliffs and block screes with their infinite hiding places are a refuge for polecats as well as the last remaining martens. The food of the polecat is varied, but its staple diet is the fieldmice, voles and young rabbits on which nearly all our flesh-eaters depend. And like most carnivores the polecat also takes frogs, beetles, worms, birds (it is not popular with owners of wildfowl collections) as well as enjoying various fruits in season.

Should you be lucky enough to meet with a full-grown polecat in daylight what you will see is a slender animal nearly two feet long, low-slung, short-legged, sharp-nosed, 'admirably formed', as the pioneer zoologist, Pennant, said in the eighteenth century, 'for insinuating itself into the smallest passages in search of prey'. Apart from a little white on its face it usually appears wholly black, but if it turns away from you, causing its dark outer hairs to separate, its thick underfur is seen to be mainly white. Caught in this position in your car's headlights it can surprise you by looking more white than black. In mid-Wales a red form used to be reported occasionally but I have seen only one red polecat in recent years.

It is not only at night that you may glimpse polecats from your car. But you are not likely to be as fortunate as a friend of mine last summer who saw not one but five polecats run in single file across a main road seven miles south-east of Aberystwyth in full sunlight. What better proof that polecats are not always solitary and nocturnal?

(1977)

FOUR OWL SKETCHES

1: Owl on a poet's gravestone

Owls are birds to some people; but they are omens to others, especially when seen in country graveyards. The other day I called at the church of Llanwnog in Montgomeryshire, a medieval building of special interest because conspicuous in its dark walls you can see blocks of reddish sandstone that were obviously brought there from the defences of Roman Caersws, a mile or so to the south.

Inside the church are an ancient rood loft and screen with carvings of foliage and winged dragons. The solid oak steps which formerly led up to the rood loft survive in the thickness of the walls. In the churchyard is the grave of Ceiriog, one of the best-known poets of nineteenth-century Wales. He lived at Caersws and was manager of the narrow-gauge railway which ran from there up to the now extinct lead mines at Van.

I was thinking about Ceiriog as I walked from the church

porch down the avenue of limes to the gate when, by a fascinating coincidence, a tawny owl flew out of the trees and perched on Ceiriog's tombstone. Doubtless the owl chose that stone because it happens to be one of the tallest there. But to see a strange bird (are not owls always strange?) standing above the poet's grave and staring at me with fixed, round, questioning eyes was a rather moving experience. Thank goodness owls to me are owls and nothing more!

2: Barn owl neighbours

This old house where we have been living for nearly thirty years used to be a farmhouse. These days the cattle have long since gone from the buildings and we have much more agreeable neighbours, a pair of barn owls. Until they first nested here two years ago these beautiful white owls had always seemed as remote as dreams as they hunted over the marshes in the twilight. But now we know a little more about them.

Their almost complete silence, for example. In fact, it was several weeks before we were sure whether they had a nest or not. Then one day I went into the building and could faintly hear the twittering voices of young ones high above my head. How different from the tawny owls which hoot so loudly and persistently and whose young ones just now are shrieking for food all night in the trees round the house.

The great moment last time the barn owls nested here was when their young could first fly. For several evenings in early July we saw four of them and their parents fluttering about in the dusk and the garden seemed full of white wings. A crucial thing about our barn owls here is that they breed in a nest-box. Otherwise the farm building is quite without suitable breeding ledges. Throughout the countryside there must be countless old buildings where barn owls would live happily if nest-boxes were provided. I am sure nothing would do more to stop the decline of these very desirable birds. All they want is a big box in a dark place.

3: Owl homes – made in Birmingham

Today two men, lurching under a load of heavy boxes, are splashing across the marshes to the pine wood. They are followed by a little girl, daughter of one of them. She carries a coil of rope. Her father has devoted the spare time of several weeks to demolishing an old hen-coop and using the wood to make boxes which they have brought a hundred miles from the industrial Midlands, setting off early so as to have a good long day in the woods near the coast of Wales.

Carefully they examine the trees, choosing those best fitted for their purpose. Then high up each tree one of them climbs, lowers the rope, and a box is attached to it. He hauls it up, sites it on the shady side of the trunk and fixes it firmly there. So the day goes on and their burden gets lighter as box after box finds a home in a tree-top.

By tea-time they have finished. The light is fading as they get into their car and roar off back towards the Midlands, happy in a day well spent. I dare say their workmates would consider that climbing about tree-tops all day is a very singular way of spending a Sunday. But each to his taste. And perhaps all her life the little girl will remember the day she spent in a Welsh wood helping to provide homes for owls and kestrels.

4: Encounter with an owl

I stand in a tree-sheltered spot where the wood meets the marsh, my gumboots in water from the melting snow. In the square mile of rushes and flood pools between the wood and the estuary nothing moves, nothing lives. It is dismal, cold and wet and there is nothing. But I wait. For this is the barn owl's hunting ground where he makes a careful patrol several times a day during winter, though in summer he is so nocturnal. So I wait, expecting every minute to see his white shape come floating lightly over the watery fields. But though I wait long he does not come and I wonder why.

Then I happen to turn round and I find the reason: he is there already, not thirty yards away just inside the wood, staring at me from a branch, a pure white owl on the red branch of a pine.

Through my binoculars I look into those large, round eyes. They have the disturbing quality of all predators' eyes but being dark seem fairly mild compared with the black-centred, yellow, penetrating eyes of short-eared owls which are really rather alarming to see at close range. Then as if feeling himself at a disadvantage being stared at by binoculars the owl turns round and flies away. But no, that describes how a crow or a pigeon would depart. I should say rather that one moment the owl is on the branch. Then he is not.

(1993)

PART FIVE

Further Afield

AFRICAN INTERLUDES

1: The Hide at Tumba

Some of my most exciting bird-watching hours came one day when we bumped across the plain in the Land Rover to a lagoon along the swamp edge three miles west of Tumba. As we reached the lagoon a crowd of birds of all sizes flew away clamouring. Then my companions left me concealed in a hide we had built the day before. I heard them start up the Land Rover and gradually the roar of their engine grew distant. I was alone in the beauty of the wilderness. I looked around at my restricted world: all I could see was this very shallow, weedy lagoon, circular, about fifty yards across, my hide being separated from the lagoon by a muddy creek about six feet wide. All about was a high green wall of bulrushes that looked to me the same bulrushes (*Typha*) that grow around pools in Europe. Above the wall of rushes rose the hazy outline of the rift escarpment many miles distant. The sky was as ever blue and without a cloud.

I waited ten minutes for the arrival of the first birds, two black-winged stilts, which were to be expected, for stilts show little fear of man and are one of Rukwa's most familiar birds. I suppose some stilts breed round the lake but by October their numbers have been greatly added to by passage birds. Perhaps these two first arrivals were uneasy at the unnatural quiet and birdlessness of the pool for they stood very still, holding themselves at their full height, very elegant with thin white heads and necks, black tapering beaks, black wings and white breasts and admirably long shanks. Then suddenly off they flew with a shrill piping, trailing their red legs behind them.

Five or ten minutes passed. I could hear an increasing volume of bird noises all round as life returned to normal in neighbouring lagoons invisible beyond the rushes. Then two large dark birds appeared flying low over the vegetation to my right. They flew past, swung round, returned and dropped to my pool, their long, down-curved, heavy-looking bills identifying them as glossy ibises. For them there was nothing sinister about a silent empty pool. They charged ponderously into the water, heads down, long beaks probing into the mud, mandibles nibbling rapidly. Occasionally they would look up for a moment and give out a deep, loud, double motor-horn sort of note. Soon they were feeding near enough to the hide for me to see the metallic gleams of green and purple that give this ibis its name.

These two pioneers were the forerunners of an invasion. Close after them came a squacco heron, a greenshank, a marsh sandpiper and several ruffs. I was glad to be able to compare greenshank with marsh sandpiper, so many writers having stressed their similarity, which is certainly very striking, for both are not only very white-looking with contrasting dark wings, but they have the same slender, graceful build, the same restless back-and-forth way of feeding, and when they rise into flight show a similar conspicuous white rump and tail. Side by side the greater size of the greenshank is obvious; apart they are best known by the difference in beak shapes, slightly upcurved in the greenshank, straight and tapering to a fine point in the marsh sandpiper. Also I found that the marsh sandpiper was a little browner on the wings, not so contrasty between black wings and white breast.

Absorbed in these details I failed to notice many new arrivals, the ruffs especially appearing with complete unobtrusiveness. At first they gathered in a creek partly out of my sight but next time I looked I was surprised to see that the initial half-dozen had grown to about forty and soon there were two or three hundred of them, dark, rotund, bowed down because very busily pecking, advancing across the lagoon, a brown moving carpet of closely packed, silent birds. Ruffs, as we found out during our trips round the lake edge that week, were by far the commonest wader of the Rukwa. There were from scores to hundreds at every lagoon and their total population in the whole valley must be enormous. I was thankful that they were so quiet for if they were a noisy bird one would rarely hear anything else. Their only noise was the roar of their wings as they burst into those sudden mass-flights occasioned by the inexplicable panics that waders suffer from, or because they really had been stooped at by one of the many marsh harriers and black kites that patrolled those lagoons incessantly. All day I could hear these explosions as ruffs rose in crowds from neighbouring lagoons, flew round and settled again.

In contrast to the silent-voiced ruffs there were plenty of waders that were noisy enough, especially the Rukwa's second commonest wader, the wood sandpiper. Wood sandpipers began to arrive when I had been about an hour in the hide but I had been hearing their shrill liquid cries all round before one walked into sight down one of the creeks. This one, and soon many more, hastened to join the other waders on the far side of the lagoon, their lively movements and bobbing sterns adding life to an already animated scene. Soon other waders came: a dozen little stints, diminutive and pale-grey, very busily probing and all a-twitter; several curlew sandpipers and ringed plovers; and two tropical plovers, the blacksmith, boldly black and white and noisy, and one white-winged plover which did not stay long, for this is more a bird of the open lake where it lives daintily stepping about floating plants in the manner of a lily-trotter. To this life it is fully adapted, for like the lily-trotter, it has evolved especially long feet, hence its other name, the long-toed lapwing.

Time passed and my bird visitors increased in number. By eleven o'clock several heron and egret species were stalking hugely among the waders. There were little egrets walking very slowly, sometimes raising bright yellow feet out of the water, then dashing forward and lunging their beak-spears in pursuit of fish or frog. With them was a yellow-billed egret, only slightly larger but quite different about the beak. And beyond them a splendid great white heron, standing half-hidden in the bulrushes, shy, watchful, only once coming into the open, one of the few birds that day which I think distrusted my hide.

But the bird most fascinating to watch was the black heron. I had never seen one before and knew nothing of its peculiar manner of hunting. It was with complete astonishment that I saw three of these birds about half the size of a grey heron glide down to the lagoon, stand watchful two or three seconds, then all three take a neat leap forward (showing bright yellow feet), bow their heads right down and spread their wings forward into a perfect inverted bowl-shape. In this weird position these three small herons began to walk slowly about the lagoon and since their heads were concealed below their spread wings they looked exactly like three little umbrellas moving about above the surface of the water. By thus shading the water they are said to be able to detect their prey more easily.

Meanwhile the glossy ibises had increased to seven and had been joined in their corner of the pool by a sacred ibis, all white except for black head and upper neck; a wood ibis, white-bodied, black-winged; and a white stork. But neither wood ibis nor stork stayed long; presumably their favourite food was not to be found there just then. Their place was taken by the most ludicrous bird of the day, an African spoonbill. He dropped heavily into the pool with a flurry of great white wings and, putting his head down, came rushing straight towards my hide, his extraordinary beak swishing heartily from side to side. Though he passed within four yards he never even looked at the hide. This swishing, guzzling creature disappeared down a creek but quite soon came charging back; and all the while he stayed, he never ceased from striding back and forth, disturbing flocks of little waders wherever he went.

I have said little about noises off. Yet they added much to the splendour of the occasion. Intermittently through the day there was a chorus of frogs rising and dying down. One frog sets another off. First there is silence. Then a frog pipes, another answers and all round they shriek at each other for several minutes till the excitement abates. A far nobler sound was the cry of the fish-eagle, described, so rightly, as epitomising the whole atmosphere of wild Africa, a lovely, laughing cry that rang far across the lagoons and marshes every ten or twenty minutes as if marking the passage of the hot hours. And there was that strangest of sounds, the indescribable bubbling of the coucals which were very common all round the lake. Flocks of unknown terns passed over repeatedly, crying unmusically. The *tew–tew–tew* of passing greenshanks reminded me of the estuary at home in Wales. Squacco herons croaked all round, a querulous harsh croak, vehement and guttural. Far more squaccos must have been hidden under cover than were visible to me; and all the time I wondered what else might be concealed in or beyond the rushes. Occasionally there was the scream of a rail, or a bittern; or I glimpsed a black crake scuttling into cover. Flocks of small birds constantly rushed by, unknown birds which I heard but never saw.

In the early afternoon I had some moments of anxiety about buffaloes. When we had reached the lagoon in the morning we had seen a long white cloud in the sky, a cloud of cattle egrets which were flapping above what was evidently a big herd of buffaloes on the move. Once in the hide and absorbed in the birds I had forgotten the buffaloes until I realized by their bellowing that they were approaching. But, hidden in the bulrushes, I had no view of the plain and it was not till I saw the cattle egrets in the sky about a hundred yards off that I realized the buffaloes were so close. I wondered what I should do if my hide lay directly in their path. Should I sit tight or should I confront them? It had sounded all right the night before when Vesey had assured us that buffaloes in a herd were quite harmless and that only individual buffaloes were dangerous because they had usually been wounded. But now I felt decidedly nervous and it was with relief that I realized that the herd was passing by along the edge of the swamps. Elephants were another worry. They were on the other side of me, out in the swamp between me and the open lake, as their occasional trumpeting indicated. I hated the thought of elephants getting interested in my presence for neither Vesey nor anyone else had quite convinced me that unprovoked elephants were harmless. Fortunately they too probably never suspected I was there.

The afternoon grew hot. The fervour of the morning's feed was over and most of the birds stood listless and silent. Only the spoonbill still raced about, the umbrellas (now eight) still crouched and bobbed, and some of the ruffs were bathing splashily, though most slept. A squacco heron stood on one leg close to my hide preening desultorily, showing me the beauty of his spread wing as he stretched himself. A group of egrets and ibises stood quite still in partial shade. Even the blacksmith plovers were hardly moving. Now and then a fish-eagle called, emphasizing the silence. I see I wrote in my notebook: 'Heavy with the heat and silence grew the afternoon of summer.' Longfellow's line had never meant so much. Mosquitos and a large kind of horse-fly now invaded my hide in some numbers, not so much to attack me as to get out of the sun, for they are shade-loving insects. In any case my head, neck and hands, the only parts of me exposed, were well anointed with insect-repellant.

An hour passed uneventfully except for a young crocodile which floated by the hide, carried slowly lakewards on the sluggish waters of the creek, his jaws set in an expressionless grin. Twenty minutes later a school of cat-fish came splashing up the creek from the lake, their mouths gaping at the surface, their heads bristling with the 'whiskers' that give them their name. But there was nothing else. The show, I decided, was over. Then along the creek in the direction of the lake came further splashing. Catfish, I said to myself, only catfish. But how wrong I was. This, in a sense, was the great moment of the day. For along that creek swam two pelicans side by side. On they came, paddling gently along until they were right in front of me at two yards range. They took in my hide with a glance, didn't like it, swept round majestically and paddled off back up the creek at speed. Now pelicans are common birds but till then they had for me been only distant birds. So it was tremendously exciting to see this pair so near. And pelicans swimming are, I think, pelicans at their most peculiar. For then the huge, pouched beak seems at its most fantastic.

A cine-photographer would have enjoyed a session in that hide, especially in the morning when so much was going on. First he could have panned round to show the total assembly of birds. Then with his telephoto lens he could have picked out each species in its turn: the pale-brown little squacco herons walking solemnly between the rushes; the greenshanks, marsh sandpipers and wood sandpipers running erratically all over the place, always sharply turning and probing; the ruffs quietly feeding all over the place with lowered backs and bowed heads; the several lovely egrets, so tall and elegant; the finely sheened plumage of the glossy ibis; the bold patterning of the sacred ibis, wood ibis and white stork; the rollicking gait of the spoonbill; above all, the umbrella-trick of the black heron. He would have needed a tape-recorder also to bring back the *tonk, tonk, tonk* of the blacksmith plover, the croak of the squacco, the deep *gerrah* of the glossy ibis, the chorus of the frogs, the water-out-of-a-bottle gurgle of the white-browed coucal.

Faced with such a concentration of birds in one locality, one is left wondering what they all feed on even though it is evident that the warmth and mineral richness of these lagoons is highly favourable to the development of myriads of small aquatic creatures. But all these birds are not in direct competition with each other. So many beaks of different lengths and shapes imply so many different depths and methods of feeding, and hence so many different kinds of prey. Perhaps, for instance, the unique way in which the black heron puts up his umbrella is adapted to the pursuit of some special sort of prey not so easily caught by any other bird.

Some days we went out across the plain east of Tumba towards where the Rungwa river comes into the lake, the Land Rover grinding slowly over the terribly rutted, hard-baked mud that gave place treacherously to soft places that often forced us to turn back and make long detours. It is true that there was, or had been, a road east of Tumba to the next abandoned Locust Control village, Kambangombi, but this road had been taken over by elephants whose footprints had made it the least motorable way across the plain. So we simply navigated across as best we could, choosing our own road and often deviating to look at animals and birds. What was most noticeable on these excursions was the wonderful eyesight of the Africans. My sight is reasonable but by the side of these chaps I felt half-blind. Time and again they spotted far-off animals which the rest of us needed binoculars to see. I never saw it more clearly demonstrated that western man has advanced into civilization at the cost of keenness of sight.

The commonest large animal of the Rukwa was undoubtedly the topi. They were everywhere in little groups, identifiable at long distances by their sloping shoulders and swept-back horns. Occasionally we saw larger groups and once, at the most easterly point we reached, the River Rungwa, there was a splendid herd of three or four hundred. Yet we did not see them at their best or most numerous, restricted as we were to this comparatively narrow plain far from their normal haunts which lay deep beneath the lake[8]. It was the same with the buffaloes. We saw 300-400 of them at times but this was nothing to the numbers recorded in the late 1950s when North Rukwa, instead of a vast lake, was a fertile plain across which the buffaloes pastured well out of reach of man. But now they were increasingly confined by this lake that year by year crept further across their world. Elephants were less inconvenienced: they like watery places and it was a joy to see them tramping off the plain into the marsh, slowly getting deeper into the vegetation until all you could see were the tops of their heads and the rhythmic swishing of their great grey ears. At other times we saw places where they had wallowed and then used nearby trees as bath-towels, leaving them smeared with mud. Their paths through the bush were well marked by their huge footprints and by trampled briers and bushes; but African elephants treat the vegetation comparatively gently and do not normally smash trees to anything like the extent Indian

---

[8] Which is of very recent origin. See below.

elephants are said to do. It is only when large numbers of them are confined in too restricted an area that African elephants are likely to do serious damage to their habitat.

Giraffe, Burchell's zebra, impala and Bohor reed-buck were the other animals we saw in quantity. Like nearly all animals they are easily approached in a vehicle, while on foot you cannot get near them except by the most delicate stalking. It is one of my strangest experiences of wildlife to have gone up to a flat-topped acacia and then found myself stared at by a giraffe whose neck and head suddenly appeared over the tree-top. Of all animals, after lions and elephants, the giraffe is, I suppose, the most popular with safari visitors. It is naturally so. For there is no animal like him, so uniquely evolved to be the supreme browsing creature, so cryptically coloured and patterned to resemble a patch of broken sunlight, so strange in his 'slow-motion' running. If I had seen nothing else in Africa I would reckon the trip worthwhile to have seen a party of adult and young giraffes standing watchful among the palms and acacias, their long straight necks all slanting at the same angle, as if they themselves were a strange group of trees leaning away from the wind.

2: The hotel at Lake Rukwa
A baobab on the steep bank above the hotel had a large and conspicuous fish-eagle's nest in its upper boughs. It evidently contained young, for one of the parent eagles, I think the female, stood on guard by it at all hours, a necessary duty in a place so infested by monkeys. Often she uttered her lovely wild laugh, her head thrown back, and this was answered immediately by her mate who spent long hours on a tree in the lake about 200 yards from the nest. The most obvious small birds round the hotel were the golden weavers which often chirped in the fringe of bushes standing in the lake. They were the usual weaver yellow but with

a splash of orange on the breast and looked bigger than most kinds we had seen. Various very small warblers threaded through the lakeside vegetation but the only one I really identified was a species, grey-green above, yellow and white below, called the yellow-breasted apalis. The Angola mourning doves (but I shall always think of them as the Rukwa doves) crooned out their song all day as they had in the heat of Tumba. And early one morning when all was quiet, a laughing dove and a red-eyed dove came to feed together under our chalet window.

But the bird most intimately associated with the hotel was undoubtedly the morning warbler. At Tumba our morning warblers had been excessively furtive but at the Outspan hotel, where they were used to people, they were much tamer. There were at least two singing males to enliven the dawn and some mornings one perched on our step as if to sing to us under the door. It was their nesting time. I watched one gather straws on the lawn and disappear with them behind the hotel. The other nest was actually indoors, in the hotel dining room which opened onto a veranda. We were having breakfast one morning when, happening to glance up, I saw a little nest on a beam that supported the thatched roof. Out of the nest protruded the unmistakable long rounded tail of a morning warbler. What was more, when we listened we could hear a delightful little sub-song coming from the incubating bird, a subdued replica of its normal song.

Along the shore one day we came to a baobab standing in two or three feet of water. If the lake went on rising much longer even that great tree was doomed for though the baobab needs plenty of water and is recorded as sending its roots a hundred yards to find it, it cannot stand prolonged immersion. So the presence of that and neighbouring old baobabs clearly indicated that no flood much greater than the one we saw can have afflicted the Rukwa valley for a long period of time. Another baobab we saw had a name hacked deeply in it. I suppose the smooth blank trunks of these trees are irresistible to cutters of initials. Even Livingstone cut his name on a baobab at Victoria Falls. Mercifully the baobab suffers less than most trees by such incisions. Though we tried to eat the great pulpy fruits of the baobab we found them distasteful. Not so the tamarind fruits. They hung in thick clusters like bunches of small narrow beans, were soft to eat and deliciously thirst-quenching.

On our last night at Lake Rukwa we had the most majestic storm I have ever seen. It had been a brilliant hot day but after mid-afternoon the sky changed rapidly. It turned grey from end to end and huge clouds built up all round the horizon. I counted seven widely separated storms along the escarpment beyond the lake, seven towering black triangles with lightning in their bellies, each with a dark wall of rain hung below. Gradually these storms expanded along the line of the hills, approaching each other and finally merging into one blue-black curtain stretching over a hundred miles round to the west and north. Vivid streaks of lightning zigzagged down from this curtain every few seconds: but at that distance no thunder could be heard. Slowly the curtain came down towards the far shore of the lake until there was no escarpment, only the long black band of storm across the lake. Below it the water was silver, meeting the dark belt of cloud in a sharp straight line. Several African canoes hastened by towards the village, the men singing songs with strange, quick rhythms as they paddled as hard as they could to escape the storm. Darkness fell abruptly. Thunder growled, thumped and crashed around the sky and lightning was now continuous. I had long desired to photograph lightning and now was my chance if ever there was one. I dashed indoors to get my camera. But already, when I came out again, there was a threshing sound out on the lake, a sound that grew quickly into a roar as immensely heavy rain advanced across the water. We leapt to the chalet for shelter and in seconds the storm broke over us. What seemed like solid rain thundered on our roof for the next four hours. The wind increased all the time. In the lightning flashes we could see white-topped waves breaking up the hotel lawn. The lake sounded like the Atlantic in a gale. We wondered what was happening to the sand-martins roosting on their floating island. Then gradually the storm passed and though it returned again and again during the night it was never quite so violent. By morning all was calm but the line of water-lettuce piled up at the hotel steps was proof of the strength of the wind. There was no need to ask what would happen to the Outspan hotel if the lake rose another two feet and then flung another such storm at it. We heard later that this in fact happened. The delightful hotel, with its fine old bougainvillea-crowned baobab, was destroyed by the rising lake not long after our visit. At the same time a hundred miles away at the north end of the lake the houses we had lived in at Tumba were also wrecked by the floods. African lakeside villages are inevitably ephemeral, but the drowning of ancient baobabs is a different matter and seems proof that the Rukwa valley floods of the 1960s were the highest for centuries.

We returned to Mbeya along that high, exciting ridge road that gave us our last views of the Usanga plain on the left and of Rukwa on the right. We stopped near the highest point of the road for a final look back towards the now far distant lake. It had been another hot day and in the north the sky was darkening for another storm; but nearer to us the great thunder-heads were still brilliant in sunlight. We looked at the far valley, this Rukwa with its two hundred miles of wilderness and we hoped fervently that its wildness and fauna would be preserved, that it would never be given up to cattle and cultivation. Thoreau's words cannot be too often repeated: man needs, and as he retreats more and more into cities he is going increasingly to need, 'the tonic of wildness', And this means not only wild country but a country containing its full and natural complement of wild creatures.

3: Kalambo Falls

Finest of all the waterfalls that fling themselves off the escarpment towards Lake Tanganyika is the magnificent fall on the Kalambo river some twenty-five miles north-west of Abercorn. Dropping over a sheer 700-foot precipice this is the highest single-leap fall in Africa, being nearly twice the height of the Victoria Falls (but only a fraction of the volume). Emerging from among the green trees the Kalambo drops as a solid band of white water which broadens slightly as it falls and then crashes in a mist of spray clouds. Not that it is ever the same from minute to minute. For apart from the main body, there are always long spumes of water coming down almost separately, none of them continuing far but sporadically shooting down alongside the main fall like white-tailed rockets that die long before they reach the bottom. The sound-pattern of the fall likewise is always changing, its roar rising or hushing with the breeze and occasionally varied by a crashing and booming as of waves against cliffs, as if the river were unsteady in its flow and now and then throws an extra spate down the fall. One day we had a great surprise when we arrived there, for the fall was quite invisible. The densest of mists, warm, thick and white, had come up from the lake and filled the whole gorge to just below the lip of the cliffs. So we stood in bright sunshine on the plateau rim and looked across a shining plain of mist that seemed almost solid enough to walk on to the other side of the gorge. There was only the muffled thunder of the fall to assure us that we had come to the right place. But soon the mist began to swirl and break, and quite suddenly it was no more than long delicate fingers reaching up from below. Cliffs appeared, then trees and in a few moments the sun was shining brilliantly into the gorge and all was sparkle and clarity.

Even without any waterfall this gorge would be a place of splendour, winding its two or three miles to the lake between high, bare, pale-brown quartzite cliffs and steep slopes sparsely clad in colourful trees, purple as they come into leaf, bright green a few weeks later. Then the eye travels down to the deep V-cleft where the river snakes along through a dark-green, rain-forest type of vegetation. Wild bananas with huge broad leaves overhang the water; there is a jungle of greenery which through binoculars appears to be a riot of tall ferns; and almost directly below, on a wide ledge just above the river, there is a massive bed of white crinums. Mary Richards would stand looking wistfully into the chasm where no botanist seems ever to have ventured, wondering what thrilling trees and shrubs she might find there if only there were a way down. Botanically the place has another attraction: as the river here is also a national frontier you can, if you can find someone with a canoe to take you across, make botanical records for both Tanzania and Zambia all in the same day.

Kalambo Falls are not only splendid scenery, they are also the site of a fine bird spectacle – a nesting colony of marabou storks. Breeding groups of marabous are only thinly scattered in Africa and though most are in trees, a few are on precipices. Although in our travels we saw plenty of marabous, especially at Lake Rukwa, we never found any nesting, except these at Kalambo Falls, but we did hear of a similar cliff colony in a gorge along the Muze river not far from Rukwa. Marabous are most often seen at their feeding places by rivers and lakes; or on plains where some dead animal can be shared with vultures. And as they are so very approachable everyone knows how ugly and vulturine the bare flesh is on their heads and necks. Presumably both vultures and marabous have evolved these bare patches because of the impossibility of keeping their head and neck feathers clean when they are forever poking into the liquefied interiors of carcasses.

It is at places like Kalambo Falls that you see marabous in a new light. Either they are far down the crags, standing by their nests like cormorants on an ocean cliff, or else they are gliding above the gorge. A marabou on the wing is a marabou transformed from something rather grotesque to a magnificent, white-bodied, leg-trailing bird with huge, black, long-fingered wings on which it silently planes and circles with perfect control. Usually to reach their nest they circle very slowly lower and lower until they are down to the right level and then swing gently on to the ledge, to stand there on long massive legs. But once we saw one come over high above the gorge and go spiralling down in a wild, feather-tearing power dive and yet reach its ledge in safety.

Marabous have a long nesting season. When we first went to Kalambo in mid November, though several of the nests contained nearly full-grown young, one bird was still carrying sticks: so they are probably present on the ledges at least from August to late January. The last time we saw them, on December 23rd, there was an unmistakable end-of-season feel about them. Hardly any were flying now. Instead they were along their ledges, about thirty of them, old and young, standing idle or squabbling listlessly over food with occasional heavy flapping of wings; or they simply crouched with wings held outspread, which is one of their favourite postures. On our final visit, on 15th February, the marabous had all gone except for two nearly full-grown dead young ones visible on one of the ledges. The great white-washed stick nests would lie empty, perhaps not even visited, until the beginning of the next season.

The marabou stork is only one of many birds of the Kalambo gorge. On our first visit we were looking down on to a yellow-billed kite gliding peaceably about 200 feet below when suddenly a peregrine shot out of the cliff straight at him, swerving away at the last instant. There followed a wild up-and-down chase, the peregrine screaming and diving with wonderful speed, the kite evading him with split second twists and rolls until he was far away down the gorge. The peregrines obviously had a nest, for after that we often saw them there, chasing away kites and eagles. By February the peregrines, like the storks, had gone and in their place had come many migrant hobbies arrowing about in the winds that came up from the lake and chasing the swifts that breed on the cliffs. Much more intimate were the red-winged starlings, like small slender jackdaws, which perched inquisitively near us in cliff-edge trees. I used to clap my hands to make them fly and show the bright orange wings that unfold from their black bodies. They would fly out over the gorge and come back to the same perch to sing out an excited squeaky song only heard in the roar of the fall because the birds were so near. All more distant birds were inaudible. You could see the clarion-voiced fish-eagles throw back their heads and yodel with mouth wide open but no sound ever came across the gorge.

Sheer precipices are unpromising localities for plants and at first sight the Kalambo cliffs look hopelessly red and bare. But look closer and you see that there are scattered streaks of vegetation which through binoculars (in such a place an essential item of botanical equipment) turn out to be fleshy rosettes of aloe leaves, prickly euphorbias sprouting dangerously over the void, patches of nindi (*Aeolanthus*) with spikes of mauve flowers, and the pink of cranny-loving kinds of gladioli. One intriguing sight at Kalambo is a fig-tree which grows at the rim of the gorge close to the falls on the Tanzanian side. Almost the whole of its roots are exposed to view because they cling to the spray-wettened face of the cliff, growing down the side of the fall for an astonishing distance.

Besides the many figs and brachystegias there were trees whose fruits looked exactly like oranges but were in fact the fruits of various species of strychnos, some of which were highly poisonous from the strychnine they contain. Yet even in this unpromising family some of the fruits are edible and these the Africans (and the monkeys) know well. It is also interesting that some strychnos fruits can be used to purify water, a fact which has been known to Africans for centuries. Some of the lovely bauhinia trees such as we saw around Mbeya also grew at Kalambo Falls, their showy long white petals like big stars hanging among the leaves. And there were the yams we had to go searching for one day. One of the pleasures, Mary Richards has discovered, of being a botanist resident in a remote part of Africa, is that she receives frequent requests for specimens of plants from fellow-botanists all over the world. One such entreaty had just come from a yam-specialist in the British Museum and so here we were prospecting the woods of Kalambo for whatever yams might be found there. After much searching we eventually found one or two – they are climbers with large, milky tubers – dug them up with great care and sent them off to London.

Throughout these woods the red-chested cuckoo repeated his three clipped notes in rivalry with the four plaintive pipes of the emerald cuckoo. But although these two voices are among the best known sounds of the bush, the birds themselves, like so many cuckoos, are among the least frequently seen of all birds. The emerald cuckoo, which lays its eggs in the nests of bulbuls, sunbirds, weavers and warblers, must surely be high on the list of the world's most lovely birds, for its head, back and breast are a brilliant, metallic green and its belly the brightest of yellows.

One November day as I went down to the falls through woods bright with yellow irises, a little bird fluttered out of a bank. Bending down I found a nest containing young. At home I would have called the bird a female redstart for it was a pale brown with a fiery tail, But our redstart does not go as far south as Zambia and in any case does not breed anywhere in Central Africa, so I sat down and waited for this bird to come back, which it soon did, standing on a twig as near as four feet away, an insect in its beak. I was then able to identify it as a familiar chat. And as it frequently came to its nest though I stood right by it I thought the bird perfectly named. It was in these woods that I had my best views of broad-billed rollers, rather strange-looking birds, not only for their broad yellow beaks but also for their very short tails, for rollers usually have long, conspicuous tails. Otherwise they had the bright chestnut backs and brilliant blue wings and tails that most of the family have.

These rollers were in small noisy flocks that cried harshly as they flew above the trees. Flying insects, though invisible to us, were evidently abundant, for the birds constantly twisted and zig-zagged about, mostly high in the air but sometimes swooping down close to our upturned faces, at which close range we got many glimpses of their flashing colours. The last time we saw them was one evening coming back from the falls after sunset. Though it was practically dark we could make out the unmistakable shapes of these rollers still weaving about the sky. With them several nightjars were diving about with great agility. The difference in the flight of the two species was very pronounced: the nightjars, arrowing about like slender sparrow hawks, made the rollers look almost heavy and crow-like in comparison. Yet before the nightjars appeared we had been admiring the rollers' deftness and agility.

The superb fall of Kalambo with its vast encircling cliffs, its deep tree-filled gorge, its silent floating birds: it was a place to return to often, and always find something new; a place to sit and think about time and eternity and the forces that have shaped great scenery. And it was a place to think about man's past as well as that of the earth. A mile up-stream from the fall, in a wide peaceful valley, the river is not recognizable as the silvery, living water that leaps into the gorge: it is slow, brown, muddy, curving without energy through a saucer-shaped depression in the land, a depression lined with the deposits of a shallow lake that occupied it long ago. Stratified one above the other in these deposits the successive living floors of the oldest known people of that part of Africa have been discovered.

Their time on earth is reckoned to have been contemporary with the last of the four ice-ages of the northern hemisphere whose probable counterparts in Africa were the four great rain-ages or pluvials. Here at this lakeside lived earliest tool-using man, caveless, his life open to the sky. But since that was a time when every rainy season brought more rain than could be drained off or evaporated during the following dry season there was a steady rise in the water levels every year. Inevitably Lake Kalambo grew deeper and wider, forcing those on its shores to abandon their camps and edge back to drier ground. They left behind them their primitive tools and other signs of how they lived – charcoals, a hearth and sharpened sticks – evidence perhaps of man first learning to skewer and cook his meat. Many times they retreated to higher ground as the waters invaded and Lake Kalambo grew to nine miles in length and three in width. And at each of their living levels they left their copious traces to be preserved in the lacustrine silt.

No lake lasts forever. Eventually the outlet stream cut through the little hills that dammed the waters, and Lake Kalambo was no more. What remained became the scene of today, the shallow basin terraced all round with alluvial clays and pebbles through which archaeologists have sliced to get their rich haul of hand-axes, picks, choppers and scrapers which, before they came along, had not been in human hands for 100,000 years or more. Faced with such a chasm of time one is left wondering at the extreme slowness of stone-age man's development, for 90,000 years later he was still using similar flake-tools and living an apparently similar life.

No archaeologists were working at Kalambo the season we were there, but their excavation was still open, the trench several yards deep and wide, cutting for fifty or sixty yards through the terraces down to a bend of the river. It looked a changeless scene: the glinting stream sliding into the shadows of the forest; tall, swollen-trunked borassus palms standing solitary; the frequent barks and yelps of tree-top monkeys; primitive, grass-roofed huts in the distance and bare-shouldered women bending among their maize. It was just the place to imagine ancient men living in isolation and oblivious of the rest of the world, perhaps only dimly aware that other similar men existed remotely elsewhere, men who like themselves were setting faltering but fateful steps on a long, long road into the timeless future.

(1967)

CONTINENTAL NIGHTS OUT

1: Nuits blanches

We British naturalists are often regretful because of the limited number of our animal species, but at least we are spared those dreadful Continental nights torn into shreds by a howling cacophony of frogs, crickets and nightingales. Having heard hundreds of nightingales lately in France and Spain I am left marvelling how this species ever got a reputation for beautiful singing. They utter a few soothing phrases, it is true, and now and then they seem about to develop a really splendid tune; but it all collapses into harshness and din. Then there are the mole crickets shrieking; and all those maddening bush crickets. I know people have written in praise of these sounds but I suspect these admirers have never been campers.

To go camping in southern Europe is not to miss a syllable of all these horrors of which easily the worst are the frogs. Only in the high Pyrenees did we find a campsite entirely free of them. Some merely squeaked and piped and were more or less bearable. But most yelled into the night with rasping, guttural voices that carried half a mile. Of course, as a naturalist, I should have rejoiced at this wealth of pulsating Continental night-life, but even naturalists like to sleep sometimes. I admit I found myself longing for the absolute night silence we get in late spring here in the Welsh woods after the owls have finished their silly season.

2: Black woodpecker

In spring, 1963, James Fisher, then a presenter of radio nature programmes at Bristol, gave £25 of the BBC's money to each of three birdwatchers of long experience to be spent by them in searching for a wild bird they had never seen before. The rules imposed were simple. 'Here's £25. Go and look for your bird. All expenditure demanded by the search must come out of the £25. No more is to be spent except in the direst emergency. The bird sought for must be declared in advance.' Elizabeth Forster of Norfolk chose to go to France to try for a flamingo. Denzil Harber from Sussex would go to Denmark for a thrush-nightingale. My choice was the black woodpecker mainly because it looked so spectacular in the bird books – the size of a crow, all-black except for a bright red top to his head, and with a beak that was said to be capable of hacking chips nine inches long out of trees.

But I took a risk in electing to go to a district in France which was right on the edge of the black woodpecker's range (it has spread westwards since then). There was also the fact that all woodpeckers, even where common, can be extremely elusive.

I drove across Wales, England and France to near Dijon, a journey that cost me much of the £25. But I had no other expenses. I took all my food from home and, to avoid overnight fees, I camped each night in roadside woods and disused quarries. Although this avoidance of official campsites had its hazards there was only one spot where I almost got into difficulties. I had driven at dusk along a track into the forest and was awakened next morning by a gamekeeper who was clearly not pleased to find me and my car deep in his coverts. I did my halting best to explain to him that I was *un observateur des oiseaux* and not a poacher after his pheasants. This mention of pheasants proved fortunate. It changed the whole atmosphere. The keeper seemed to find the idea of his being a keeper of pheasants quite amusing. His reserve, he assured me with some pride, was for the hunting of wild boar and roe deer. After that he became really affable and told me about some of the birds of the forest and how *le milan royal* (red kite) and *l'autour* (goshawk) were getting scarcer year by year. Then off he went through the trees leaving me to have my breakfast in peace, if I can speak of peace when ten thousand frogs were shouting themselves hoarse in a nearby swamp.

I explored that countryside for several days – a gently beautiful land with pinewoods on the hills and wide cornlands between. The wildflowers were spectacular, especially the orchids: long stretches of the lanesides had lady and military orchids in full bloom. Along the forest edges there were crested tits and often the stuttering little song of Bonelli's warblers. All week the weather was perfect for sleeping out and I never unpacked my tent. But the absence of black woodpeckers was worrying and

I was wondering whether to make a quick dash to the Vosges mountains or perhaps the Jura.

But I decided to stay where I was. Then on almost my last morning I lay listening to the dawn chorus in a woodland of beech and pine. I could hear hoopoes, quails (in the field outside), cuckoos, blackcaps, orioles and blackbirds imitating orioles rather well. It is a magical moment when you wake up in a strange forest and have no idea what you may hear or see next. That dawn, as I lay there, I heard a startling noise high in the trees: *kok-kok-kok-keear*. Then I saw the bird which had produced it, looking very large and black as it came flapping over my clearing a few yards above my face. That was how the black woodpecker came into my life. I lay a few moments listening but he didn't come back. Then I heard a loud *klonk-klonk* of beak on hard wood about a hundred yards off. So I got out of my bag and went through the trees as quietly as I could. Soon I saw him, high up a pine, the great black woodpecker with his red crown, banging away at a dead branch. I watched him for several minutes. Then he saw me and away he went, not undulating like the smaller woodpeckers, but flying almost floppily like a jay. And that was how the black woodpecker went out of my life, for I have never seen another.

(1993-1995)

The tree-frogs in southern France have to be heard to be believed. When I first came to live in Ariege, in the middle of one night I walked down to the bottom of the garden in my dressing gown thinking a car alarm had been set off. It was a tree-frog, and it carried on like that until dawn. I wholly agree with Bill about the nightingale's song. That of the blackcap, for example, is far more tuneful, clear and poignant. But try getting our Keatsian fellow-countrymen to agree to this notion. Do the English ever think for themselves?

TICK-HUNTING IN ANDALUSIA

When Thoreau withdrew from society to live in his hut in Walden Woods his solitude was often disturbed by callers. But only in the warm season. In winter he was left almost entirely alone with the trees, the few birds, the frozen pond, and the deep Massachusetts snow. Then he was visited only by the most devoted and determined such as his friend who was a poet: 'The one who came from farthest to my lodge, through the deepest snows and most dismal tempests, was a poet. A farmer, a hunter, a soldier, a reporter, even a philosopher, may be daunted; but nothing can deter a poet, for he is actuated by pure love. Who can predict his comings and goings? His business calls him out at all hours, even when doctors sleep.'

Penny and I felt like that when, before we came to Ynys Edwin, we were living not far away in a little hillside cottage called Felin-y-cwm, a mile up the narrow, wooded valley of the Einion stream. On winter nights we, like Thoreau, were tucked up 'as snug as a meadow mouse' and seldom had visitors. Yet through the darkness, sometimes trudging through snow drifts, there was one who came up over the mountain track and down to our door. And he, as if to give truth to Thoreau's words, was a poet. R.S. Thomas, then vicar of our parish, came to chat about many things: but above all about wild birds. For they are a very special part of his life.

Now poets, the good ones, occasionally get literary prizes. And it happened one day that R.S. Thomas was granted a bursary that carried with it the condition that it had to be spent on foreign travel, the idea being, I suppose, that visiting other countries broadens a writer's mind. But I fear that R.S. Thomas took a somewhat narrow view of what would broaden his: he saw it as an opportunity of adding to his life-list of birds. 'Tick-hunting' is what birdwatchers call it. You carry a card with a list of all the birds on it and you happily tick them off as you spot them. A fatuous occupation, you may say, but it gives people a lot of pleasure and is quite harmless unless, as sometimes happens, too many birdwatchers want to see the same bird and pursue it to the point of harassment.

On receiving his travel award R.S. Thomas resolved to go and see the birds of southern Spain. (He had been reading that inspiring book *Portrait of a Wilderness* by Guy Mountfort.) And he generously invited me to go with him as a passenger in his car. Because the grant was not enormous we would need to keep our expenses down by taking most of our food with us and by camping. So it came about that one morning in late April we set off for Andalusia.

As our ship began to move down the Solent from Southampton we began putting ticks on our cards. Herring gull, cormorant, oystercatcher... In mid-Channel a few more commoners... in Cherbourg a crow and a starling. (Even the most soaring lists need these bread and butter species to get them off the ground.) The only choice birds we got that first day were a barn owl and a nightingale, both heard over a frugal supper at our camp near Rennes. Next day, heeding the call of the south, we drove across Brittany without stopping to look for birds. But by chance we got our first touch of glamour – a golden oriole near Saintes – before we camped on the Landes coast at Arachon. And there is nothing like a golden oriole for putting northern birdwatchers in good spirits and convincing them that the golden age is beginning. No golden age for us next day, however. It was a day that should have carried us well into Spain but because of a Montagu's harrier and other events it did not. Heading south we saw a signpost on our right, 'La Route des Lacs', and what tick-hunter short of waterbirds could resist a lakeside road? So fate diverted us from the Bordeaux-San Sebastian highway into a quiet coastal road that led with promise through open heathlands and scattered groves with an occasional hint of sand-dunes far on our right. It was then that we saw our Montagu's harrier floating over the heather and we rejoiced, for this is a rare bird nearly everywhere. We stopped. Since this wild, apparently unpeopled land had harriers it probably had other good birds. So though we were going to fall far behind our strict schedule we felt we must spare this Arcadia a little while. We got out and walked along the road. In a few minutes we had seen a Dartford warbler and had gazed enraptured up into a tree at our first Bonelli's warbler. Next moment we were being arrested by a French military officer for spying on a military base. (It was there all right, this base, but in the excitement we hadn't spotted the rather small notice-boards.)

All that sunny morning we were interrogated by the commandant of this top-secret defence establishment; and then re-interrogated all afternoon by the civil police especially summoned from Bordeaux. It was an agonizing waste of our precious holiday. But it had its amusing moments. As when we were being questioned outside the base headquarters soon after we arrived. Suddenly R.S. Thomas stepped out of the group and raised his field glasses to stare intently up into a tree. 'Woodchat shrike,' he said after a few moments. And taking out his bird-list he solemnly ticked it off. We spent the next ten minutes explaining to the military police what a bird-list is and what a woodchat shrike is and pointing to its picture in a book. How thankful we were to the *Field Guide* for giving us the French names of birds. All the same, anyone who thinks his French is good should try explaining the mysteries of bird-ticking to a group of suspicious French military police. To our captors this incident probably appeared a clever piece of acting and convinced them that we really were dangerous spies. Or maybe it just confirmed them in their belief that all the British are mad. Though the proceedings ended at last in handshakes and genial goodbyes, one fact could not be altered: we had lost a whole precious day. That night we got no farther than a camping place by a pine-surrounded pool called Lac Leon, many miles short of where we had intended to be.

Next morning we entered Spain along the coast road and kept carefully to the main highway all the way to Burgos. Spanish military police, we decided, would be even more difficult to deal with than the French ones. All that day, because we hardly ever stopped, we only got nine ticks on the list: but one was for a species new to us both, an evasive little bird that spluttered out an unfamiliar loud but cheerful phrase from a thicketed streamside and which we eventually identified as a Cetti's warbler. That was the day the corn buntings began. To us, coming from West Wales, a few corn buntings along the wires were a novelty at first. But when, down that long road to Burgos, we realized that there was a corn bunting on the wires every few hundred metres, they soon began to get tedious. There were plenty of wire-perching species we wanted to see – shrikes, chats, flycatchers – but no, practically every bird on the wires all that long day was a corn bunting. We had not dreamed there were so many in all the world.

It was from Burgos southward, and especially after Valladolid, that life began to change, that we felt we had crossed an invisible frontier. The early morning in our camp under tall poplars at Burgos gave us wrynecks laughing among the branches: and a wryneck is a good enough start to any British birdwatcher's day. In the same place serins choroused among the leaves and another valued tick went down for the spotless starling. We passed through Valladolid and Salamanca on a memorable day that soon gave us quail, little ringed plover and crested and short-toed larks. Overhead the first black kite came circling. And we felt we were getting into the real south when we began to see frequent hoopoes flapping across the road and scintillating bee-eaters perched along the wires. A red-roofed town with white storks on chimney pots and rows of lesser kestrels along the walls was for us a new species of town. We only needed a roller, we said, to convince us that we really had reached southern Spain. And before we got to Salamanca we saw one, a joyous dazzle of blue as it dropped from a wire to snatch up a beetle off the ground. Soon afterwards a pure-white bird that came beating across the sky seemed an authentic touch of Africa – a cattle egret, a bird that lives in some numbers in Morocco and Algeria but has only the slenderest hold on Europe, mainly here in south Spain.

When you've reached far enough into Spain to tick off your first eighty birds you begin to find new species much harder to come by. But the trickle you do get are nearly all good quality. So on 1 May, still motoring, we saw our first red kite gliding high over the road. Stopping awhile we heard the delicious song of a woodlark, now become so rare a sound in much of Britain. Among roadside birds was a small colony of great grey shrikes; farther on a black-eared wheatear; then one of Spain's most exclusive and beautiful species, the azure-winged magpie, seen briefly as it slipped away into a thicket.

So we came to Andalusia and to Seville, its chief city. On 2 May, however, there was a heat-wave. We could hardly breathe, there was an annihilating confusion of traffic and, of course, no birds. None, that is, except the swifts that arrowed back and forth across the burning sky and were presumably a mixture of common and pallid swifts, two species that are indistinguishable overhead. Thankfully we took the coast road from Seville towards Huelva along the north side of the Guadalquivir marshes, turning off at Almonte for El Rocio through scented plantations of pine and eucalyptus. The bridge at El Rocio, a place known to birdwatchers all over Europe, gave us squacco heron, night heron and little egret. Then we entered a different world – of wide sands and aromatic unfamiliar bushes and scattered trees – the strangely beautiful, wild world of the Coto Doñana, once a hunting reserve of the Dukes of Medina Sidonia but now a wildlife refuge, thanks to the World Wildlife Fund and the efforts of many private individuals.

Through all our five days on the Coto Doñana, which is in the hottest corner of Europe, the north African desert chose to breathe at us with a fiery breath. If it is like that at the beginning of May I never wish to go there in the summer. Coolest places were the estuary marshes (called *marismas*) which stretch flatly away to an infinite horizon in the south. And the benign air of the *marismas* could be felt also in the heathy oak-scattered margins of the estuary: but the farther we wandered from the water the hotter it was. Still, the cork oaks shed a deep shade and escape from the sun was easy enough. It was seawards where the real heat lay in wait. For between the heathlands and the sea stretches one of the wildest dune areas in Europe, mountainous ranges of sand going away ridge beyond ridge towards the invisible Atlantic, as if a chunk of the Sahara had escaped across into Europe.

Though days were hot the nights were cool in our tents under tall, ancient gum trees. But to anyone thinking of camping in this region I would emphatically recommend a mosquito-proof tent if you want a night's sleep. True, Spain's mosquitoes are not malarial. But there is nothing else in their favour and there are millions of them. Yet though their tormenting keeps you awake there are compensations. Through the darkness across the *marismas* comes the 'oomp-ooomp-oomp' of many bitterns; from the heathlands you hear the delicious wailing of the stone curlew and the 'tok-tok-tok' of red-necked nightjars; and in the trees overhead the passage of the night hours is registered by one of nature's machines, the Scops owl, which yelps its changeless 'kee-wick' every two seconds through the whole night, or so it seems. It is well to make the most of these noises because they come from birds very difficult to find by day. When you wake at dawn next morning to the song of the oriole and other splendid birds do not be over-hasty to shower ticks upon your card. For in the top of the gum-trees overhead roost several spotless starlings and the first thing they do when they wake up is to practise their repertoire of imitations. Not that they need much practise. The average spotless starling is immaculate, if I may so put it, in his renderings of the songs and calls of orioles, curlews, wood sandpipers, redshanks and many others. It is all very confusing.

It was the *marismas* we looked at first. From a distance they seem a vast green plain but when you get to their edge you see they are shallow water, weedy with rushes and crowfoots. Everywhere there are birds flying. Whiskered terns, very lovely with their near-white wings and their pure-white cheeks and breasts, circle over their nesting colonies with rasping cries. Separate, but not far away, scores of black terns also wheel and chorus above their nests, their voices higher and more gentle than those of whiskered terns. Gull-billed terns, gleaming white and with distinctive black beaks, pass occasionally from remoter colonies. Everywhere are moorhens and common coots: but the crested coot, an African species that breeds in Europe only in south Spain, is far less easy to find. And you need to get close to it before you see the distinguished red knobs on its head (they are often far less pronounced than those inflated, red balloons depicted by some bird artists).

In the midday heat the *marismas* were drying and retreating. Daily the margin of hardening mud grew wider and shore birds were beginning to nest. If we walked near the water there was constant harassment by angry stilts calling 'yik-yik-yik' as they flew over, trailing long drooping red legs behind their elegant black and white bodies. Pratincoles, too, were nesting there: they swooped around like small dark terns calling 'kirrit, kirrit'. On this same bare ground short-toed larks also had their nests. And always in the upper air there was a traffic of birds to and from their colonies in the cork oaks. Grey herons, spoonbills, egrets, sometimes a stork: out they flew to far feeding grounds in the *marismas* or flapped more heavily home. Occasionally marsh-harriers passed; and nearly always somewhere in the sky, there were circling, diving and whinnying black kites.

The mixed heronries were incomparably beautiful. We could see them from far off, for the gleaming birds sitting on their crowded nests made whole trees look white. Getting closer we began to hear them too: a chorus of squeaks, murmurings, croaks and moans interspersed with sharp comments from the jackdaws that also nest in these heronries. Because an often used ride passed close to the colony the birds were quite used to human visitors and sat stolidly on their nests as we watched and noted the carefully organized social structure of the colony. Little and cattle egrets occupied the lower and middle levels of the branches. Above them nested the spoonbills, spread out in a splendid rank all over the rounded tree top, their fine mane-like crests waving in the breeze. And with them the few grey herons ever watchful but not, I think, as wary as ours in Britain. But if any of these flattish or rounded trees had an isolated main stem overtopping the rest, then on this pinnacle was placed the huge nesting platform of a single pair of white storks who seemed to take no heed at all of the noisy multitude below. But they kept a wary eye on every circling kite, either red or black. For kites can change in a flash from birds that float harmlessly aloft into darts that come plunging at anything that looks like food. And that something could be an infant stork.

These woodlands among the *marismas* are the home – almost the last remaining – of one of Europe's noblest and rarest birds, the Spanish imperial eagle. Several were nesting on the Coto Doñana reserve the year we were there and occasionally, chancing to look across the forest, we saw a pair circling above the trees – big, black-looking eagles with bold white bands on their shoulders. Always they were remote and we were content that they should be so. Such rare, shy and wild-spirited eagles are better without man's company and all they need is the preservation of their solitudes. The people of Spain have a marvellous opportunity of earning a conservationist accolade by making a real effort to keep this precious eagle away from what looks dangerously like the road to extinction.

One morning I sat quietly in a glade among the oaks noting the various utterances of the birds: the ceremonial bill-rattling of the storks (if that can be called an utterance) as they changed over duties at the nest; the grunting of spoonbills that seemed to be some sort of alarm-cry; the rasping chatter of great spotted cuckoos as they chased each other wildly through the woods. Occasionally I glimpsed azure-winged magpies, golden orioles and hoopoes in the treetops – all creatures of delight but very fleeting and not nearly as satisfying as the many warblers that were nesting in the bushes all around my clearing. There was a Sardinian warbler with his distinctive black cap, white throat and red eye-ring; a sub-alpine warbler, known by his grey head, pink breast and white moustache; and a rufous warbler, red-backed, white-breasted with a full, reddish, white-ended tail. Up in the trees lived two other warblers more easily heard than seen: the melodious warbler which at treetop height is extremely like a willow warbler and has the same restless way of threading through twigs and delicately picking off insects; and the orphean warbler which looks rather like a blackcap but whose song is thrush-like in the repetition of its phrases. I count it among my most valued memories of Andalusia, this perfect May morning spent with the warblers among the cork oaks.

For these warblers the world, as they find it on the Coto Doñana, is a coloured and fragrant tangle of cistuses, pistachios, halimiums, junipers, tree heaths, brambles and gorse. It is pierced in all directions by trails of deer and boar. And there are wide spaces adorned by red gladioli, blue irises and a purple-brown orchid called *Serapias lingua*. So flowery and scented a place, lit with such radiant sunlight, seemed a perfect haunt for butterflies: yet there were surprisingly few and they were mostly painted ladies which, lovely as they are, can be met with almost anywhere in Europe, Asia or Africa. Had I come all the way to Andalusia, I wondered, to see only painted ladies? And that was the moment when my first Queen of Spain fritillary chose to alight in a sandy hollow close to where I was sitting. It settled with closed wings that showed off their tawny, silver-spotted undersides – a lovely insect that had at last become a reality instead of a creature I had seen all my life only as a picture in books. But a few minutes later I dropped all thought of butterflies when, with loud scufflings and gruntings, a female wild boar came bursting out of the yellow-flowered halimium bushes followed by three piglets. A family of wild pigs was something else I had never seen before and what surprised me about them was that though the mother was covered with long black hair, the young were distinctly red and prettily marked with dark horizontal bars. Why these habitually nocturnal animals should have been hastening through the scrub in the broad light of day I do not know. All I can say is that as they passed at only five feet distance they never even saw me sitting with my back against a cork oak. I stayed there some time in the hope (vain as it turned out) that some predator had disturbed this wild boar family and would soon come along on their tracks. A Spanish lynx for example. For this large, over-persecuted cat, as for the imperial eagle, the Coto Doñana is one of the few remaining refuges. Distinguished from the lynx of north Europe by lines of heavy spots, the Spanish lynx is a beautifully marked animal. But though I looked for it everywhere I never found more than footprints in the sand. We were shown one cooped up in a pen outside the former hunting lodge that is now the Reserve's headquarters but this merely left me sad and angry, the way I always feel in zoos.

The savanna-like heathland dotted with cork oaks does not end abruptly at the edge of the *marismas*. Between the two zones stretches a broad damp margin of rushy pastures that slope very gently to the estuary. Here we added two further warblers to our list, neither of them easy to observe. One was Savi's warbler which makes a reeling sound in thick cover and would be passed over as a grasshopper warbler if it could sustain its song instead of always stopping and starting. The other warbler was the fan-tailed, at four inches Europe's smallest warbler. It is also Europe's only grass warbler (the genus Cisticola), that numerous group of species so characteristic of Africa, India and south-east Asia and so notorious for causing headaches over their field identification. The fan-tailed warbler, which in Europe is found only in the south, is spread across much of Africa down to the Cape, across Asia to Japan and over the Pacific to the north coast of Australia. It looks rather like a small sedge warbler with a short tail, and since it spends most of its time skulking in deep grass and rushes it is easily missed. But in the breeding season its song-flight draws attention to it. It mounts high above the ground calling 'zit-zit-zit' (hence its other name of zitting cisticola) as it passes over in jerking flight. But up there against a bright sky this tiny brown warbler can be difficult to see. Most of the time it is just a wandering sound somewhere in the sky. And where

fan-tailed warblers are abundant their zitting can be so persistent
a background noise that, along with the risping of grasshoppers
and the hum of bees, you eventually cease to be aware of it.

Chateaubriand once remarked that forests came before man
and that deserts followed him. And at the Coto Doñana you see
plenty of evidence that he was right. The arid, semi-desert scrub
of the heathland has all the look of secondary vegetation coming
in the wake of destroyed forest. Then if you cross this heathland
towards the sea you come literally face to face with real desert,
a great wall of loose silver sand with 200 square miles of dunes
and all the winds of the Atlantic behind it, a wall that advances
eastwards implacably, smothering everything in its path. It is
both spectacular and frightening to see this high wave of sand
breaking right over the crowns of not one but whole groves of
mature stone pines. How long, you can't help wondering, before
the whole Guadalquivir estuary and marshlands will disappear
under range after range of dazzling, near-white sand that already
peaks up to form, at 340 feet above sea-level, what may well be
the highest dunes in the whole of Europe.

Not that these dunes are a continuous and uninterrupted
stretch of loose sand. Out in the desert there are pinewoods that
somehow manage to survive; and they are the favourite nesting
place for the short-toed eagles that prey on water snakes, ladder
snakes and Lataste's vipers, all of which are said to be numerous.
The pines also attract many small migrant birds that come down
to rest as they might visit an island in the sea. In the dunes, too,
we were told, lived the Thekla lark. This, in Europe, is a very local
bird and the Coto Doñana was the only place we knew for it. But
when we read that the Thekla was almost indistinguishable in
the field from the crested lark I decided I was not going to fry
out there in the dunes looking for so unsatisfactory a fowl. So I
opted for another day on the *marismas*. But R.S. Thomas wanted

his Thekla lark and is a man of determination. With the sun burning in a cloudless sky I watched his tall, straight figure get ever smaller as it reached the crest of a far dune and disappeared into the desert like some Old Testament prophet who would never again be seen on earth. But that evening he duly turned up having satisfied himself that he had seen his Thekla lark. I, too, had had my moment. I had seen a small pink cloud of flamingos moving westward far out over the *marismas*.

Sometime in the fairly recent past the Guadalquivir had a delta with many mouths. But now blown sand has bottled them all up except one and practically obliterated the former delta landscape. The line of one of the lost channels is still to be traced in a string of attractive pools along the eastward edge of the dunes, pools that are the haunt of many plants, birds and animals. Here we glimpsed through the bulrushes a purple heron on her nest; we heard the harsh squawk of the crested coot; saw our first ferruginous ducks and red-crested pochards; but failed to see white-headed duck, marbled duck or purple gallinule, all three of which you need a slice of luck to find there.

From the Coto Doñana, when the air was clear, we looked inland across the *marismas* to the alluring Sierra de Ronda whose ragged summits rise against the eastern sky to nearly seven thousand feet. So because the coastal region was so hot and the mountains looked so cool; and because our bird-lists were most in need of mountain species, it was to the uplands we decided to go when we left Doñana.

The Ronda mountains cover nearly a thousand miles of harsh and broken country, much of it arid limestone, a thinly populated region with far-scattered villages and one or two spectacular, high-level towns. Of the villages I especially remember Grazalema, so attractive with its terracotta roofs, white-washed walls and narrow streets. From its remote mountain shelf Grazalema looks to wild and distant sierras and is itself dominated by a pallid thousand-foot crag of creviced limestone, a crag noted for its especially beautiful narcissi: but you have to be there in April to see them. If you are a connoisseur of country towns you will travel far in Europe before you find one more striking than Ronda, an ancient place set well over two thousand feet above the sea and cleft in two by a three-hundred-foot deep gorge spanned by a massive eighteenth-century bridge that is a triumph of engineering. On this bridge you can be happy for a long time watching choughs, swifts and lesser kestrels playing in the wind. You may see a peregrine, a vulture or some exciting eagle wheeling round; or merely the rock-sparrows nesting in cracks in the masonry. And if there are no birds at all it is still a wonderful place, this great chasm in the crumbling sandstone, with the old town far above and the torrent called Guadalevin a thread of silver far down in the shadows.

Till recent years there have been few good roads through these mountains and many awful ones; but tourism is changing all that. Good or bad, these roads lead you across delightfully rocky and open country that is still quite flowery. But for how much longer? For the ever-nibbling goats that have no equal as destroyers of vegetation roam everywhere in large herds. No doubt they have played a key part in reducing the once far-spreading cork-oak forests of these uplands to the small relict patches you find up there today. The same with the Spanish fir (*Abies pinsapo*) whose world distribution as a native is restricted to north-facing slopes of these Ronda mountains. Very distinctive because of its short stiff needles, this rare conifer, though such a lime-lover, grows well when planted even on acid soils in Britain, as you can see in the National Trust garden at Bodnant in north Wales where one was planted in 1876 and now makes a tree about a hundred feet tall.

Camping in these mountains was pure delight after the Coto Doñana. For up here the nights were cool and entirely without mosquitoes. We dropped into sleep listening to nightingales, red-necked nightjars, common nightjars (and the inescapable goat-bells) and we woke at dawn to the harsh shouts of great grey shrikes, the gentle cooing of turtle doves and the song of melodious warblers (which to me are not remarkably melodious, achieving something between the rich song of a garden warbler and the scratchy tune of a whitethroat). One of our camps was near an escarpment where the limestone had weathered and shattered to form a precipice full of caverns and deep fissures. And here many vultures were nesting. We scrambled up from the road to the foot of this great crag up steep slopes rough with block scree and oak bushes and for once were grateful to the goats. For the oak there was the Kermes oak which, though reaching only a few feet in height, was quite as prickly as holly and made a jungle that would have been quite impenetrable if goats had not criss-crossed it in all directions by their trails.

Two kinds of vulture were breeding on these cliffs: griffons mainly and a few Egyptians. The huge griffons perched prominently along the rocky skyline, managing to look aloof and indifferent yet never, I think, really taking their eyes off us. Occasionally they sailed out to circle slowly over us with rarely a flap of their vast square wings. But when a goat-herd came following his flock across the scree a griffon swooshed down with a thunderous *woomp* of wings a few yards above the man's head. Then the bird went straight back to its crag to resume its silent, unemotional pose. The Egyptian vultures were even less demonstrative: but they were more beautiful to see gliding along the pale rock face, their black and white plumage gleaming in the sun's bright light. To me their outline against the sky and the stiff way they held their wings suggested some huge and strange sort of fulmar. We had a final moment of excitement as a new bird came sailing along the cliff top. A large raptor which, from below, had a white head and body contrasting with long dark wings. Then it banked to show a clear white bar down the centre of its back. It was our first Bonelli's eagle. A species of the southern fringe of Europe, and much better known in Africa and India, this beautiful eagle is one of many birds of prey that are in urgent need of protection in Europe.

Below the vulture crag we came upon a splendid lizard. For anyone who knows only the darting little brown lizards of Britain it is one of the most delightful shocks of natural history suddenly to be confronted with a lizard that is well over two feet long, brilliantly green and generously spotted with bright yellow and blue. You really do feel you're getting near the tropics. But it did not wait to be admired, this gorgeous ocellated lizard. A quick scuttling movement, a rasping of claws against bark and it was away up a tree trunk and gone.

Then, soon after, a snake crossed our path, much to R.S. Thomas's delight. He is, I would say, a particularly snake-conscious man. Before even going to Spain he evidently did some herpetological homework because he had several times relieved the tedium of motoring across Spain by giving me lectures on the snakes we might encounter in Andalusia. He spoke often of the terrors of Lataste's viper and I think he was disappointed we had met so few. Even on the Coto Doñana we had hardly seen the tail of one disappearing into cover. But now at last here was a most satisfactory serpent nearly four feet long right at our feet and giving us a leisurely view of itself as it moved slowly off. It was slender and medium-brown with two thin dark lines going parallel down the length of its back. Joining them at regular intervals were many short cross-bars: hence this species' name, the ladder snake. Like all European snakes, the vipers excepted, the ladder snake is non-venomous.

To us who know the chough as a precarious species clinging to the mild fringes of western Britain and Ireland, it was a revelation to see how abundant the bird is in these warm southern mountains. We found nesting pairs in many places and near El Burgo saw a large flock of presumably non-breeders rising and plunging as if in a ballet dance in the breezes funnelling through a gorge. Here spotless starlings chorused cheerfully about their nest-holes in the cliffs (till then we had seen them only on houses and trees); and male rock-buntings, cleanly stroked with black lines across their silver-grey cheeks, perched stolidly on boulders and repeated toneless notes with true bunting persistence. Another new bird for us was the black wheatear, a really aristocratic-looking member of its family because of its superior size and the eye-catching splash of white on its rump and tail that contrasts so perfectly with the solid blackness of the rest of the plumage. Red-rumped swallow and alpine swift completed our mountain tally. About our identification of the pallid swift we continued to feel uneasy: we saw many 'possible probables' without ever being able to swear that they were not common swifts.

Goats had not eaten all the wildflowers. A shrubby grey sage with purple-pink flowers (*Phlomis purpurea*) was an adornment to many a slope; and occasionally a whole hillside was gay with cistus flowers, some all-white, some white with chocolate centres, some purple-red. Man orchids and late spider orchids were frequent and one wet place was solidly purple-red over many square yards with the tall and elegant loose-flowered orchid (*Orchis laxiflora*). Dry stream-beds were pink with oleanders. Tall, white-flowered asphodels and equally attractive stars-of-Bethlehem graced the roadsides. Viper's bugloss spread lavish purple-blue patches on banks. A cream and pink figwort called *Bellardia trixago* stays in my memory as an especial joy. So does the remarkable *Scilla peruviana* which has a rounded mass of violet-blue flowers rising from wide, green, strap-like basal leaves. Two bindweeds were colourful: *Convolvulus tricolor*, delicately pale blue white and yellow; and *C. altheoides* which is a bright purple-pink. Most spectacular was a giant fennel whose great yellow umbels towered over our heads. Most curious was the dwarf fan palm, Europe's only native palm but which is a mere fountain of leaves at ground level, lacking any trunk to bear them aloft. Most alarming was the sight of prickly pear escaping into the wild along mountain roads. We thought with dread of its rapid and devastating colonization of thousands of square miles of eastern Australia's sheep pastures and wondered if the delectable Sierra de Ronda were doomed to a similar fate.

With regret we left these fair mountains for the long drive north. But one last Andalusian splendour was promised – a roadside lake where we had been told we might see flamingoes, a lake which, when we first sighted it across the plain, seemed a thoroughly domesticated sheet of water. For it was overlooked by a sizeable village and there were fields of barley and sunflowers all round, olive groves farther back and men shouting to their mules as they tilled the nearby crops. Not a place for flamingoes, we reckoned. We had always thought of them as belonging to the greater wildernesses of the world, not to roadside lakes with herds of goats in the foreground. But it doesn't do to romanticize too much about birds and wild places. It's not only sparrows and starlings that will accept man on intimate terms. A dotterel may delight in a pool outside a steel-works. A peregrine may nest on a skyscraper. Wagtails will roost on a city railway station. And a warm salt-lake rich in plankton will be found by flamingoes no matter how tamed its surroundings.

So, when we looked through our binoculars at this unpromising pool, there, prominent in the foreground, were our flamingoes, three hundred of them wading in a shallow bay at the nearest end of the lake. Large and mainly white, with an S-shaped neck occasionally visible, they were at that range very swan-like. They did not become real picture-book flamingoes till we were much nearer and could see the patch of bright crimson each carried on its wing and the strange shape of their beaks when heads were lifted. But most of the time they kept their long, thin necks vertically downwards and their heads under water as they sifted the mud; so that they looked like a close-packed crowd of headless round white bodies each supported by three long legs. That night we camped at the lake edge with the flamingoes near by. Until then we had not realized how noisy they are. We fell asleep to their goose-like honking, heard it several times during the night and woke to it again at dawn.

The lake had many other birds. Migrant spotted redshanks, greenshanks, ruffs, knots, sanderlings, dunlins and wood sandpipers foraged round the drying margins with dozens of stilts and avocets. Along shingle bars extending into the lake scores of Kentish plovers were obviously breeding. Pratincoles swooped low over the water taking flies with the utmost grace. High above them circled a pair of gull-billed terns. Coot, mallard and pochard were everywhere. There were a few gadwall and, at last, the marbled duck we had failed to find at the Coto Doñana. Great reed-warblers sang in the rushes; fan-tailed warblers lisped unseen in the air; quail called their three quick notes in the fields; calandra larks sang loud and clear all around us; crested and short-toed larks rose into flight as we walked round the water's edge.

Given a whole year at this lake an observer would, I think, record a wonderful selection of Europe's birds. It is one of those rare and special places whither birds seem called from the four ends of the earth. Long may it remain thus unpolluted and unexploited. In north Europe a water so abounding with life would be a well-wardened bird sanctuary. In south Spain who knows what may happen? You have only to see the devastating effect of the holiday industry on the coast to realize how precarious could be the future of inland waters also. So I pray that inspired by success on the Coto Doñana, the conservationist movement in Spain will go on gathering strength and be able to safeguard many of the other places known to be rich in animals, birds and plants whose future is threatened by developments of every description. Andalusia alone has very many choice areas that would make superb nature reserves. Indeed the whole province should be given special status as a conservation area before it is totally ruined by tourism, rice fields and a hundred other undesirable changes.

(1975)

PART SIX

Reflections on Nature
and Conservation

DUNELAND DELIGHTS

The ordnance map shows us Morfa Harlech whose name stretches in capital letters across the whole flat land overlooked by Harlech castle. The Welsh word *morfa* is a marriage of two words: *mor* (the sea) and *fa* (a place). My dictionaries variously translate it for me as sea-brink, salt-marsh, bog or fen. And as you look across its flat expanse, where only in our day houses have begun to venture, you can easily picture the whole stretch from Harlech to the estuary of the Dwyryd as once being continuous marsh, several square miles of wild saltings, creeks and fens; though I daresay we would have to go back a long way to find a Morfa Harlech that was entirely marshland.

Today a very different Morfa exists. Man has long since laid hands on the place, ditched it, drained what he can of it and bit by bit extended his fields towards the sea. A great haunt (we may suppose) of wildlife, of plants, birds and other creatures of marsh and water, has been tamed. Some of it has become pasture land. Some of it has served as a military training ground. And now some of it is being planted by the Forestry Commission. But still a choice and sizeable fragment remains, a bit of former wilderness that not even busy-fingered twentieth-century man has found fit for his use. This is the salt-marsh and sand-dune area tucked away in the north-west corner furthest from habitations and now a National Nature Reserve. Here naturalists, especially botanists, can be truly happy[9]. Not that they are likely to see anything very rare unless by chance the dune helleborine, which was reputedly discovered a few years back, but which no one has been able to find since. But what these dunes and marshes offer is variety and profusion: so many different stages of dryness and wetness from arid dune-top to deepish water; so many different aspects producing, for instance, a different flora on the south and north sides of the same dune; so many different degrees of acidity or non-acidity from the leached soil of the dunes to the lime-rich hollows of the dune slacks.

For flowers at their best go to the *morfa* at full summer, when you can walk in the sunlight through the shining plumes of the downy-oat grass and the common blue butterflies flutter away all about you. On the dunes you will find not an array of large showy plants but low and carpeting sorts, gems you must bend to see: yellow dune-pansies; that tiniest dandelion, the smooth cat's ear; the common and the slender centaury; sea-milkwort; field gentian; stork's bills of every size; a good variety of trefoils; thyme, hound's tongue, sea-holly, blue fleabane, both the dune spurges, burnet rose and a great many more delights. And everywhere the sharp fragrance of sand-dunes. Or if you like more primitive plants there are adder's tongue, moonwort and horse-tails.

It is not in the dunes but in the marshes that colour is extravagantly splashed, in the acres yellow with irises. If there

---

9 Birdwatchers less so, since the Crown Estate Commissioners, in their wisdom, for over thirty years have leased to a local wildfowlers' association the shooting rights all along the NNR foreshore and into the Dwyryd estuary – one of the great U.K. winter gathering grounds for geese, ducks and waders, in consequence of which their populations here have declined drastically. Attentive readers will readily surmise how Bill might have viewed this. (See pp. 196-197.)

were nothing else on this *morfa* it would be worth a visit to see these irises and the hundreds of black-headed gulls that burst in a white explosion from them as you approach. And among their nests you find other plants: three kinds of aquatic speedwells; red rattle of bush-like stature; common and lesser water-plantain; pale yellow stars of the square St. John's wort; and pond-weeds, sedges and rushes.

Then there are the orchids. Our wild orchids have a great following of enthusiasts. Some of them are seekers of what is rare among orchids: monkey, military, ghost, lizard and so on. Morfa Harlech is not for them. But if you rejoice in profusions, deluges of orchids no matter how common, if you like those species that nature casts at your feet with uninhibited generosity, then go to Harlech.

First in time come the green-winged orchids of May, mostly red-purple, a few pinks and whites: all about six inches high, profusely scattered in the rough of the links[10], thinning towards the dunes. As they fade, the marsh orchids are beginning and it is these that are this *morfa*'s greatest delight, and also its greatest despair, these seldom straightforward, sometimes unidentifiable marsh orchids.

These we are told may be species in the act of evolving, striving for stability of form; but, insufficiently distinct from one another for the normal rough and tumble of inter-specific rivalry, they end by flowing into one another and the result is a bewildering infinity of hybrid forms. Here the lovely little deep-coloured *purpurella* of the north meets the taller, paler *praetermissa* of the south. Here the parents stand side by side and around them proliferate their intermediate offsprings. This would be fairly simple if it were all. But the *incarnata* orchis can scarcely be

---

[10] The Royal St. David's golf course lies between the lower town and the dunes.

ignored at Harlech, for this is the most abundant marsh orchid of the whole place. And it too hybridizes with the rest.

Finally, to make confusion further confused, both the heath spotted and the common spotted orchids are here, crossing with the marsh orchids and with each other. It is hardly surprising that often the greater task is to find not the offspring but the original parents of these mixed relationships. Frequently no parents exist, having been crowded out by their descendants long since, for often the intermediate forms tower up with hybrid vigour to reach over two feet in height and carry six or eight inches of glorious purple spike.

But perhaps hybrids are not to your liking. If not, you may turn with relief to the assurance of more solid species. *Orchis incarnata*, for instance, though I mention it as sometimes hybridizing, is for the most part pure at Harlech and from the golf-course nearly to the edge of the salt-marsh its brick-red variety, *coccinea*, is in scores in every marsh and dune-slack. With them you will see rosettes of sharp leaves in crowded hundreds and these later on will produce the other orchid wonder of this place: countless spikes of the lovely marsh helleborine. Also there are the twayblades and the deliciously scented butterfly orchids. Then, but in most years uncommonly, you may find on the drier slopes a few bee orchids and rather more pyramidals, Finally, September brings a handful of autumn ladies' tresses.

I have many birdwatching memories of Morfa Harlech; of, for instance, a perfectly still evening at midsummer, the only near sound being the hiss of the spring tide making haste across the sands. In the foreground the dunes and dune grasses are cut out almost in white against the great blue arc of mountains that curves round from Llŷn to Hebog and on to Snowdon, Cnicht and Moelwyn, then round to the Rhinogydd close in the east. Overhead is endless lark-song; in the distance are faint exclamations of nesting redshanks and the incessant far-off wailing of the black-headed gullery. I lie watching stock-doves in courtship around their nest-holes in the sand. From another burrow a shelduck waddles forth and, taking wing, flies down the sands to meet the tide. Then a dozen curlews come high across the sky. In silence they head out to the estuary and seem to be about to cross over when, dramatically, the flock explodes and each curlew comes yelping earthwards in a wild power-dive, corkscrewing down like a stricken aeroplane, with a violent sound as of tearing feathers. All land simultaneously on the sands, immediately fold away great beaks under their back feathers and stand in silence to wait for the tide.

And I remember a mid-winter day. This time I am lying hidden in the marram on a dune-top overlooking the gullery-pool. Now the gulls of summer are dispersed, perhaps wintering far to the south and the pool has no other occupants. Brilliant blues, greens and chestnuts flash in the sun off the heads and wings of mallard and teal splashing and scuttering in courtship play. Even more colourful are a group of shovelers feeding half out of the water just below me. A shelduck, a pintail drake, some pochard, a few coots, moorhens, a dabchick… there seems hardly room for such a crowd on so small a water. Then, like yachts appearing round a curve of the river, four wild swans, three whoopers and a Bewick's come swinging round a bend of the dunes, and they too somehow find a place on the pool. I ask myself: could there be any more intense experience of life, movement and colour than this?

(1958)

TO THE LIGHTHOUSE

A soft April dusk and the lightest of airs off the Atlantic. A mist almost drizzle cools our faces as we stand on top of Bardsey's mountain. There will be no stars, no moon tonight. So there will be shearwaters, for it is only on black nights they come to the island. We stand and listen. Behind us, down on the low south end of the island, the lighthouse begins to flash its night-long message out to the Irish Sea shipping lanes. At first there is nothing to be heard except the rustle of the tide moving through the sound, and the capricious slap of water against cliffs five hundred feet below. It is one of those too-rare moments of utter tranquility. We think of wind and ocean and the slow dissolving of rocks through the measureless years. Then an ancient voice speaks, a faint caterwauling high in the blackening sky, and in a few minutes the air is full of primal sounds, wild cooings, sobbings and wailings. The shearwaters have arrived for their nightly courtship play. But as we listen a figure climbs up to us out of the darkness. It is the warden of the island's bird observatory. He thinks that with this mist there might be work for us bird-ringers at the lighthouse.

Half an hour later, by permission of the principal keeper, we stand on the lighthouse balcony that is built out into space around the lantern. A parapet of steel keeps us from the drop below. As the mist thickens into fine rain we wait for the coming of the night birds. We stare into the darkness, listening to the moaning of seals and watching the play of the light's successive white beams across the island. At first nothing happens. We speak of other lighthouses: of the South Stack at Holyhead, our next neighbour north; and beyond it the blinding light of the Skerries which brings safety for ships but death to migrant birds. We think of Skokholm's kindly light to our south, kindly because red, so not alluring to birds of the night. Then we remember Heligoland as it was in the time of the great German ornithologist, Heinrich Gatke, who died in 1897.

For over half a century Gatke pioneered lighthouse bird-watching and thrilled the ornithological world with an account of his life's observations that has lost none of its excitement with the passage of sixty years. In *Heligoland as an Ornithological Observatory* bird-migration takes on real grandeur. British bird observers speak of rushes of birds involving hundreds, sometimes a few thousand. But on Heligoland, thirty miles off the German coast, Gatke witnessed clouds, deluges, cataclysms of birds. Year after year, in spring and autumn, migrants rained upon Heligoland in numbers beyond human calculation. On the night of October 28th, 1882, he saw such a phenomenal passage of the tiny goldcrest that he could only compare it with a snowstorm. Twenty-four years before, he had spent a calm autumn day watching a slow, majestic procession of birds of prey passing over to the south hour after hour. The number of birds Gatke saw was not more remarkable than their variety: by the time he published his records his tally for the island was almost four hundred species. Nor was it only birds he saw from his lighthouse. It attracted moths in prodigious multitudes. He described how in August, 1882, silvery moths, for four nights in succession, passed the lighthouse in millions.

Gatke's work sent others off on the lighthouse trail and it was not long before lighthouse-keepers round the coasts of the British Isles were being asked to report on birds seen or killed at their lights and to send corpses of unknown birds for identification. The results were revealing. It began to be realized that many more of our common species were migrants or partial migrants than had been dreamt of. The magnitude of the passage of birds up and down the coasts of Britain to and from north Europe came as a surprise to those who had witnessed only visible daytime migration which is usually on a trifling scale in Britain compared with night movements. Finally, the lighthouse records indicated that many species of birds, formerly reckoned very sporadic or quite absent in Britain, actually pass along our coastlines annually, landing for short rests only on small islands and remote headlands, and therefore escaping detection unless picked up dead at the foot of some lighthouse tower.

Since these lighthouse discoveries the era of the bird observatory has arrived and now many vantage points around our coasts are manned by enthusiastic amateur birdwatchers. Their findings have confirmed the work of the lighthouse pioneers and have illuminated it with fresh observations and new ideas. Meanwhile the lighthouses continue to attract hordes of migrants which is all very well for science but can be hard on the birds which, dazzled by the light, may crash into the tower on nights of poor visibility.

So we stand on Bardsey tower, all Gatkes for a night. For a whole hour there is nothing visible except the endless play of the five white beams sweeping round and spearing away into the darkness. Then we begin to see the birds. Or rather we see silver balls come swinging round in the beams to disappear instantly behind us. We catch faint unfamiliar cries, the unknown calls which birds use only on migration. And now a warbler is fluttering at the glass beside us like a moth at a lamp. The warden gently closes his hand over it and puts it into a string-top bag where it will lie quietly for the rest of the night; for once completely dazzled like this a bird may go on beating against the glass till it drops in exhaustion. Next day the bird will be released with an identity ring on its leg. Sometimes the intense glare of the light will upset the delicate emotional balance of these spring migrants. They may burst into song, or spread wings and tail in courtship display, or even play with nesting material.

More and more silvery shapes twirl past, the air is full of whispered cries, and now we are all kept busy taking the fluttering birds from the glass. So the night hours pass; hours of a dream-like experience when we hardly know whether we wake or sleep, a prolonged experience of strange beauty in which we have seen, almost touched, the mysteries of migration and its elemental forces. At last dawn pales in the east, the grey island begins to take shape, and quite suddenly there are no more birds.

(1957)

ON THE NAMING OF RIVERS

1: Rivers have ancient names

Our local river, the Dyfi, is a stream of great beauty and interest. Having a wild little temper it has managed to keep most human settlements at a distance and so has kept itself sweet-smelling and unpolluted for all its thirty miles. Often fishermen from the town come and spend a whole day alone on its banks and having caught nothing go home contented and refreshed. What further proof is needed of the close links that must have existed between primitive man and rivers? And since for thousands of years the life of early man was intimately bound up with rivers, it is not surprising that we have carefully preserved some of their names from the earliest times of which we have any word-memories.

So even in districts of England where nearly all place names are of German, Norman or Danish origin, the prehistoric names of some rivers survive (Avon, Dove, Exe and so on). In Wales, as in the other fragments of Celtic Europe, all the ancient names are still preserved and are in everyday use. Not only names such as Hafren (Severn), Gwy (Wye), Dyfrdwy (Dee) and Wysg (Usk), but countless other place names which probably date back into pre-Roman times nearly as far as the river names themselves, their preservation having been assured by that astonishing phenomenon, the long duration and continuing survival of the Welsh language.

2: All that glitters

One day I was in the Golden Valley in Herefordshire and it was raining. The woods were leafless, black and wet. Fields were sodden. Streams were overbrimming. Dark hills rose round and disappeared into darker clouds. I stood under a holly hedge sheltering not from the rain, for that was inescapable, but from the gusting south-west wind. As the water trickled down my neck I wondered how such a place ever came to be called 'golden'. The beaches of Tahiti I could believe are truly golden: but except for a fortnight in late summer when the corn is ripe, could this dark dripping valley under the Black Mountains ever be golden?

I looked down at the River Dore coming down full and fleet from upland Wales. I began to speculate about the name of this stream. Because, I said to myself, nearly all the streams along this border – Lugg, Teme, Arrow, Severn and the rest – have names of Welsh origin, presumably Dore has come from the Welsh *dŵr*, meaning water. Maybe our Norman masters back in the eleventh century, indifferent to the niceties of philology, heard the word *dŵr* but wrote it as 'd'or' and the valley has glittered with false gold ever since? So from floundering through waterlogged fields I blundered into the bogs of place-name etymology. Is there any more dangerous ground for the untutored than that?

3: A sacred stream in Wales

Some rivers have definite sources but I can't think that anyone could claim to have discovered exactly where the Welsh river Dee rises. Looking for it the other day I followed the stream back till it was only a foot across but found then that it originates nowhere in particular. Instead it comes oozing out of a wide peatbog along a hundred tiny channels. Or you could say it really springs out of the black cliffs of the mountain above. No matter, it's a good quiet spot reached only after a long uphill plod with no path to help you as you stumble over the tussocks of purple moorgrass.

In an earlier, simpler age than ours when rivers were gods, the Dee was the sacred stream of north Wales. But, mercifully, the Welsh have not perpetuated this tradition. Otherwise we would probably now have some crackpot shrine erected at the head of the river like the one the French set up last century at the source of the Seine showing a statue of a water nymph reclining in a fake grotto behind an iron railing with a souvenir shanty nearby. Instead, the source of the Dee remains entirely natural, or as natural as the ever-nibbling sheep allow any place to be, a place of heather, cotton-grass and reindeer moss and the wild moorland stretching round for miles. Long may it so remain.

(1993)

Two years after Bill's death, following his lead, I went to look for myself for the source of the Dee – the Welsh name of which, Dyfrdwy, means 'water of the divinity.' It rises in the wide boggy basin of Waunygriafolen, one of the wildest places in the Welsh uplands and one of Bill's favourite botanizing sites. By dint of following the stream into this morass and at each dwindling fork taking the most substantial branch, it brought me to a last pool close beneath the cliffs of Dduallt. And around this pool, the remains of a simple, ancient chapel-shrine orientated west-east, invisible until you stumble right across it. It's one of the regrets of my life that Bill was no longer around to share a find he would have appreciated – though he certainly had the sense of the true source: 'it really springs out of the black cliffs of the mountain above'.

SILENT SPRING, 1963

If you are looking for stimulating ideas on the link between food and health you will find them in the current number of that excellent quarterly, *Mother Earth*, the journal of the Soil Association. There are several cautionary articles on the dangers of using pesticides and chemical fertilizers. (In Australia insecticides caused schizophrenia as well as physical breakdown in workers in orchards.) These articles leave me more than ever alarmed by the scientists' excessive confidence in the safety of their chemicals when, in fact, so little is known about the true as distinguished from the guessed-at safety levels of any chemical doses.

And so we come to *Silent Spring*, by Rachel Carson, excellently reviewed in *Mother Earth*. This book will, we pray, be a best-seller in Britain as it is in America. The silence of Rachel Carson's spring is the silence that will come to the world when we have killed off all the singing birds with insecticides. It is a silence that symbolizes all the horrifying effects on nature and on ourselves by the mass onslaught by poison that man is now launching on the earth. So far we have only seen a shadow of what could come unless the reckless madness that has got into our scientists, our agriculturists, our horticulturists and our forestry experts is checked pretty soon[11].

---

[11] As I write, in May 2015, the BBC tells us of an application to the newly-elected Conservative U.K. government by pharmaceutical industry lobbyists to have lifted the ban on the neonicotinoid pesticides proven to be responsible for the catastrophic decline in bee populations, with its devastating ecological effects. It would be unsurprising if, 52 years on from the publication of *Silent Spring*, Big Pharma and agri-industry's wishes were granted. What Rachel Carson and Bill will be saying to each other as they wander through the Elysian fields is not hard to guess. The 'reckless madness that has got into our scientists, our agriculturists, our horticulturists and our forestry experts' is still rampant, and historical precedent over the last fifty years tells us that a financially-implicated right-wing government is unlikely to muster the resolve to rein in their destructive excesses.

Finally, whenever the topic of *Silent Spring* comes up it's surely proper to mention the crucial research work of Derek Ratcliffe into the eggshell-thinning of raptors, that underlay much of its ferociously apposite rhetoric.

DDT 1970

So 1970 comes and DDT begins to go. It is a promising start for a special conservation year. If DDT conquered malaria somewhere, then all credit to it. But now that we have non-persistent insecticides that will do the job, let us shed no tears over DDT and all other unpleasant substances that have been showered wholesale on fields and forests, poisoning everything within range, and have been washed into the rivers killing fish and fish-eating eagles and so down to the sea, until the farthest limits of the ocean and its animals are now polluted.

What a fantastic degree of pollution the world accepts before doing anything about it! The totally dead Lake Erie, 10,000 square miles of it: most people who live by it apparently accept its death as an inevitable part of progress. This attitude is at the heart of the matter. It was the nineteenth-century champions of progress who convinced the western world that it was heading towards its 'manifest destiny'.

This is the philosophy that has persuaded the twentieth century to believe that all scientific and technological progress is good for us. Dissenting voices from Thoreau onwards were for a long time few and scarcely heard. Thoreau said: 'They may go their way to their manifest destiny which I trust is not mine'. Now, suddenly, the world is full of Thoreaus. Everyone talks of pollution not progress. May they keep it up loud and clear.

DOUBLE STANDARDS IN EUROPEAN CONSERVATION YEAR

Undoubtedly European Conservation Year is the year in which we British really ought to try not to be such hypocrites about nature conservation. Take birds. Our record in bird protection at home is excellent. Apart from a few nasty birds and some that have the misfortune to be classed as fair game, all our birds are protected by stringent laws. Yet we quite happily take advantage of the fact that other countries fail to protect their birds. We allow our cage-bird industry to import thousands of birds annually from all over the world. And it's the same with animals. What is worse, we know full well that for every animal or bird that gets here alive a vast number die in being caught or transported.

Similarly with plants. We have many local laws forbidding the uprooting of our wildflowers. Yet botanists and gardeners who would never uproot a choice British plant will quite cheerfully come home with a load of exquisite foreign plants. One horticultural journal recently had an article describing how a score of British gardening enthusiasts pillaged their way through the wild flora of another country. Joyously the author related how they collected a large number of plants wherever they went, their delight culminating in the final triumph when 'the Customs allowed us through each with our plastic bags containing the spoils of a truly enjoyable tour'. We must learn to be better Europeans than that.

(*1970/1993*)

THOUGHTS ON CASTELL Y BERE

The other day I was at Castell y Bere, the medieval castle between Cader Idris and the sea. How changed, how face-lifted it is compared with what it was a few years ago. It used to crouch concealed upon its mound, a mysterious ruin quite buried in trees and undergrowth. But now it has had the full Ministry of Works treatment. The site has been laid bare, the old walls have received a most generous application of cement and now they stand conspicuously white and scrubbed-looking above the valley. One can only hope that this antiseptic look is but temporary and that lichens, moss and ferns will be allowed to tone it down. At the moment you might be forgiven if, from a distance, you mistook the site for the beginning of a new power station.

The trouble we go to in order to preserve our ancient monuments! Yet the oldest and most remarkable man-made thing in Wales is commonly scorned even by some Welsh people. I mean the Welsh language, a tongue so ancient as to make the oldest of the so-called monuments seem like something reported in yesterday's paper. Just because a language is not something you can see and touch and plaster with cement and put an officious little fence around and charge sixpence for admission, it is allowed to rust and rot away while we go to enormous expense to shore up the castles of medieval tyrants.

(1993)

BOYS' TOYS

Air-gun manufacturers would not have welcomed my [*Guardian* country] diary for 10 December 1966. In it I sent seasonal best wishes to all parents who resisted little Willie's plea that he might be given an air-gun for Christmas. Air-guns, I wrote, might be all right if used only on proper targets but they seldom are. We all know what happens; sooner or later, they are used against sparrows, starlings, blackbirds, thrushes and other birds of garden and hedgerow. Few of these victims are shot cleanly. Most are injured and die slowly. To buy little Willie an air-gun, I reckoned, was to start him off on the wrong foot. As he gets older his little air-gun becomes a despised toy and he goes and buys himself a more powerful one. Then he ventures deeper into the countryside and does greater damage to wildlife. In a countryside in which more guns are firing than ever before in history it seems time that a beginning be made to reduce their number. Not that I blame little Willie for wanting a gun. He is conditioned from an early age into the notion that firing a gun is a manly form of behaviour. Anyway, who can censure him for eventually going in for blood sports when he has before him the example of some of the Very Best People forever murdering grouse and pheasants for amusement?

(1975)

... or hen harriers, if it comes to that.

H FOR THE HORROR OF A TETHERED HAWK

Another face of the exploitation of wildlife was the revival of falconry. I received a letter from a Shropshire falconer asking me if I could help him to get a young peregrine. I pointed out to him that peregrines were protected birds, that they were apparently declining and that in any case I felt that a peregrine, the quintessence of wild freedom, should stay wild and free and not be tethered to a block of wood for someone's amusement.

In 1961 we began to count the number of peregrines breeding in Britain. It was a census whose results were to shock the bird-watchers of this country as never before. For it showed that quite suddenly the peregrine had suffered a truly catastrophic decline in numbers. Though we didn't realize it at the time this peregrine census was a turning point in the history of natural history. Till then only a minority of naturalists were deeply involved in conservation. But the sudden decline of the peregrine, quickly followed by severe losses in other creatures, caused by widespread use of agricultural pesticides, taught us all how suddenly and totally the world of nature can be threatened in the technological age. From then on many naturalists began to devote most of their time and energies to conservation and have gone on doing so.

(1975)

181

Note that unequivocal view of falconry! 'Exploitation of wildlife'. Anyone who has watched, for example, the sky-dance of the goshawk in its courtship ritual – as Mark Cocker and myself did recently at Bury Ditches near Clun – must surely be appalled at the thought that such a gloriously wild free creature could ever be caged and made subject to human will.

OYSTERCATCHERS MASSACRED

From time to time nature conservationists suffer major defeats. A few years ago we lost the battle of Cow Green and so a part of Upper Teesdale in County Durham, with its botanical treasures, was flooded. This winter in Wales we have lost the battle of Burry Inlet and thousands of oystercatchers have been shot by permission of the Secretary of State for Wales and the Ministry of Agriculture.

Why? Because the birds are allegedly reducing the number of cockles in an area where cockling is a local industry. But if cockles have declined, what proof is there that oystercatchers are responsible? It could be pollution of the water by the local tinplate factories. More likely it is because the cockles are being over-fished by man, just as whales are.

There is another point. Even if oystercatchers are reducing the cockle population, will this shooting produce any reduction of oystercatchers in Burry Inlet? Will not their place be taken immediately by oystercatchers from less favourable breeding grounds? Who better than the Ministry of Agriculture to know that the shooting of woodpigeons is a futile exercise? And what about rabbits? In pre-myxomatosis Pembrokeshire millions of rabbits were trapped every year. But this only encouraged the rest to breed more enthusiastically to keep the numbers up. Surely it should have been proved conclusively that oystercatchers were responsible for a reduction in cockles before these horrible and probably futile killings were allowed. Whatever happened to British justice?

For South Wales oystercatchers 1973, read South West badgers 2013. DEFRA, as it now is, has never needed much excuse to bring out the guns. And we could add the Welsh Assembly's willingness to grant licences for shooting mergansers on Welsh rivers. Culling anti-environmental ministers might be a better conservation tactic.

A FIFTY-FIVE-YEAR-OLD CARTWHEEL[12]

Few men these days can make a pair of cart-wheels, a pair so exactly alike that they would run sweetly together and continue to do so year after year. The perfection of such wheels results from the judgment inherited by craftsmen down the generations. And now the craft dies fast, for a young wheel-wright is a rarity in the countryside, especially one who can tyre a wheel as well as make one. The tractor-driving farm-hands of the future will not even know what timbers are needed for a wheel: ash for preference for the felloes, oak, nothing but oak, for the spokes, elm for the hub. Perhaps the very word felloe is doomed to disappear or become a mere book-word. If so, people will soon forget that it was usually pronounced 'felly'.

I suppose the most striking difference between the products of individual craftsmanship and those of mass-production is in the length of time they endure. Motor vehicles are not intended to last many years. Farm-carts may last for generations. Recently, a farmer near here took a cart-wheel to be re-spoked by a local wheel-wright. The wheel-maker recognized the wheel as his own

---

[12] Take a look at *The Wheelwright's Shop* (1923) by George Sturt ('George Bourne'). This and Sturt's other writings, particularly *Change in the Village* (1912), form an interesting alternative discourse to Bill's early writing.

work and on separating the felloes was able to point to his initials in the joint and the date 1904. Which demonstrates both the age of our wheel-wright and the quality of his work.

(*1993*)

HEDGEROWS

That we live in hedge-grubbing days is a sorrowful thought because hedges and their banks offer a last hope of survival for whole societies of mammals, birds, insects, wildflowers, mosses and lichens – the ancient forest's relict fauna and flora. Hedges are not only shelters: they are also highways along which wildlife makes its way from one patch of woodland to another. So to destroy a hedge is to break a living chain. Though it is true that hedge clearing has been most severe in eastern England, the practice has also affected parts of Wales, especially in the east and south. Not that hedge-clearing is new. It went on all through the nineteenth century with increasing momentum as farming machinery came more and more into use. In 1910 a Welsh border naturalist wrote: 'This cutting down of hedges goes on year by year. I am anxious to note whither the red-backed shrike will resort for nesting'.

You don't have to be a naturalist to love hedges. Their long history, their beauty and their fragrance make them one of the chief glories of the countryside. Where would many of our wild roses be without the hedges to grow in? Perhaps best known in Wales are the dog rose (*Rosa canina*) and the downy rose (*R. tomentosa*), but the field rose (*R. arvensis*) is, except in the south and east, not nearly as abundant as it is in much of southern England and the Midlands. Many other roses are locally well represented, their identification frequently a challenge.

When we look at hedgerow trees we find that many of them look happier out there among the fields than in the competitive world of woodlands. Oaks in hedges can spread their great boughs and look magnificent. True they shade out the shrubs below, causing a gap in the hedge which then has to be fenced: but cattle, summer and winter, are glad for their shelter. For standard trees the farmer's preference is often for ash because it lets in more light and allows the hedge to flourish; or in some parts of Wales, elm is the hedgerow favourite. Or was until 1970 when a strain of Dutch elm disease of unparalleled virulence was accidentally introduced from America, a disease which is still spreading because there is no way yet discovered of stopping it. In Wales the county of Gwent was the first to suffer because the beetle-borne disease spread in from Gloucestershire which it probably reached from Avonmouth, a port which handled American elm logs in the 1960s. The hot summers of 1975 and 1976 brought out brood after brood of the elm-bark beetle (*Scolytus scolytus*) and so hastened the epidemic. In north Wales it first occurred in common elm around Wrexham, Caergwrle and in the Clwyd valley. Throughout the 1970s it continued to spread and before the end of the decade was ravaging wych elms also.

Beech hedges, so stolid in gales, are not uncommon in Wales and are typically set across exposed slopes and over ridges in treeless districts. Some beeches are not planted as hedges but as broad windbreaks and these, when mature, make safe nesting trees for ravens, rooks, buzzards and sometimes kites. Often beech is just one species among many along a hedge and then it may have been planted by nature rather than man. For, given enough time, nature will enrich a hedgerow with many trees and shrubs and their number may therefore indicate the antiquity of the hedge. So the most historic hedge in a district may also be the most interesting ecologically.

What of the smaller trees of Welsh hedges? Certainly among the commonest are blackthorn (*Prunus spinosa*) and hawthorn

(*Crataegus monogyna*), mostly planted by man, some sown by roosting birds. They are immensely valuable for wildlife not just for their millions of berries but also for the insects that eat their leaves. And their thorns protect many a bird's nest. Some thorn hedges may be centuries old, marking medieval boundaries which can be traced on early maps or in documents. Holly too can be ancient and has the added virtue of evergreenness to protect winter roosting birds. But it is hazel that must be by far the most abundant hedgerow shrub and it is understandably popular for it makes a tough and lasting barrier and is most easily laid. It is a valuable wildlife plant, its leaves and nuts supporting many animals. But it has no love of high ground and therefore the last hedges up the slopes usually contain more birch, rowan, hawthorn, sallow and here and there an aspen. In the summer, sallows and aspens, even in the uplands, are always worth searching for caterpillars of hawkmoths, prominents, kittens and puss moths.

In modest numbers elder trees (*Sambucus nigra*) have found their way into hedgerows. People have always welcomed them (in a guarded way) and still use the flowers and fruit to make drinks, face-creams, eye-lotions and internal cure-alls. But I doubt if anyone now makes elderberry ink as the eighteenth century poet Twm o'r Nant did when a schoolboy in Denbighshire in order to teach himself to write. Botanists are very fond of the elder: its bark is the chosen home of unusual mosses, and best in this connection are the most elderly of elders because they have had more time to gather their mosses, Naturally, being so choosy, some of these mosses are rare. One called *Pylaisa polyantha* discovered in north Wales in the 1830s does not seem to have been seen again until it was refound on a venerable elder near Bala in 1976. So long live the elder, a very special tree. Not that many are likely to be singled out for destruction. Our ancestors never dared to cut down a tree so vibrating with magic and this fear is still strong among country people.

Other trees of hedges are much more local. Field maple, so abundant in much of southern Britain, is little known in about three quarters of Wales. It stretches, mainly with the lime-rich soils, in a narrow arc round the north, east and south. Its wood is hard and its constitution hardy, for it reaches 375m (1,250 ft) in Denbighshire. More familiar along some hedges is bird cherry (*Prunus padus*) which is passed by unnoticed most of the year but is conspicuously beautiful when its white racemes stand among the leaves of May. I usually think of bird cherry as a tree of the south Wales limestone – the waterfall region of the upper Nedd, the Brecon Beacons and Gwent. But it is well distributed, if always local, in mid Wales and northern districts as well. Then there is wild pear (*Pyrus communis*), a tree of unknown history. Did man bring it here or did it precede him? It lives very shyly among the hedges and thickets of Gwent but nearly everywhere else it is totally absent.

Two aliens, one a shrub, the other a small tree, are locally dominant in Welsh hedges: willow-leaved spiraea (*Spiraea salicifolia*) and common laburnum (*Laburnum anagyroides*). The spiraea you will have no difficulty in finding: it borders many a roadside in the Bala-Ffestiniog region and is a delight from June onwards when its pink flowers are showing. Its history in Merionethshire is clear enough: it was introduced by the owner of the Rhiwlas estate near Bala, R.J.Ll. Price, who was famous for the encouragement of local industries and other innovations. ... Around Bala spiraea is called 'spriars' (I don't guarantee the spelling) by Welsh speakers. There is also a tradition that it was sent to R.J.Ll. Price by Welsh settlers in Patagonia as a token of their esteem. Not that it is a South American plant: it is a native of eastern Europe and Asia.

Probably long before the spiraea hedges were planted in Merioneth the laburnum hedges had begun to appear in south Cardiganshire, adjacent parts of Carmarthenshire and Pembrokeshire and in other districts. Laburnum had been grown in Wales since at least the seventeenth century and as a hedge plant it must date from the development of cottage and commercial nurseries which began at the end of the eighteenth century. These nurseries were encouraged to produce hedging plants by premiums offered by local agricultural societies. By 1810 Walter Davies was writing in praise of laburnum hedges: 'Its leaves in times of scarcity have been found an excellent forage. Cattle and sheep are exceedingly fond of it'. Which is curious because some authorities tell us that laburnum is toxic in all parts, not merely in its seeds. Farmers I have spoken to never seem to have heard of its poisonous reputation. Some of them do not value it much because it isn't very stockproof. Others like it for its hard wood which makes lasting fence posts and also because when its stakes are set in the ground they readily take root.

Doubtless the popularity of laburnum rested mainly on its willingness to grow in places where hedges were difficult to establish. Deep-rooted against gales, laburnum hedges, though common enough in valleys, are especially characteristic of rather high, bleak country. 'No tree', wrote W.J. Bean, 'is better adapted to our climate'. It is also reputed to have the enormous advantage of being disliked by rabbits and therefore did not need to be protectively fenced in its early years. The history of these hedges would make a fascinating research project for anyone willing to delve into old estate and farm records and into the early development of tree nurseries. There seems to be no Welsh word for laburnum other than *tresi aur* which is a translation of 'golden chain'. Certainly overgrown hedges of it are a splendid sight when miles of them are in flower in June.

(1981)

NIGHT ON A DESERT ISLAND

It was on a sun-filled afternoon in late July, 1961, that I landed on Cardigan Island amid a clangour of anxious, aggressive herring gulls that swooped at me to protect their young ones crouching in the scurvy-grass along the cliff-top.

The sea was calm. The boat had swayed in the tide-race, but it slid smoothly in between the rocks of the island's landing creek and let me jump out with my tent and my rucksack. Then it backed out gently, turned its bows towards the mainland, and in a minute was gone round the point, leaving me alone to explore the island.

As every new island should, this one had several quick surprises for me. First there was the lushness of the grass. From the mainland the island had looked burnt and thirsty, but now I found that the brownness that capped the whole top of this cliffy island was due only to the heavy seeding of the grasses. For the grass itself was deep and springy and lovely to polish your feet on. That, and a complete absence of gorse, inspired my first act: I cast off my sandals to give my feet 24 hours' freedom.

My second surprise was to find a natural well, for the boatman had told me that no one had ever lived or ever could live permanently on Cardigan Island because there is no drinking water.

My third surprise was to find clear traces of earth walls in straight lines and curves that suggested fields of some far antiquity. Then on top of one of the island's two hills there was what seemed the remains of a tumulus or some other sort of man-raised mound. Finally, an unpleasant find: there were rat-holes, dozens of them, round the cliff-tops wherever there was soft earth for burrowing, enough to chill any hope of finding puffins or shearwaters breeding there, for it is particularly those birds that nest in holes that are preyed on by rats.

How, I wonder, did the dreadful brown rats get on to this otherwise delectable island? Could they have swum across from the mainland, attracted by the smell of the island's bird cliffs? For at the lowest tides the channel narrows from 200 yards to less than half that distance. If you doubt that rats are so enterprising you may prefer the shipwreck theory, in support of which I can offer you the 6,500-ton liner *Herefordshire*, which was being towed from the Dart to the breakers' yard in the Clyde. She tore adrift from her tugs in heavy seas on 15th March, 1934, and was deposited by a north-west gale on to the north-west corner of the island. She clung to the rocks, so I was told, long enough for any number of rats to get ashore and then quietly slid into the sea, where she lies to this day in no great depth of water.

Let me give you a few of the island's measurements. The length east to west is just under half a mile; the breadth just less than a quarter-mile; it is almost completely surrounded by sheer cliffs, but none is much higher than about 100 ft.

There are a number of caves at sea-level, but I could not climb down into them to see how far they extended. Some of the rock is beautifully gnarled and honeycombed and so shattered and contorted that the earth must have gone through some agonizing moments producing it. Of the two highpoints (you rise only gently to them from the flattish top of the rest of the island), the higher is 172 ft, the other (where my alleged tumulus is) being a few feet lower.

In my 24 hours there I walked right round the island several times. I listed all the birds I saw (there were 24 species) and all the plants I could find (some 40 different sorts). Besides gulls there were shags and a few cormorants and oystercatchers nesting; a fulmar flew close round the island; six kittiwakes stood on the north cliffs, five adults and a young one. I saw gannets, razorbills and guillemots off-shore.

Three kinds of birds sang: skylark, rock pipit and meadow pipit. The crow tribe was well represented: dozens of jackdaws and a pair each of ravens, carrion crows and choughs. Earlier this century puffins used to nest on the island, but as from some other Welsh islands they have now gone. (Enter rats, exit puffins?) I lay awake till after midnight and woke several times before dawn hoping to hear night birds such as owls or shearwaters, but there were none.

The other living creatures were a mixed bag. There were a few grasshoppers, woodlice and ladybirds. I saw three kinds of butterfly: meadow brown, small copper and grayling; and there were six-spot burnet moths. In the sea there were seals that quietly watched me all day, and once a score of dolphins rolled and leapt among the white-topped green breakers a few yards from the rocks. Finally there were the sheep: 21 small, nearly black, horned sheep called Soays, a primitive breed said to date back to the Vikings. The flock on Cardigan Island was put there a few years ago by the West Wales Field Society. Soays may be the nearest we have to true wild sheep in north Europe and wild their behaviour remains, for they went bounding off to the other end of the island whenever they saw me. It was only by the use of a telephoto lens that I was able to get anything of a photograph of them.

So there was one animal of distinction – this fine-horned, ibex-like primitive sheep grazing on what are perhaps the fields of primitive man. For birds of distinction I would choose the choughs whose cheerful voices woke me soon after dawn. A plant of distinction? Yes, I think two: first the vernal squills that must have been a sheet of blue in May and which had now gone to seed. For my second plant I would choose the tree mallow, a splendid species that belongs so much to the islands, even the isolated stacks, of our rocky western coasts and is often, as on Cardigan Island, the only plant that gets anywhere near to being a tree, growing tall and rather woody and producing large leaves and big pink flowers in defiance of all the salt sea-winds that blow.

That night I unrolled my sleeping bag on a soft bed of grass in a hollow circled by a low bank that I like to think was a hut-circle. But even if it was no such thing, someone had made it and I am sure a very long time ago. For a while I sat in the still warm dusk watching the four bright flashes of Strumble light 18 miles to the south-west. But Bardsey's light, which I had hoped would shine nearly 50 miles to the north, was either lost in cloud or too low on the horizon to be visible. Then I lay awake under the stars watching the play of grasses very close to my face and hearing the very softest wind swish through grass, the very slightest rustle of water against rock: sounds you miss in the daytime.

Waking in the night I heard oystercatchers piping to one another, the calls of passing redshanks and the occasional unaccountable alarms of the gulls rising up in sudden shouting bursts into the dark sky, them slowly subsiding. I also heard a gnawing close to my ear and discovered that a rat had got into my rucksack and was helping itself to a packet of sandwiches.

When I woke in the morning as the choughs called and bounced through the air over me I was conscious first of grasses shaking wildly against racing grey clouds. There was an autumnal touch in the light twitter of passing finches. I felt the wind stronger over the island and heard a heavier sea than that of the previous night. I stood up to see white water breaking all round the rocks and spray flying far. I looked at the creek, the one possible landing place in this island of rocks, and saw the waves surging heavily into it. If it was like this on what was merely a breezy summer day, what, I asked myself, was it like in winter?

By the afternoon, when the tide had ebbed, the waves fell

a little and when the boat came I was able to fling my pack and then myself into it. Quickly on the south-flowing tide we slipped through the narrow sound. We looked up at the south cliffs gasping with summer; at three young cormorants on a nest, their mouths agape and their throats vibrating to get air; at the sea-beet hanging great seeding heads from the ledges. Then the island was behind us and soon we were entering the Teifi river and our boat was dancing through the wavelets of the bar.

(*1961*)

BIRTH OF A BIRD RESERVE

The years have gone since Penny and I came to live at Ynys Edwin and there have been many changes, especially after the death of Hubert Mappin who had owned Ynys-hir estate (which includes Ynys Edwin) since 1929. He was a retiring, gentle, kindly man in whose hands Ynys-hir with its woodland, marshes and estuary had retained a tranquility and wild beauty now rare in a countryside steadily being degraded by conspicuous chalet parks, ill-concealed caravan sites and by houses and other buildings out of character in rural Wales.

Hubert Mappin loved gardens, trees and the world of nature. And honey bees. Many a summer's day I saw him with bees all round him as he bent over an open hive, sometimes wearing no protective veil, his arms and hands quite bare, mumbling to the bees as all truly bee-mad people do. ('Bee-mad' is not derogatory – it describes those rare souls who handle bees by instinct and seem to enjoy mysterious affinities with them.) You will not be surprised to hear that such a man as Hubert Mappin had little use for blood sports. I dare say in his younger days he had done some shooting (this was almost inevitable with his country gentleman upbringing) but by the time we knew him he had long outgrown all that. By then he was keeping Ynys-hir virtually as a private nature reserve (as far as this was compatible with farming) and I remember him angrily turning the otter hunt off his stream. It was because he knew that Penny and I shared many of his views about the countryside that he invited us to live at Ynys Edwin. And for seven years before he died I often helped him to warden his domain by turning back wildfowlers who came trespassing across to the estuary.

His death was the start of an anxious period. What would now happen to Ynys-hir? We had two thoughts to give us some comfort. We knew that his widow, Patricia, wanted if at all possible to keep the estate just as he had made it, retaining its quiet beauty and its status as a wildlife refuge. Further, we were consoled by the knowledge that with his dying hand he had signed a covenant empowering the National Trust to safeguard the place against the worst forms of commercial exploitation. At least that would prevent Ynys-hir, if it had to be sold, from falling into the hands of developers and speculators, the smartest of whom had immediately begun to make inquiries. Come what may, the oakwoods would not be felled and replaced by conifers, which is what happens on so many estates that fall into the hands of financiers. Nor would the fields be covered with caravans or chalets.

The decision came at last: the estate was to be sold. But it would go if possible to someone sympathetic to conservation. But who? Ideally all estates that are wildlife refuges should pass into the hands of wildlife trusts. I am thinking especially of low-fertility areas whose reclamation for agriculture is highly expensive and then produces only third-rate land on which vast amounts of fertilizer must be squandered for evermore. Cors Fochno, the peat bog behind Borth, is an example of such an area. Its centre is a National Nature Reserve whose value as a wildlife habitat depends on the drainage being almost nil. Yet round its margins men and machines are always trying to wring the water out of this great acid sponge that would be far better left as a haven for sundews, the large heath butterfly and geese that graze there in the winter. A modern Welsh historian has written that the draining of the marshes of Malltraeth, Porthmadog and Cors Fochno was 'beneficial to everyone'. But with this learned author I totally disagree.

Too often when wildlife-rich estates come on to the market their value is far beyond the resources of the local naturalists' trust. So it was with Ynys-hir. But, we wondered, what about the Royal Society for the Protection of Birds? Patricia Mappin proved sympathetic to this idea. And in due course the R.S.P.B.'s director, Peter Conder, came from the society's headquarters at Sandy, Bedfordshire. He arrived on a March day of raw east wind. The world was grey and shrivelled; there was no sky; the oakwoods were black and lifeless; a dismal haze hid the estuary and its flocks of wildfowl; and the Dyfi-side hills that should have stood up as a splendid background were lost in the filthiest murk. Not a day we would have chosen to show off the charms of the estate. I took Peter round, trying to make up for the gloom and absence of birds by giving him a word-picture of what Ynys-hir is like on better days.

As we got near their clump of Scots pines our pair of ravens rose and circled impressively, proudly trumpeting their ownership of the site, for after eight years they were still using their old nest. We watched them as they flew across the sky at speed to chivvy off a buzzard that had floated too near. Beyond the pines, as we walked along the ridge of Ynys Feurig, a lovely pale hen harrier sailed closely past. And, final touch, when we went to look at the heronry, there was a peregrine perched on one of the herons' tallest pines. Maybe these fine raptors helped the cause.

For despite the east wind and the gloom, Peter Conder had no difficulty in seeing the possibilities of the place and went away full of enthusiasm. To buy Ynys-hir the R.S.P.B. successfully launched an appeal, an important contribution to which coming from the West Wales Naturalists' Trust.

So most of Ynys-hir estate became an R.S.P.B. reserve. A blow had been struck for conservation and by coincidence another occurred at about the same time: the neighbouring Dyfi estuary was declared a National Nature Reserve by the Nature Conservancy. This means that although, in deference to long tradition, wild-fowling is still permitted in the wide, seaward end of the estuary, the narrower head of the estuary adjoining Ynys-hir estate has become a refuge where wildfowl are fully protected. So two sanctuaries exist in mutual support, an arrangement that suits all concerned. The conservationist, though perhaps unable to understand why people want to go shooting, is happy that they can't shoot everywhere. The wildfowler is contented because he appreciates that refuge areas are essential to the future of wildfowl stocks.

He also knows well enough that every evening plenty of duck will quit the refuge to go off and feed in the surrounding countryside. To get there they have to fly over the guns that lie in wait. It's the same at dawn; the wildfowlers are there again, awaiting the return flight. Men who gladly leave their warm beds to go and lie in a mud-hole in the darkness of a winter estuary amid snow and east winds in the hope of getting a shot at a duck, such men are clearly possessed by some extraordinarily powerful and primitive urge. I am torn between admiration of their hardihood and despair that they feel it necessary to destroy what is so beautiful and innocent.

If they always killed cleanly I might more easily accept it. But, shooting in near darkness, they cannot see to recover all they cripple[13]. (Many have no dog with them.) It is left for those of us who come along the estuary in daylight to pick up here a duck and there a wader scuttling wretchedly along a creek with a broken wing. There are also the many victims who fly on, carrying in their flesh lead pellets that may well bring gangrene and slow death.

What, I wonder, is your attitude towards words like 'reserve' and 'sanctuary'? 'Bird sanctuary', though still in popular use, has long been out of favour among conservationists, especially those who like to think of themselves as scientific. I was once at a conservationists' meeting that almost unanimously rejected the word 'sanctuary' on the grounds that it was 'emotional'. But I believe there is not enough emotion in the conservation movement. Certainly we need all the science we can get. But we need to have feelings as well. So to my taste 'reserve' is chilly and uninspiring and is far too much like 'preserve' which suggests pheasants and guns and gamekeepers' gibbets. I prefer 'sanctuary' which implies genuine respect for wildlife. But call a place what you will, reserve or sanctuary, it still needs defining for the naïve sort of visitors (mercifully they are few) who, having arrived at Ynys-hir reserve look around with genuine puzzlement at the wild scene, all this woodland, marsh and estuary where the birds are just as keen on not being watched as they are in most other

---

[13] Nor indeed can they always identify what they shoot, so rare and protected species fall foul of their bloodlust. And perhaps some of the shooters do not even care? In 1988 I found a red-throated diver on the saltings of the Dwyryd estuary, shot and cast aside by a man whose car displayed the bird-brained dog-badge of the British Association for Shooting and Conservation (sic!) That same organization, in 2013, sought to lease from Crown Estate shooting rights over the Dwyfor estuary – a wholly inappropriate site for their activities. In this instance, and for the time being, they were averted by a concerted press campaign from local naturalists and residents. But the shooters will try again, here and elsewhere, and their resources and sympathy for them among the political right are huge.

places. I think what they expect, these people, is that as soon as they come through the gate they will see tame and amicable birds advancing from all sides with greetings, song and general goodwill. They seem quite surprised when they look across the saltings and see two thousand ducks and not one with its wings clipped and eating corn from a bucket. This is an inevitable way of thinking in a world increasingly littered with wildfowl collections, country zoos and safari parks.

But people can learn. Some of them, after all, have never really seen wild birds before. In a way they know that such creatures exist because they've seen them on television. But I suspect they keep them in a special place as part of their television dream world and don't relate them to the living world at all. Even when you take them into a hide on the estuary and show them wild ducks and waders at a few yards range they see them framed in a viewing slot that has something in common with a television screen. The scene is still not quite real for them. So they poke an arm at full length through the slot to point out a bird and are disappointed when the bird flies off in alarm. The birds on telly behave themselves better than that. But most reserve visitors are quite sophisticated. They know that a wild bird can both see and hear acutely and they enter a hide as it should be entered – with the respect with which they would go into a church.

I can imagine a few, a very few, of my readers getting increasingly impatient at this point. These are the anti-reserve-visiting school. Why, they demand to know, why allow people to come to reserves at all? If you create a bird reserve, they say, then it should be what it claims to be, a place truly reserved for birds to enjoy in peace and not be gawped at by people. So, they would argue, an estate like Ynys-hir was better as it used to be – private, secluded, a genuine bird sanctuary where people seldom intruded. Undoubtedly there is some merit in this argument.

But realities have to be faced. How much public support would there be for wildlife refuges if people were never allowed to visit them? And the fortunate truth is that, provided reserve visiting is arranged on sensitive lines, then many people can enter and see yet not intrude. Miracles can be worked with hides and screened approaches and a little education on how to behave. There is the additional safeguard that in a properly run reserve only about a third of it need be frequented by visitors and then only on carefully selected trails. Another third should be visited only by the warden and his helpers. And the last third should hardly ever be visited by anybody. So perhaps the word 'sanctuary' could be retained for this specially reserved area.

When I have tried to explain to people who are new to the idea that a bird reserve is not a zoo but a place where wildness is everything, then I often see their minds swing to the other extreme. They immediately assume all that needs to be done in a bird reserve is to make a few hides with trails between them and then sit back and let nature play. So I find myself giving a lecture on reserve management. I have to explain why it is that a nature reserve, far from being left to nature, can be a place where man intervenes quite often. A bird reserve warden looks at his pools, his marshes, his woods, his hillsides and sees that they are changing all the time, that the vegetation is always on the move and that some species, if there is nothing to check their growth, are sure to be elbowing out others. This may be good or it may be bad for those birds particularly in need of protection. So crucial decisions must be made. The warden has to determine at what stage he must try to hold the vegetation in suspension. In order to check a reed bed that is invading a pool, or brambles rollicking through a wood, or gorse prancing across a field, he and his workers go to work with bill-hook and scythe and so take on a job that will need to be repeated year after year.

To illustrate these problems of vegetation control I have taken people through the woods at Ynys-hir and told them how the oak is under ferocious attack by the sycamore. They look up at the trees, oak and sycamore growing so quietly together some halcyon morning, and clearly they find it hard to accept the reality behind the idyll: that the trees are engaged in a long and desperate struggle that will end only when one or the other falls away in disease and death. Their roots fight underground for the soil's nutrients. Their leaves compete for light. And in high winds their branches lash at each other as if in anger. Then I explain that, for various reasons, the alien sycamore is spreading far more rapidly than the native oak and, if permitted, must ultimately turn our oakwood into a predominantly sycamore wood.

'But what's wrong with that?' visitors have asked.

I have then tried to explain why most conservationists are unenthusiastic about the sycamore. Admitted it is a handsome sturdy tree, good for wind shelter, and that in April it roars with bees from dawn to dusk, so eager are they for its nectar. But against it are grave accusations. Except in its brief flowering time it is a poor tree for insects: very few caterpillars eat the leaves of sycamore compared with the multitudes that grow fat on oak leaves every June just when countless small woodland birds need lavish supplies on which to feed their young. And there is also the disadvantage that sycamore casts so deep a shade that hardly any shrub survives below it; and a woodland bird reserve needs a wealth of under-storey shrubs for birds to nest in.

Sometimes as I speak of these things a grey squirrel comes rippling along the trail. My visitors understand about grey squirrels and how they have 'driven out the red squirrel' (the expression is always the same). I am therefore able to make the parallel: just as an alien squirrel ousts a native squirrel, so an alien tree (the sycamore was introduced from south Europe) threatens a native tree. Not that I am entirely anti-sycamore. Every kind of tree adds variety to the woods and, after all, we do see birds feeding in sycamores at times. So I hope that Ynys-hir will keep some of its biggest sycamores even though they scatter their winged seeds far through the wood. Once on the ground they are not eaten as avidly as acorns are by birds and animals. And when they germinate, the young sycamores are better able to survive in the woodland shade than are infant oaks. Hence their success in life.

One of the splendours of Ynys-hir is the oakwood called Coed Penrhyn (Wood along the Ridge). It clothes the rocky spine that is the reserve's central feature and which looks north across former wetlands to the estuary. It is barely a mile long, this wood, but even so is one of the largest surviving fragments of the Boskus de Lissecoed[14]... As such it is precious. And it owes its survival to the devotion of a long line of owners and especially to Hubert Mappin who held on to Coed Penrhyn when it had become fashionable (the fashion continues) to clear away oakwoods and replace them by conifers. For he was well aware that an oakwood is richer in wildlife than any other land habitat and that in keeping his oaks he was providing a sanctuary for birds and mammals, not to mention myriads of smaller creatures that depend on oak leaves, oak bark, oak wood or acorns for their livelihood.

I have often taken R.S.P.B. members down the woodside to the stile at the bottom where, clear of the trees, the view is across the marsh to Ynys Edwin. Perhaps the month is May, the morning delicious and the gnats and horseflies of summer not yet thought of. Everywhere there is birdsong because birds are

---

[14] Boskus de Lissecoed (literally 'Forest of Courtwood') is the name given to the former forest that stretched all round the hill-skirts of north Cardiganshire. Its reduction to the relict present state was almost certainly attributable to the lead-mining industry in these hills, with its incessant demand for charcoal for use in smelting.

more numerous along the bushy edge of a wood than within the shade of the trees. Willow warblers, pied flycatchers, blackcaps, thrushes, tree pipits, wood warblers, redstarts, garden warblers, blackbirds, nuthatches, woodpeckers – all in their special idioms add beauty to the hour. From the oaks of Coed Penrhyn we venture into the quaking peat bog to see the flowers peculiar to wet places: strange insect-eating sundews of three species, the great sundew (in its greatness it towers up to no more than a few inches) being the most attractive of the trio; bog rosemary creeping shyly among the sphagnum mosses; asphodel, its leaves only tiny green swords so early in the season; heath spotted orchids almost thinking of flowering; attractive rushes, sedges and stately grasses. My visitors are delighted by it all. Simply walking a few yards across a bog – something they had never dared to do before – has opened their eyes to new wonders. Till now a bog has been no more to them than a squalid, dangerous mire that ought to be drained. But now it has become a world of delight.

On the peat bog I have also pointed out to the visitors the menace of the rhododendrons that stand all around like a wall. But no, a wall suggests something stationary; and the rhododendrons of Ynys Edwin bog move ever forwards like a dark green tide as their seedlings spring up before them in the sphagnum moss. If we do not have willing hands to help us fight back this threat we would soon lose the entire marsh under the sort of jungle that has invaded the adjacent Scots pinewood, most of which no one had been able to get into for the past twenty years, so total was the interlacing of the long, tough, curving branches of the rhododendrons. If only rhododendrons were rich in birds! If even one rare species found a refuge in those dark shadows, how we would treasure these thickets – the product of a century's growth. But the bleak truth is that very little bird life ever stirs in all that dense cover except when in some winters we get a vast invasion of roosting starlings.

It was Sir Uvedale Price of Hereford and other landowners who in the late eighteenth century succeeded in popularizing in Britain this *Rhododendrum ponticum* that we now aspire to eliminate almost entirely from our Ynys-hir woodlands so that sunlight can enter and encourage less stifling, more bird-full trees to spring up instead. But we must not think too harshly of Sir Uvedale and his fellows. They were gardeners with undying enthusiasm for picturesque landscapes; and a few rhododendrons clumped tastefully here and there no doubt helped their design. The mischief came after them in the nineteenth century when the pheasant-rearing craze really began to scourge the British countryside and landowners planted rhododendrons all through their woods as shelter for their pheasants in winter.

Contrary to what some may suppose, the life of a bird-reserve warden is far from being that of a solitary stroller through wood and marsh, communing with nature like a Romantic poet. Truly a warden needs to love his fellow men, for people are visiting reserves in ever-increasing numbers. Most come simply to see and learn about birds. But there is another quite numerous group (without whom life for me would be impossible) who come to help. In all weathers and at all seasons they arrive at Ynys-hir, at their own expense, to give their time and energy with unfailing cheerfulness. I have had marvellous aid from young and old – voluntary wardens who stay a week or several weeks; school groups who come partly to help and partly to pursue field studies; the Young Ornithologists' Club; the Conservation Corps; students from the University of Wales; scouts and guides both British and foreign; local residents sympathetic to the cause; Outward Bound and adventure school parties, both civilian and from the services. One of their main tasks is the clearing of the rhododendrons which, when we began work, covered about fifty acres. For me this flow of practical aid is one of the most cheering faces of modern society. And when I see these volunteers all working happily at their tasks, I wonder how many more people would be willing to give a hand in the countless conservation schemes that are in progress all over the country if they only knew how much their help would be appreciated.

Life for the warden and his helpers at Ynys-hir is far from being entirely taken up with swiping at sycamores or being nasty to rhododendrons. There is scope for more direct forms of creativity. Trees to be planted, for instance. We are growing alders for siskins that will come for seeds in winter; Scots pines at the heronry to replace in years to come the tall trees the birds breed in at present. And we are adding to the birches, hazels, hollies and hawthorns that are already here. As a monument to optimism we have even put in hornbeams for the hawfinch, even though that desirable bird is entirely absent from the district. (Birdwatchers of the twenty-first century ticking hawfinch off your lists as you stand under the great hornbeams of Ynys-hir, we send you greetings!)

In the woods we have also provided nest-boxes. I suppose there are a few ecological purists who would sniff at our nest-boxes as quite unnatural. And certainly they have had their effect on our bird population – a noteworthy increase in pied flycatchers for instance, no bird being more addicted to boxes. I have often claimed, though I admit that I have never actually tried it, that if, in the critical week of the year when boxes are being so fiercely squabbled over, someone were to stand in Coed Penrhyn holding a box up over his head he would soon get a pied flycatcher excitedly popping in and out of it. All right, I'm exaggerating; but I speak truth when I say that the more boxes we put in our woods the more pied flycatchers come and breed here. So we wonder how many we could attract if we provided 1,000 boxes instead of the present 150? Clearly there must be a limit somewhere but with our fifty pairs of flycatchers I'm sure we are not yet near it for there are several woods and spinneys that have not so far been provided with boxes. Meanwhile I doubt if the artificial increase in pied flycatchers has done anything to upset the ecological balance. True, they compete with other small birds for food but the oakwood's caterpillar harvest is so generous every year that there seems more than enough for all. Certainly the nest-boxes give much pleasure to our human visitors who come far to see this engaging flycatcher, so confiding and watchable, showing off his neat black and white plumage as he sings enthusiastically among the buds of early May. Then there are the blue tits, great tits, nuthatches, redstarts and tawny owls that are all happy to lease our boxes for a season. We should be thankful. Elsewhere in the world we might not be so fortunate. As when a friend of mine put up nest-boxes on trees in an African national park: not a single bird ever went near them! (But will African birds eventually learn the use of boxes?)

For a wide view of Ynys-hir in its estuary setting under the shapely line of the Meirionnydd hills you cross the main road and follow paths through the bracken up the hill called Foel Fawr where the reserve reaches its highest point. Here among the grey rocks are the nesting places of wheatear, whinchat, tree pipit and many a strong-voiced wren; and some nights the purring of nightjars comes through the mothy darkness. Choicest wildflowers of the hills are the insect-trapping butterworts that in May hang purple flowers on neatly curved stems. Then in July the elegant little ivy-leaved bellflowers open pale blue cups half-hidden in the grass. Summer also brings crimson-purple sheets of bell heather and swiftly passing dark green fritillary butterflies; and family parties of ravens playing in the wind over the summit rocks. The brackeny slopes tilt sharply down through birches and oaks into the dingle of the hastening Einion that soon drops over Furnace Falls, then flows on to form a beautiful margin along the lower levels of the reserve. Here in recent years mergansers have begun to breed, hiding their nests in the banks. Here, too, are grey wagtails, dippers, and sometimes the flash of blue that is a kingfisher. Slowing between banks of tidal mud the Einion joins the Dyfi under the motte called Domen Las (Green Mound) on which in the twelfth century the defenders of south Wales built a wooden fort to challenge invaders from the north. Then perhaps for many centuries after the fort had decayed the mound stood bare until, I would guess, early in the nineteenth century, some owner of Ynys-hir thought fit to crown the knoll with Scots pines that stand today. To him we are grateful: for the weather-battered old pines now house the nests of two or three dozen pairs of herons who come and go all day in slow, grave flight. Under the trees in holes in the banks of the mound several pairs of shelducks have their nests. And what bird brings more life and colour to the river-bank than shelducks?

Despite being so varied Ynys-hir had long lacked one habitat especially precious to wildlife and that is freshwater pools. There were a few marshy fields and there were often floods in winter: but no permanent open water apart from the river. So into one of the fields a few years ago we brought a mechanical digger and a bulldozer and, during the summer drought, we gouged out a hollow as dry as a moon crater. But if there was no water visible in this hollow there was plenty just below. It was truly frightening to see the five-ton bulldozer working delicately down through the silt a few inches at a time until it was supported only by a skin of floating, tremulous clay and looked certain to disappear at any moment into deep and watery depths. But at last the job was done, the thunder of the machinery died away and the hollow was left to fill slowly in the autumn rains. By the first Christmas it was a real pool with an island in the centre; and wigeon were beginning to visit.

Nature gave us a nod of encouragement while we were making this first pool. When the job was only half done, a pair of oystercatchers arrived from somewhere and nested on the island, though they did well to recognize it as such since there was not yet a drop of water anywhere. We felt this was a true benison upon our efforts because this was the first time that oystercatchers had ever been known to breed at Ynys-hir. And it was for just such birds as oystercatchers, ringed plovers and little terns that we had planned this island. They are special birds of stony beaches; but hardly anywhere along the shore these days can the birds have peace because people and dogs are there all day and every day throughout spring and summer. So on our island we laid a carpet of plastic bags to stifle the weeds; then on top a layer of pebbles to resemble a beach. It is up to the birds to do the rest. So far, apart from the one pair of oystercatchers, only common sandpipers have nested on our island. But in experiments like this you live by faith.

When spring came we planted sedges, aquatic grasses, pondweeds and Amphibious bistort in the shallows of the pool: all plants that provide waterfowl not only with cover but also food, for their seeds are nutritious. Meanwhile the water, which for long months had been clouded with silt, began to clear and look healthy. Soon we were cheered by the sight of our first water beetles, water snails, pond skaters, water boatmen and dragonflies. Then, in the mysterious way fish have of finding their way to new waters, three-spined sticklebacks appeared. And it wasn't long before the dabchicks came to dive for the sticklebacks. Still, it was not until we saw the first herons and kingfishers that we began to feel our pool had truly arrived.

Since then other birds have dropped in one after another; and to date ten species of duck and a dozen waders have been seen at the pool.

Lately a new pool has been excavated nearby. But while the first was made oval with one large central island, the second pond has an interesting, five-lobed shape (with several islets) to provide a maximum length of shoreline. As this is a pool expressly aimed at attracting waders, we made it shallow all over in the hope that, come August and September, at the height of wader migration, it will be partly dry and provide an interesting pattern of wet mud and puddles for ruffs, stints and sandpipers both common and rare. Dreams? We must wait and see.

I admit these pools are only small affairs, a mere 150 yards across, but they are a start, the first steps in the creation of a mosaic of ponds and marshes of differing sizes, shapes and depths that I hope will eventually change the face of some of Ynys-hir's sea-level land. In any project you have to begin somewhere: and in the drainage-mad days in which we live it is good to have reversed the trend however minutely, to have actually ripped up a few drainage pipes and held back a little water from flowing too hastily away. But let me assure any farmer who may have recoiled from this last sentence in horror that most of Ynys-hir's fields are farmed and thoroughly drained. To be drowning some fields and draining others may sound a little odd. But then we live in a time when farming and wildlife-conservation are, we trust, beginning to learn to live together.

Meanwhile at the other end of the reserve we plan wetlands of a different character. These, we hope, will be a chain of lagoons amid reed swamps where water birds, for centuries bereft of nesting places by drainage schemes, will be able to breed once again. We should remember that the bittern, for instance, was once familiar to Welsh country folk as *aderyn y bwn* ('the booming bird') – sufficient evidence that it nested widely in Wales, for it is only when on its breeding grounds that this strange cousin of the heron draws in his great breaths and then, exhaling with all his might, lets the surrounding marshland have the benefit of his splendid voice – the farthest carrying bird sound in all nature. The bittern, after a long absence from Britain, returned to nest in East Anglia in 1911. Now it breeds not only in the east but also in the west, in Lancashire and Anglesey. The question is: will this spread continue? And the answer is that it probably will if more wetlands with extensive reed-beds can be provided. It is going to be a crucial test for conservation, this problem of creating more wetlands in a world in which lowering the water table has become a national preoccupation.

As with bitterns so with harriers. They, too, like to nest in reed beds and no doubt once did so in many parts of Wales. The fortunes of harriers have fluctuated in the last few decades especially those of the hen harrier and Montagu's. In the 1950s there were in some years perhaps ten pairs of Montagu's breeding in the coastal counties of Wales. Since then they seem to have almost completely ceased to breed in Wales: which is hardly surprising since they are being increasingly shot for fun on migration during the great autumnal bird slaughter that goes on every year in many south European countries and on the Mediterranean islands. But meanwhile the hen harrier, formerly an extreme rarity, is slowly gaining ground. (The hen harrier winters in Britain and so avoids the hazards of a journey across south Europe[15].) As we struggle to create our reed beds at Ynys-hir it is inevitable that these beautiful, long-winged raptors float

---

[15] It needs to learn to avoid royal estates in Norfolk, and Dark Peak grouse-moors too – in both of which there are records of these beautiful birds being shot or their nests destroyed in recent years – by 'some of the very best people', of course, to adopt Bill's ironic term for these brutes.

in and out of our thoughts. Someday, maybe, we shall see their exciting courtship flights above our marshes in spring.

The shortage of wetlands and therefore of breeding places for bitterns, bearded tits, harriers, spoonbills, godwits, ruffs, avocets and other desirable birds is only one way in which the British countryside is out of balance. The excess of pheasants in so many places is another symptom of malaise. I am happy not to have known Ynys-hir early this century when its woods were given over to pheasants. I'm sure the buzzards and sparrowhawks didn't survive here long in those days. I can easily picture the nineteenth-century coverts tyrannized by some ruthless gamekeeper; and gibbets hung with putrifying hawks along with rows of white owls, brown owls, stoats, weasels and polecats. How different today. All this spring there has been not a single call of a pheasant to threaten my peace of mind, Instead four pairs of lovely buzzards circled and wailed over the woods. And three pairs of sparrowhawks nested safely. Tawny owls filled the trees with their music. We have frequently seen peregrines, merlins, hen harriers, kites and barn owls. Raptorial mammals have abounded. It is all so very healthy, having such a robust team of predators to keep the pheasant in his place, his proper place as a bird of crake-like secrecy, hiding in reed-beds and other dense cover and hardly ever raising his voice in self-advertisement. So different from the half-tame, crowing multitudes that are fussed over by an army of keepers on Britain's shooting estates and are the chief reason why birds of prey, especially the larger sorts, are rare in England. Take the buzzard for example. Buzzards are protected birds, but only on paper. They thrive abundantly in those parts of Wales where pheasant-rearing is little practised; and there is no doubt that these areas produce enough young buzzards to populate the woods of England in not many years. Probably every autumn there is a liberal dispersal of buzzards eastwards from Wales, youngsters eager to colonize new districts. But what is their fate? It is rarely possible to prove anything. But there is every reason to suspect that gun, trap and poison still do some very dirty work every year in many an English covert. Pheasants there are big business and big business has no conscience. The continuing (but surreptitious) use of the dreadful pole-trap, which ensures a slow death by torture and which has been illegal since 1908, is evidence of this.

Predators kill other birds besides pheasants, which means that Ynys-hir will never raise battalions of wild ducks or go in for rearing geese as our wildfowling neighbours would like us to do. But what we shall achieve, if all goes well, is a varied and healthy community of animals, birds, plants and trees living together with as much balance and harmony as can be hoped for in a small area islanded in a world where wildlife is increasingly on the defensive. As for people who have to live in that world, more pressingly as time goes on they are going to need 'the tonic of wildness' (I never tire of quoting Thoreau's apt phrase). And I hope that if they come to Ynys-hir reserve they will have a genuine experience of wildness either in the birds they see and hear or in the trees and wildflowers. Or simply in the place itself which I trust will always retain something of the wilderness quality of its former days.

In writing about this one nature reserve I hope that I have said something applicable to wider fields. Not every wild place can become a nature sanctuary but everywhere a little can be done to help our native plants and animals. Often it needs only a thought at the right time and a thicket, a short length of hedge, a single bush or a tiny pool can be saved – habitats minute in themselves yet whose preservation is a lifeline perhaps for a thrush, a butterfly or a colony of frogs and toads. At the other end of the scale are the big areas of land and water, maybe whole districts of mountain, moorland, downland, forest, lake or sea coast. Here the problems of nature conservation get involved with other issues – the preservation of landscape beauty, the organization of National Parks, the management of water resources, the agricultural use of land, the future of forestry plantations, the damming of estuaries or the building of power stations.

When you see the storms of controversy that can suddenly rage over a hitherto peaceful stretch of countryside because someone proposes to build an airport, open a mine or create a reservoir then you realize what almost complete chaos there is at the heart of affairs. You see that although there are planning departments everywhere (some of whose officials really do carry a light in a very dark world) the overall picture is one of an ill-controlled free-for-all in which developers and their supporting financiers are always seeking some new field to adventure in. There is not yet any sufficient guiding philosophy of how the countryside should be treated. Perhaps there never will be, never can be. Perhaps the conservationists must always be an impotent minority moaning their little protests as the oil tide blackens the beaches, as the estuaries vanish behind barrages, as the orchid meadows give place to improved grasslands, as the lichens die on the tree trunks through foul air, and as the oaks go crashing to make way for the Sitka spruces. Perhaps we are doomed to struggle on, saving a little patch here as we lose a greater one there, fighting a battle that is already lost. As the world's resources shrink, as human populations grow more and more like a pestilence, are the pressures on us all and on our land likely to get less? If not, what are we to do? These are vast questions which mere individuals are powerless to cope with. And governments, who could achieve something, do as little as they can get away with doing and then vote another few thousand millions to promote the next stage in the sacred cause of economic growth. What they never tell us, because they think only short-term thoughts, is where it is all leading to, this economic growth, in terms of the squandering of natural resources and the blighting of our habitat. We know we are going to have more people, more houses, more cars, more motorways, more aircraft, more airports, more factories, more goods of all sorts, more towns. But in our overcrowded Britain where are they all going to be put? And what hope is there of saving anything of ultimate value to the spirit of man in terms of natural beauty and wildness; or of health and sanity in the real meaning of these words?

The hope, the one hope perhaps, is in a vast increase in public concern for the ecological well-being of the earth. And though up to now the signs of such a revolution are small, they certainly exist. Trickles of thought are approaching each other from many directions and they could flow together at last as a stream with force enough to burst through the accumulated debris of wrong ideas that have landed us in our present mess. Modern man's naïve faith in perpetual economic growth and ever more industrialization is beginning to be shaken, More and more people are realizing that we cannot go on over-exploiting our finite resources for ever and that we've got to put the brakes on somewhere.

But, politicians tell us, without growth we get mass unemployment. They are probably right. And always will be as long as our economy hinges on making motor-cars, aeroplanes and power stations; and getting oil and coal and other minerals out of the earth. Yet are these things truly necessary? When I look round I see everywhere enormous works that need doing, works that would really improve the quality of people's lives, works to improve the environment, all sorts of tasks of rehabilitation of people and places that at present are left largely to volunteers.

I would say that there is positively no need for anyone to be unemployed for centuries to come, there is so much to be done in our towns and cities and throughout the countryside. You will object perhaps that this would be 'unproductive' work and could not be paid for as the economy is run at present. If this is so then clearly we need a new sort of economy. And the sooner the better because as things are the world about us is becoming more and more uninhabitable. Only a completely new social philosophy, based on conservation and a genuine concern for the health of the environment, of man and the whole world of nature, can give any hope that life in the twenty-first century will be worth living for anybody.

Certainly in any rehabilitation of the countryside I would like to see many more nature reserves. Not just for the sake of conserving wildlife, which is hard-pressed enough, God knows, but for man himself whose plight is far more desperate than that of many animals. Since I have been warden of a bird reserve I have become increasingly interested in the people who come to visit it. They may think me a very queer sort of bird (seeing my aquiline nose they probably class me among the raptors) but I in my turn find some of them totally fascinating. So many of them show signs of stress, in their faces and in their words; and, unconsciously, it is more than wildlife that they are looking for in a nature reserve. Without realizing it they are seeking, I think, some way back to a simpler, more natural type of living. They seek it instinctively, like salmon ascending a muddy estuary to find sparkling water near the sources of a river. So I am prepared to believe that the greatest beneficiary of nature reserves will prove in due time not to be nature after all, but man.

(1975)

PART SEVEN

Envoi

THE SUN WARM ON MY ARM

Wherever I went the normally dry and springy hillside turf squirted water from under my boots. But what else to expect after a month that left us with twenty inches of rain. Never mind, the sun shone now. Sunshine. Something we had almost forgotten about. But now here it was, a cloudless blue sky and the sparkle and glint of sunshine on tree and rock and grass.

I had walked several miles up the valley, up through oak dingles loud with waterfalls and then up hawthorn-scattered slopes. I had passed the last inhabited house (there are only two in all the valley) and now, alone with the sheep, the gorse and the heather I had reached the highest house of all, a house where not even the oldest man in the parish remembers anybody living, a roofless house empty perhaps a hundred years but its walls still intact, a house with russet hills all around except where it looked down its valley to a perfect view of the far-off Dyfi estuary.

The most tattered peacock butterfly imaginable – a miracle how it could fly – settled by me on the doorstep. So near the end of its life yet clearly enjoying every second of that splendid sunshine. And so time passed. Only a near-dead butterfly, a house in ruins, the gurgle of a stream in the bracken, a raven croaking and somersaulting overhead, the sun warm on my arm.

(1993)

Select Bibliography

Thoreau (Witherby, 'Great Naturalists' series, 1954)

A committed and perceptive tribute to the life and writings, and a useful personal addendum to the authoritative biography by Robert D. Richardson (*Thoreau: A Life of the Mind*, University of California Press 1986. Richardson's biography of Emerson is also required reading for Thoreau addicts.)

The Birds of Cardiganshire (co-author). (West Wales Naturalists' Trust, 1966)

The Snowdonia National Park (No. 47 in Collins' 'New Naturalist' series 1966)

A replacement for NN13, *Snowdonia* (1949), by North, Campbell & Scott, and a better book in almost every way.

The Kites of Europe (American Museum of Natural History, 1967)

Birds and Wild Africa (Collins, 1967)

Exploring Wales (Faber, 1970)

An enjoyable and knowledgeable peregrination around all the old counties of Wales, disarmingly obsessed by inscriptions on old bridges. The favourite Welsh guidebook of all those who are fortunate enough to possess a copy.

Woodlands (Collins Countryside series, 1974)

The third in a cheap-and-cheerful series that was second cousin to the New Naturalist volumes. Intelligently organized and engagingly written, Bill's contribution is a thoroughly worthy primer to woodland and all aspects of its wildlife and ecology. Not easy to find, and well worth it when you do.

Pathway to the Wild (Faber, 1975)

Rare now, and one of the high points of Bill's literary achievement. Substantially represented in the present volume. What isn't included here is very well worth seeking out.

The World of a Mountain (Faber, 1977)

For the younger reader (deadly phrase!) Exemplary of its type.

The Natural History of Wales (No. 66 in Collins' 'New Naturalist' series, 1981)

Definitive and splendidly readable account of its subject. Good first editions now becoming quite valuable.

Snowdonia (David & Charles, 1987)

Wales (The National Trust, Gomer, 1991)

Wildlife in our Welsh Parish (Eglwysfach Women's Institute, 1993)

A Welsh Country Diary (Gomer, 1993)

Indispensable – the best of his *Guardian* pieces.

Wildlife, My Life (Gomer, 1995)

A kind of autobiography: exact knowledge, much lyricism, few of the disclosures a modern audience might demand (thank heavens!)

Welsh Country Essays (Gomer, 1996)

Don't be put off by the floppy, large-format paperback – contains some of the best of his early writing, in particular the essays for *Country Life*.

Wildlife Safari: the Life of Mary Richards (Gomer, 1998)

A dignified and richly-informed biography of one of his closest botanical associates and mentors. It tells an extraordinary life-story.

See also:

The Dublin Magazine, January-March 1955

'The Vertebrate Animals of Cardiganshire', in the *Cardiganshire County History* Vol. I (UWP Cardiff, 1994)

Introduction to *Wood Engravings* by Gertrude Hermes. (Gregynog, 1988)

'Choughs' in *Tomorrow is too Late* (Macmillan, 1990)

The Countryman, Summer 1996

A Year in a Small Country, ed. Jon Gower (Gomer, 1999)

There are also many contributions to wildlife and nature magazines, to publications such as *The Manchester Guardian, The Guardian, Guardian Weekly, Country Life, The Countryman* and *The Dublin Magazine*, and a wealth of holograph material in the National Library of Wales's William Condry archive (which also contains E.H.T. Bible's nature diaries and writings) – I leave you to explore these as you will.

Acknowledgements

My thanks above all go to Penny Condry for her unstinting support for this project, and for permission to re-print Bill's writing, of which she is copyright-holder. I'm indebted to Gwyneth Lewis, finest of our national women poets, for her luminous and enthusiastic foreword, and to Arthur Chater for information and guidance. I'm also grateful to Bill's previous publishers: H.F. & G. Witherby; Collins; Faber & Faber; and Gomer Press. My especial thanks to Ceri Wyn Jones, English Language editor at Gomer for his unwavering enthusiasm for this project and his scrupulous editing. Many other people too numerous to list here have communicated enthusiasm, preferences and recommendations about Bill's writing over many years. To all of them I offer my appreciation. Without their dialogue this book would not have come about. To Conor Gregory, Janet Wolf, Paul Evans and Mark Cocker I owe personal thanks for emotional support, advice and close reading of drafts. And it goes without saying that I stand forever in debt to Bill himself for his knowledge and kindness, friendship, guidance and genial irony and humour. To those of you who were not privileged to know him, I hope this book serves as introduction. To his many surviving friends, may it act as reminder of the remarkable man they knew.

The Annual William Condry Memorial Lecture

Taking its cue from a hint by R.S. Thomas on an apt way to commemorate Bill, every year since 2008, on the first Saturday in October, an English-language lecture by an eminent authority on a natural history theme is held at Tabernacl/MoMA in Machynlleth. Information about this, along with an archive of texts of past lectures, can be found at:

www.thecondrylecture.co.uk